Research
on
Teaching

THE NATIONAL SOCIETY
FOR THE STUDY OF EDUCATION

Series on Contemporary Educational Issues
Kenneth J. Rehage, Series Editor

The 1979 Titles

The Principal in Metropolitan Schools, Donald A. Erickson and
Theodore L. Reller, Editors
Educational Environments and Effects: Evaluation, Policy, and Productivity, Herbert J. Walberg, Editor
Research on Teaching: Concepts, Findings, and Implications,
Penelope L. Peterson and Herbert J. Walberg, Editors

The National Society for the Study of Education also publishes Yearbooks which are distributed by the University of Chicago Press. Inquiries regarding all publications of the Society, as well as inquiries about membership in the Society, may be addressed to the Secretary-Treasurer, 5835 Kimbark Avenue, Chicago, IL 60637. Membership in the Society is open to any who are interested in promoting the investigation and discussion of educational questions.

Research on Teaching

Concepts, Findings, and Implications

Edited by

PENELOPE L. PETERSON
University of Wisconsin, Madison

&

HERBERT J. WALBERG
University of Illinois at Chicago Circle

McCutchan Publishing Corporation
2526 Grove Street
Berkeley, California 94704

ISBN 0-8211-1518-9
Library of Congress Catalog Card Number 78-62102

Printed in the United States of America

Cover design and illustration by Catherine Conner, Griffin Graphics

Series Foreword

The current Series on Contemporary Educational Issues includes two companion volumes that deal directly with classroom instruction. This volume, *Research on Teaching: Concepts, Findings, and Implications,* edited by Professor Penelope L. Peterson and Professor Herbert J. Walberg, reports on several inquiries into classroom instruction that focus particularly upon studies related directly to teaching. The book provides helpful insights contributing to an understanding of how the actions of teachers influence the outcomes of the instructional process. Because various approaches to the investigation of teaching are used, the book has methodological as well as substantive significance for persons working in the field of education.

The second volume, *Educational Environments and Effects: Evaluation, Policy, and Productivity,* edited by Professor Walberg, brings together a number of studies that provide data on the effects of environmental influences on educational achievement. In that volume Professor Walberg has included reports of investigations that deal with environments outside the school, as well as with various aspects of the environment within the classroom. Both volumes serve to illustrate that various approaches can be used to study how educational achievement is influenced by environmental factors.

The National Society for the Study of Education owes much to Professors Peterson and Walberg for their work in collecting and editing the reports contained in these volumes, and to each of their colleagues without whose contributions the books would not have been possible. We are indeed pleased to have both volumes in the series.

Kenneth J. Rehage

for the Committee on the Expanded Publication Program of the National Society for the Study of Education

Contributors

David C. Berliner, Professor and Head, Department of Educational Psychology, University of Arizona

Hilda Borko, Instructor of Education, University of California at Los Angeles

Christopher M. Clark, Assistant Professor of Educational Psychology and Senior Researcher, Institute for Research on Teaching, Michigan State University

Richard Cone, Program Administrator, Joint Educational Project, University of Southern California

Walter Doyle, Associate Professor of Education, North Texas State University

Maurice J. Eash, Dean, College of Education, University of Illinois at Chicago Circle

N. L. Gage, Professor of Education and Psychology, and Director, Program on Teaching Effectiveness, Center for Educational Research at Stanford, Stanford University

Chen-Lin C. Kulik, Senior Research Associate, Center for Research on Learning and Teaching, University of Michigan

James A. Kulik, Research Scientist and Associate Director, Center for Research on Learning and Teaching, University of Michigan

Ronald W. Marx, Assistant Professor of Education, Simon Fraser University

Donald M. Medley, Professor of Education, University of Virginia

Penelope L. Peterson, Assistant Professor of Educational Psychology, University of Wisconsin at Madison and Faculty Associate, Wisconsin Research and Development Center for Individualized Schooling

Barak V. Rosenshine, Professor of Educational Psychology, University of Illinois at Champaign-Urbana

Nancy Atwood Russo, Educational Evaluator, System Development Corporation, Santa Monica, California

Richard J. Shavelson, Associate Professor of Education, and Head, Research Methods and Evaluation, University of California at Los Angeles

Robert S. Soar, Professor of Education, University of Florida

Ruth M. Soar, Gainesville, Florida

Harriet Talmage, Professor of Curriculum, Instruction, and Evaluation, University of Illinois at Chicago Circle

Herbert J. Walberg, Research Professor of Urban Education, University of Illinois at Chicago Circle

Philip H. Winne, Assistant Professor of Education, Simon Fraser University

Robert J. Yinger, Assistant Professor of Education, University of Cincinnati

Contents

Introduction and Overview

Penelope L. Peterson and *Herbert J. Walberg*

In our lives it sometimes becomes necessary to take stock: to think back over the past, to catalog our successes and failures, and to evaluate our efforts to date. Such an evaluation suggests how and where to expend future efforts. In a field of research, investigators find it necessary to make the same kind of assessment. They gather together research studies that have been conducted, review the results, and evaluate the findings to date. Then, based on their evaluation, they decide how and where to expend their research efforts in the future. In applied fields such as education, moreover, such efforts can affect not only research but also practice.

This volume takes stock in the field of research on teaching. The effort is timely because of the growing concern among parents and taxpayers that our schools are not teaching children the basic skills. Newspapers abound with reports of declining test scores and with stories of high school graduates who cannot read or do division problems. Educators and parents wonder: Do teachers make a difference? What can teachers do to teach children the basic skills? Such questions deserve responses—perhaps direct, perhaps a reconsideration of the questions themselves. This book attempts to provide some answers to these and other pressing questions about teaching. In addition, as implied above, it is also addressed to re-searchers themselves and concerns the history of empirical research on teaching, its present status, and possible future directions.

OVERVIEW

This volume is organized into three parts. Part One summarizes where research on teaching has been. The authors review several decades of research on teaching and discuss findings and implica-tions of past research. Part Two, which describes where research on teaching is today, gives examples of different types of studies in research on teaching. Part Three explores where research on teaching is going and presents and discusses possible new directions research on teaching might take.

Reviews of Research on Teaching

In the first chapter, Donald Medley traces the history of empirical research on teacher effectiveness through four phases and sum-marizes the findings. In the first of the phases, effectiveness was assumed to be a consequence of personality traits or characteristics of the teacher. Then, effectiveness was conceived of as a function of the teaching methods. In the third phase, research focused on the relation of behavior—what the teacher does—to pupil learning. Effectiveness, in the final phase, has been regarded as depending on the mastery of a repertoire of competencies and the ability to use these competencies appropriately.

Barak Rosenshine briefly reviews the history of research on teacher effects and goes on to describe in detail a recent cycle of research that has focused on variables such as content covered by students, time spent on relevant academic tasks, and quality of instruction as reflected by students' achievement. He introduces a concept called "direct instruction," which "refers to teaching activities focused on academic matters where goals are clear to students, time allocated for instruction is sufficient and continuous, coverage of content is extensive, the performance of students is monitored, questions are at a low cognitive level and students pro-duce many correct responses, and feedback to students is immediate and academically oriented." His conclusion is that direct instruction is more effective than more open approaches for obtaining achieve-ment gains in reading and mathematics in the early grades.

Penelope Peterson further examines the research related to direct instruction. She argues that, after reading reviews of recent research on teaching, the reader may be convinced that direct instruction is the most effective way of teaching. But a closer look at the research literature suggests that this conclusion is too simplistic. Direct instruction may be effective for attaining some educational objectives or outcomes, but not others. It may be effective for some kinds of students, but not others. A review of studies that compares direct instruction with more indirect, open, or nontraditional approaches leads to the conclusion that the effectiveness of each approach seems to depend on the kind of student being taught and the educational outcome to be attained.

Whereas the first three chapters review past research on teaching at the elementary and secondary levels, the one by James Kulik and Chen-Lin Kulik reviews research on college teaching and its effects on students. After an overview of fifty years of research on alternatives to the lecture method in college teaching, the Kuliks summarize the findings from the extensive recent literature on personalized systems of college instruction and conclude their chapter by defining some general characteristics of college teaching that promote student achievement.

Studies in Research on Teaching

Robert and Ruth Soar describe four studies of emotional climate in grades three through six. In the studies, which provide examples of what Medley earlier called "the third phase" of research in teaching effectiveness, teacher behavior was systematically observed, coded, and related to student achievement. The findings are described with respect to teacher management of pupil tasks, behavior, and thinking, and the implications of the findings for teaching are discussed.

David Berliner, in "*Tempus Educare,*" describes a study of three time variables: allocated time (the time a teacher provides for instruction in a particular content area), engaged time (the time a student spends engaged in instruction in a particular content area), and academic learning time (the time a student is engaged with instructional materials or activities that are at an easy level of difficulty). To illustrate the great differences among classes in terms of these time variables, Berliner presents data on mathematics from four second-grade classes and data on reading from four fifth-grade classes. His conclusion is that many teachers could improve their effectiveness by recognizing the effects of these time variables and by reorganizing classroom practices to maximize teaching and learning time.

Hilda Borko, Richard Cone, Nancy Russo, and Richard Shavelson describe four experimental studies of how teachers make decisions. The research shows that effectiveness may depend upon a teacher's ability to select and use the appropriate teaching strategy at the appropriate time. The first study examined the accuracy of teachers' estimates about students and the effects of these estimates on teachers' instructional decisions. The second one investigated teachers' planning related to instruction in reading and mathematics. The third study looked at the planning done by teachers with respect to classroom organization and management, and the fourth explored teachers' interactive decisions about classroom management in the context of a reading lesson. The authors summarize their findings and discuss possible educational implications.

Although past research on the effectiveness of teachers typically has not focused on curriculum, the appropriateness of certain teaching strategies or competencies clearly depends on the subject matter. Harriet Talmage and Maurice Eash discuss four evaluation research studies of curriculum, instruction, and materials. The studies serve to illustrate a paradigm for investigating the effects of curriculum, instruction, and materials on learning environments. Talmage and Eash present the significant findings of the studies and suggest implications for research and practice.

Directions in Research on Teaching

Walter Doyle, in "Classroom Tasks and Students' Abilities," suggests that research on teaching is on the threshold of a fundamental conceptual reorganization. He argues that future efforts should include four features. First, research should include the concept of reciprocal causality—not only do teachers affect what students do, but students affect what teachers do—in classroom relationships. Second, researchers should take an information-processing view of the strategies students use to navigate classroom environments. Third, the research should examine the possibility that different types of students might do better under different instructional conditions. Finally, researchers should take an ecological approach to the study of classrooms. It is the ecological approach to research on teaching that Doyle goes on to describe, indicating the possible findings and implications of such an approach.

In "Perceptual Problem Solving," Philip Winne and Ronald Marx offer an information-processing view of the strategies that students use to learn in classrooms. Thus, they illustrate how future research on teaching might develop Doyle's second feature, information processing. In particular, Winne and Marx explore how students' perceptions of teaching affect how they learn by citing instances where teaching may hinder or aid the student. They argue that future research on teaching should be able to explain how learning occurs as a result of teaching and that, in explanatory statements about the processes of learning, traditional paradigms used in research on effectiveness should be modified.

Christopher Clark and Robert Yinger also present an information-processing view in their chapter, "Teachers' Thinking." They assume that what teachers do is affected by what they think and that the study of their thinking will lead to an understanding of the processes that guide and determine their behavior in the classroom. Since this concept is relatively new, little research has been conducted. Clark and Yinger review the limited research, which has focused on four topics: planning, judgment, interactive decision making, and implicit theories or perspectives. Then they summarize the findings and point out possible directions for future research.

In the final chapter, N. L. Gage addresses the question: Should research on teaching be conducted at the general level or at the specific level? If research on teaching is pursued at the general level, then researchers will search for concepts and findings that apply to all subject matters, all kinds of things to be learned, and all grade levels. On the other hand, if research is pursued at the specific level, researchers will establish firm generalizations about the best way to teach one kind of thing using specific curriculum materials intended for a particular grade level. Researchers could then determine the degree to which the findings could be generalized to other learning outcomes, subject matters, and grade levels. Gage presents evidence for both positions. He concludes by hypothesizing that teaching behaviors, including methods, styles, and techniques, will fall into a hierarchical model, ranging from the highly general to the highly specific.

PERSPECTIVES

We, the editors, are grateful to these authors for their syntheses of concepts, findings, and implications in the several areas of research on teaching. The chapters, as a whole, appear to refute opinions occasionally voiced in recent years that variations in teaching make little difference in student learning, that educational research is too inconsistent to contribute to policy and practical implications, and that empirical research in education is unsystematic, undisciplined, and unscientific.

It seems fair to say, however, that gains over the decades were achieved in small, irregular steps, rather than in giant strides. Centuries of educational wisdom, experience, and common sense have contributed to the current base of practice, but it was not enlarged dramatically by any single piece of research nor markedly advanced during a particular, brief span of time. And sometimes a generation needs to rediscover for itself teaching insights well known not only to John Dewey, William James, and E. L. Thorndike but also to Plato and Aristotle.

The important gains, those that broadly advance the understanding and practice of teaching, are likely to derive from an explicit, testable theory; from a cumulative program of research by a single investigator or team; from a synthesis of comparable, replicated studies of independent investigators; and from sustained, reflective criticism of past work. These are the standards by which the authors were selected to contribute chapters. Such selection in no way implies unanimity in point of view; indeed, the contrary was intended. Representation of diverse approaches was intended from the initial conception of the book in an effort to acquaint readers with the variety of systematic views to be found in past, current, and future empirical research on teaching. Since the authors confined themselves, by editorial request, to specialized topics and approaches, readers of any given chapter may find it useful to remind themselves of the need for balance and coherence in thinking, feeling, and acting—the ancient triumvirate of philosophical psychology.

There are, of course, causes other than the teacher that bear upon the classroom learning process, among them, subject matter, social-psychological properties of the class, administrative and financial characteristics of the state, district, and school, and educationally relevant qualities of the community and home environments of the students. Such considerations are represented in a companion volume, *Educational Environments and Effects: Evaluation, Policy, and Productivity,* which was edited with similar intentions and is a part of this same series.

What is offered in the chapters should also be viewed in a context larger than social and behavioral research. Education in its best sense balances scientific findings against other considerations; science alone might make the teacher a mere technician who follows prescribed strategies that obtain empirical results. Science can quantify some important educational means and ends and can establish or probe their causal relations, but it cannot claim to be the sole authority when assessing the morality of the means nor the value of the ends. A democratic society requires the involvement of citizens, legislators, parents, and students, as well as the contributions of our colleagues in the arts and humanities, in assessing issues of policy and value.

PART ONE
Reviews
of
Research on Teaching

1. The Effectiveness of Teachers

Donald M. Medley

The effect of schooling on the individual pupil depends to a considerable extent on who his teacher is. This is an assumption that should not need much defense in a volume addressed to teacher educators. During the early years of a pupil's school life, in particular, the teacher is the point of contact between the pupil and the entire educational enterprise, and all of the effects of the money and effort expended on education must be channeled through the teacher to the learner. Personnel costs themselves represent so large a share of the day-to-day cost of education that the best hope for improvement in cost-effectiveness lies in improving the effectiveness of the teacher.

There are two important ways to improve the effectiveness of teachers. One is by improving the way teachers are evaluated, and the other is by changing the way teachers are educated. Either type of change can result in improvement only if it is based on accurate information about differences in the behavior patterns of more effective and less effective teachers, and the only reliable source of such information is sound research.

In the past, the impact of research in teacher effectiveness on either the evaluation or the training of teachers has been slight. Both important enterprises have been operating without any firm research base, owing in part to a failure of communication and in part to the inconsistency and incomprehensibility of most of the research findings.

In this chapter, I shall begin by attempting to ascertain why this gap in communication exists. Next I shall try to reduce that gap by reporting a set of findings that are both consistent and comprehensible. Finally, I shall discuss the implications of these findings and the future of three activities—maintaining the learning environment, making use of learning time, and improving the quality of learning activities—as they relate to the improvement of teaching.

RESEARCH ON EFFECTIVENESS: THE PAST

The history of research into the effectiveness of teachers reflects a gradual evolution in the researchers' conception of the nature of that effectiveness, which has largely determined the nature of the research as well as the nature and usefulness of the findings. At first, effectiveness was perceived as the consequence of certain personality traits or characteristics possessed by the teacher, and research was geared to identifying those traits. Later, effectiveness was seen not so much as a function of characteristics of the teacher but of the methods of teaching used, and research focused on methods of teaching. Then, effectiveness was seen as mainly dependent on the climate the teacher created and maintained in the classroom. More recently, effectiveness has been viewed as mastery of a repertoire of competencies, and, finally, there has been increasing emphasis on the ability to deploy these competencies appropriately, that is, on professional decision making.

Characteristics of Effective Teachers

The very earliest research set out to describe the characteristics that differentiated more effective teachers from less effective ones. [1] Techniques for the measurement of mental abilities, personality traits, attitudes, and similar factors were virtually nonexistent, and so early researchers asked pupils to describe effective teachers they had known. The analytical process essentially involved collating and comparing such descriptions, and the output took the form of lists of traits attributed to teachers regarded as effective. One of the best-designed studies of this kind listed four characteristics named by at least 10 percent of the students questioned as distinguishing the teacher from whom they learned most from the teacher they liked best. The four characteristics were: "makes greater demands of students," "has more teaching skill," "has more knowledge of subject matter," and "has better discipline."[2]

In later studies the opinions of expert judges of one kind or another were studied. The best example of this type of research was surely the *Commonwealth Teacher-Training Study,* in which the top six characteristics listed were good judgment, self-control, considerateness, enthusiasm, magnetism, and adaptability.[3]

By 1930 the teacher rating scale had come into widespread use as a device for evaluating teachers. In one study, 209 such scales were located and analyzed to give some idea what educational leaders regarded as characteristics of effective teachers. The most frequently mentioned characteristics included cooperation (helpfulness, loyalty), personal magnetism, personal appearance, breadth and intensity of interest, considerateness, and leadership.[4]

It is important to realize that all of these lists characterized teachers *perceived* as effective. In no instance was any evidence adduced to show that teachers possessing these characteristics were actually more effective in helping pupils achieve any of the goals of education than teachers who lacked them. Insofar as they describe anyone, they describe the teacher who *looks* effective. It is difficult to see how such lists as these (with the possible exception of the one obtained from students) could be used in the planning of programs for training teachers, even if it could be demonstrated that teachers who possessed the characteristics were, in fact, more effective than ones who lacked them. It is what a teacher *does* rather than what the teacher *is* that matters. What a student in a preservice teacher education program needs to learn is not what he should *be* but what he must *do* in order to be effective.

Since most of past research input into teacher education appears to have come from this kind of research, most of the knowledge base concerned with teacher education is questionable. Some of these findings are undoubtedly valid, but just as many are not. There is no reliable way of telling one from the other, except to do sound research.

Effective Methods of Teaching

Early in the history of educational research, there appeared a form of study usually referred to as "methods experiment." In a typical methods experiment, two or more classes were taught by different methods, and the mean gains in knowledge of the classes taught by each method were compared to find out which method was most effective. It was presumed that such research would provide the knowledge base for a course in which preservice teachers could learn the "best" methods of teaching. The results of methods experiments have tended, however, to be either inconclusive or to contradict the results of other methods experiments. The reason seems to lie in a single technical defect common to this type of research.

Almost every methods experiment that I have found in the literature was designed to use the pupil (rather than the teacher) as the unit of analysis. As a result, no valid generalization to teachers other than those who actually took part in the experiment could be made. In order to make such generalizations possible, many teachers (the more the better) would have to teach by each method, so that an accurate estimate could be made of the consistency of the results obtained by different teachers using the same method. This has rarely been done.

Behaviors of Effective Teachers

As it became apparent that sound research in teacher effectiveness must focus both on teacher behavior (what the teacher does) and on pupil learning (teacher effectiveness), the kind of research called "process-product research" became more widespread.

The focus of process-product research was not on teacher characteristics as such, but on stable behavior patterns that have been referred to as "teaching styles" or "dimensions of classroom climate." The notion of stability is central here: the method of the research is to observe behavior in teachers' classrooms on random occasions, looking for behaviors that are stable across observations. Variations in behavior from one occasion to another are treated as errors of measurement, without regard for whether the variations reflect differences in the teacher's purposes on different occasions or chance variations.

It is odd to note that systematic observation of behavior in the classroom as a means of studying the nature of effective teaching was uncommon before 1960. Stevens seems to have been the pioneer user of the method,[5] and her work was not widely imitated for forty or fifty years. As early as 1930 Barr and others advocated the use of criteria of teacher effectiveness based on measured pupil gains rather than on expert opinion,[6] but nobody seems to have paid them any heed.

Finally, the development and active dissemination by Flanders, Amidon, and others of "Interaction Analysis,"[7] the publication of the first *Handbook of Research on Teaching,*[8] and other factors led to a proliferation of process-product studies. The publication in 1971 of Rosenshine's review of fifty such studies presented evidence that at least some aspects of teaching style or classroom climate are related to pupil learning.[9] Research in teacher effectiveness had at last found a method that worked. The patterns of behavior identified as distinguishing effective and ineffective teaching included clarity, variability, enthusiasm, task-oriented or businesslike, criticism, teacher indirectness, student opportunity to learn criterion materials, and use of structuring comments.[10] It should be noted that, in addition to having been shown to relate to pupil learning, most of these patterns could conceivably be modified by appropriate training.

Competencies of Effective Teachers

The development of a model for teacher education called *competency-* or *performance-based teacher education* had important implications for research in teacher effectiveness. This model assumes that the effective teacher differs from the ineffective one primarily in that he has command of a larger repertoire of competencies—skills, abilities, knowledge, and so forth—that contribute to effective teaching. The number of such competencies is seen as large, so large that no one possesses or needs them all. Some are seen as interchangeable, in the sense that equally effective teachers may possess somewhat different sets. Some are seen as basic competencies that every effective teacher should possess.

What distinguishes competencies from the stylistic behavior patterns identified in process-product research is that a competency is used only under certain circumstances. The ability to ask higher-order questions is a competency; clarity is not. There are times when higher-order questions are inappropriate, when the teacher who can ask them should not do so; there is no time when clarity is inappropriate. Research in teacher competencies must take account not only of how teachers behave, but when and why they behave as they do.

This is where the methodology of research in teacher effectiveness seems to be today. It involves three variables: measures of teacher effectiveness based on pupil learning, measures of teacher behavior derived from systematic observation of classroom interaction, and information about the teacher's intention or purpose.

From this brief sketch of the history of research on the effectiveness of teachers, one reason why research has had so little impact on teacher education becomes quite clear: so many of the findings have been either irrelevant or inconsistent, or both. To borrow a phrase Charles Silberman once used in a similar context, the teacher educator who examines the research is likely to conclude that there is less there than meets the eye. Is he correct in this conclusion? Has research in teacher effectiveness yet produced any findings that the teacher educator cannot afford to ignore?

RESEARCH ON EFFECTIVENESS: THE PRESENT

Despite its shortcomings, some of which have already been mentioned, process-product research can produce, and has produced, reliable information about the nature of effective teaching. When teachers are visited by observers trained to record their behavior accurately and objectively, appropriate analysis of the records reveals stable differences between the behaviors of teachers who are more effective and those who are less effective in helping pupils grow in basic skills as well as in some affective areas.

This statement is based on a recently completed monograph in which I examined 289 empirical studies of teacher effectiveness. The study was undertaken under the assumption that, if certain criteria of quality were applied to the results of these studies, most of the apparent contradictions and inconsistencies in them would disappear. The first of these criteria had to do with the definition of effective teaching employed.

Defining Effective Teaching

The daily process of teaching is concerned with specific facts, principles, vocabulary, and so forth, which the pupil is expected to retain long enough to pass a test. It seems logical, therefore, to assess teacher effectiveness on the basis of how much of this content a teacher's students master in how brief a period of time, with allowances made for relevant characteristics of the particular group of students being taught and other factors affecting pupils' learning that are beyond the teacher's control.

Acceptance of this concept of effective teaching greatly facilitates research on the effectiveness of teachers. Measures of gains of this kind are relatively easy to obtain and to administer, and detectable gains can be produced over a relatively short period of instruction, so that how effective a teacher is can be estimated in a week or even a day. But teachers are not hired to cram information into students' heads to be retained just long enough to enable them to pass objective tests. Teachers are hired to educate children, to produce important, lasting changes in their behavior, not short-term changes in test scores. Teachers are supposed to teach children to read, to communicate, to reason, to become happy, productive, responsible members of this democracy. In accomplishing these things, it may be necessary also to teach them a great deal of content, most of which they will forget almost immediately. The teaching of these facts, principles, and the like is, however, a means, not the end, of education.

The longer the period over which the student change is measured, the more likely it is that the change measured will be lasting and important. And it is the teachers who produce permanent changes in pupils who deserve to be called effective. There is no evidence that teachers adept in producing quick gains are also effective in producing permanent, important changes in pupils.

Among the 289 studies examined, only those in which teacher effectiveness was measured in terms of student gains over several months were regarded as valid studies; all others were discarded.

Describing Competent Behavior

A second quality sought in each study had to do with the measurement of teachers' behavior. Since the aim of process-product research is to describe effective teacher behavior in terms accurate enough to form a basis for training novice teachers to behave that way, it is critically important that a research study yield accurate and objective descriptions of the behaviors of the teachers studied.

Many studies employ rating scales as measures of teacher behavior. After observing a sample of a teacher's behavior, the rater records his estimate of that teacher's score on each dimension of behavior to be studied. Such a rating does not constitute an objective description of the behavior of the teacher being rated. Two teachers may receive identical ratings on a dimension although their behaviors were quite different. The ratings contain no record of what either teacher did, although that is what the study is supposed to determine.

To be useful in a process-product study, then, what the observer produces must be a record of what he observed, not an evaluation of it. The proportion of studies that use rating scales is decreasing. Most modern studies use systematic observation schedules, on which observers record frequencies of behaviors falling into predetermined categories. Among the 289 studies examined, only those that used such procedures, or others that yielded clear descriptions of teacher behavior, were retained.

Establishing the Generalizability of Findings

The analysis of the relationships between measures of classroom behavior (process) and gains in student learning (product) in a study is an important step. A strong positive relationship is interpreted as evidence that effective teachers tend to exhibit the behavior more often than ineffective ones, which suggests that teachers who wish to become more effective should increase the frequency of the behavior in their own teaching. Such a suggestion is worthless unless it is supported by evidence that the same relationship would have been found if a different sample of teachers had been used. Among the 289 studies, any that failed to present such evidence were discarded.

Revealing Important Relationships

Studies that possessed the three characteristics just described— valid measures of teacher effectiveness, intelligible descriptions of teaching behavior, and evidence of generalizability of findings—were examined for process-product relationships strong enough to have practical importance.

How strong must a relationship be before the behavior may be said to have an "important" relationship to teacher effectiveness? For the purposes of the review in question, it was decided quite arbitrarily that the minimum overlap in variance should be 15 percent, which corresponds to a Pearson product-moment correlation coefficient of ±.387.

Only relationships that survived all four of these criteria were reported in the monograph. The number of such relationships was 613, and they all came from just fourteen different studies. Approximately 95 percent of the 289 empirical studies of teacher effectiveness originally located yielded no results usable according to all four criteria.

The fact that over 600 important and dependable relationships were found in these fourteen studies is encouraging. Even more encouraging is the fact that many of these relationships were verified in more than one of the studies, a fact that further justifies their being referred to as "dependable."

Collating Data from Different Studies

The means by which related findings from different research projects were brought together for comparison is illustrated in Figure 1-1, which shows how relationships between praise and teacher effectiveness were categorized. The data of the study were presented in forty-three forms similar to this one with each form showing all of the relationships between a single process variable and various criteria of teacher effectiveness.

The process variables used are listed at the left of the form and the product measures of teacher effectiveness at the top. Each relationship is represented by a letter (L, H, or M) located opposite the process variable and below the product measure involved. The letter "L" indicates that the frequency of the behavior was lower in classrooms of effective teachers than in those of ineffective teachers, the letter "H" indicates that it was higher in classrooms of effective teachers, and the letter "M" indicates that the frequency of the behavior in the classes of effective teachers was in the middle—that it occurred more often in some classes taught by ineffective teachers, and less often in others. In what way the teacher was effective, and with pupils of what socioeconomic status, is indicated over the column in which the letter is located.

Figure 1-1 shows, for instance, that "all adult praise" was more common in classes in which first-grade pupils of low socioeconomic status showed high gains in arithmetic in the first grade. It also

Behavior item	Grade	Pupils of low socioeconomic status						Pupils of high socioeconomic status						Source symbol
		Reading gains Complexity		Arithmetic gains Complexity		Affective gains		Reading gains Complexity		Arithmetic gains Complexity		Affective gains		
		Low	High	Low	High	School	Self	Low	High	Low	High	School	Self	
All adult praise	I													SK 398a
Positive motivation (with language experience method)	I	H		H	H									
Positive motivation (with language experience method)	II		H											
Positive motivation (with skills-centered method)	II	L												CRAFT OScAR
Public praise as motivation for others (self-report)	II-III	H	H					H	H					BE Q39
Praise in pupil-initiated work contacts	II-III		H						L					BE P133
Ratio of praise to praise-plus-criticism (in reading groups)	II-III	H	H					L	L					
Ratio of praise to praise-plus-criticism (general)	II-III	L	L	M				M	M	M				BE Q155
Praise after pupil response	IV									L	L			GG

Note: For definitions of the abbreviations used in the last column, see the original monograph.

Source: Donald M. Medley, Teacher Competence and Teacher Effectiveness: A Review of Process-Product Research (Washington, D. C.: American Association of Colleges for Teacher Education, 1977).

Figure 1-1

Sample of form summarizing data on the relationship between praise and teacher effectiveness

indicates that the "ratio of praise to praise-plus-criticism (general)" was smaller in classes of pupils of low socioeconomic status with greatest grains in reading, but intermediate in value in classes of pupils of low socioeconomic status where gains in arithmetic were greatest.

At the right of the figure are symbols identifying the project that reported each relationship. It should be noted that three different studies reported that praise was high in classes of effective teachers of grades one, two, or three, and low in the classes of ineffective teachers. Inconsistent results were found in one study, in classes taught by one method. It is interesting to speculate about what this means, but it is the high agreement between findings in different research projects done in different parts of the country with different samples of pupils that constitutes the major finding of the study.

The Structure of Effectiveness

One largely unanswered question about the nature of teacher effectiveness is whether a teacher who is effective in producing one kind of gain with one kind of pupil may also be expected to be equally effective in producing other kinds of gains with other kinds of pupils. Is teacher effectiveness general, or specific to the kind of pupil taught and the kind of outcome measured? This point is of particular interest as it applies to cognitive versus affective outcomes. Do teachers who produce relatively rapid gains in reading and arithmetic do so at the expense of pupils' attitudes toward school or their self-esteem?

The findings reviewed in this study contain information relevant to this question, in the form of pairs of relationships found in the same study between one process measure and two different measures of teacher effectiveness. If both relationships are Hs, or if both are Ls, they may be said to agree, that is, to indicate that the same pattern of behavior is effective in producing both kinds of outcomes.

There were ninety pairs in which one outcome was cognitive and the other was affective. In sixty-six pairs, or 73 percent, both outcomes agreed, indicating that almost three-fourths of the time the same pattern of teacher behavior that maximizes pupils' achievement gains also has a positive impact on student affect. Pupils tend to like school best and to have highest self-esteem in classes where they are learning most about reading and arithmetic. A similar analysis indicated that there was little detectable difference between effective patterns for teaching reading and arithmetic, or for producing gains on tests of high or low complexity.

When relationships of eighty-four pairs based on the same outcome in classes of different socioeconomic levels were compared, only 38 percent of the pairs agreed. And 62 percent (two-thirds) were opposite in sign. Most of the behaviors found to be effective with pupils of low socioeconomic status were found to be ineffective with pupils of high socioeconomic status, and vice versa. These data come from just one study, and so they cannot be taken as conclusive, but the implication is disturbing. If optimal strategies for teaching the two kinds of pupils are opposite, a teacher with an integrated class (one containing both kinds of pupils) must do what is wrong for half the class while doing what is right for the other half. The only way a teacher can even look effective is by ignoring half of the class, which is not a healthy situation for either teacher or pupils.

Characteristic Behaviors

A study of the 613 relationships reported in the forty-three tables of the monograph reveals a number of relationships of particular interest because they are verified in several different studies. Table 1-1 presents these results in the form of parallel descriptions of the behaviors of effective and ineffective teachers of pupils of low socioeconomic status in the primary grades as observers saw them. In studying the table it is important to bear in mind that each point in the table is supported by a strong relationship (at least .39) replicated in at least two independent and soundly designed and executed studies. The risk that any of them will be disproven by future research is slight. This point is emphasized because the profile of the effective teacher that emerges is not entirely consistent with the general consensus of how a good teacher behaves, or with the way teacher educators train teachers to act.

The *learning environment* found in the effective teacher's classroom agrees with the general belief. It tends to be orderly and psychologically supportive, and to be maintained with relatively little effort on the teacher's part. The environment in the class of the ineffective teacher, on the other hand, is characterized by disruptive pupil behavior, which requires more effort on the part of the teacher

Table 1-1

Differences between effective and ineffective teachers of disadvantaged pupils in the primary grades verified in two or more independent studies

Teaching function	Behavior of teachers	
	Effective	Ineffective
Maintenance of learning environment	Less deviant, disruptive pupil behavior Fewer teacher rebukes Less criticism Less time spent on classroom management More praise, positive motivation	More deviant, disruptive pupil behavior More teacher rebukes More criticism More time spent on classroom management Less praise, positive interaction
Use of pupil time	More class time spent in task-related "academic" activities More time spent working with large groups or whole class Less time spent working with small groups Small groups of pupils work independently less of the time Less independent seatwork	Less class time spent in task-related "academic" activities Less time spent working with large groups or whole class More time spent working with small groups Small groups of pupils work independently more of the time More dependent seatwork
Method of instruction	More "low-level" questions Fewer "high-level" questions Less likely to amplify, discuss, or use pupil answers Fewer pupil-initiated questions and comments Less feedback on pupil questions More attention to pupils when they are working independently	Fewer "low-level" questions More "high-level" questions More likely to amplify, discuss, or use pupil answers More pupil-initiated questions and comments More feedback on pupil questions Less attention to pupils when they are working independently

Source: Medley, Teacher Competence and Teacher Effectiveness.

to cope with it and which generates more than the average amount of rebuking and criticizing behavior from the teacher.

Use of pupil time does not conform to the general notion among educators, however. It is in the ineffective teacher's class that time spent on "academic" activities is lowest, that there is the most independent and small-group activity, and that the class spends the least amount of time organized in one large group with the teacher. The research clearly indicates that this is how a classroom looks in which gains in achievement, as well as the pupils' feelings about school and about themselves, are lowest.

The effective teacher devotes more class time to academic activities, with the class organized in one large group, and devotes less class time to small group activities and independent seatwork than the ineffective one.

Nor does the *method of instruction* resemble the stereotype of the profession. Teachers who ask the most high-level and the fewest low-level questions, teachers whose pupils ask more questions and get more feedback from their teachers, teachers who tend to amplify or discuss pupil-initiated comments most are the ones who are least effective. Teachers who use more low-level questions and fewer high-level ones, whose pupils initiate fewer questions and get less feedback, who tend not to amplify or discuss what pupils say—these are the most effective teachers.

The final point of difference in the table suggests that, although more effective teachers devote less time to pupil seatwork, they supervise pupils engaged in seatwork more closely than ineffective teachers do.

RESEARCH ON EFFECTIVENESS: THE FUTURE

The primary goal of the National Institute of Education has recently been defined as "educational equity . . . a state of affairs in which race, sex, and SES [socioeconomic status] of a student no longer predict educational achievement."[11] This is a goal worthy of adoption by all institutions involved in education, one not only important but urgent.

Findings similar to those shown in Table 1-1 are highly relevant to this goal, and have clear implications for preservice and in-service teacher education, for teacher evaluation and accountability, and for future research in teacher effectiveness as well. In view of the urgency of the problem and of the broad empirical base that underlies the findings (the chances that future research might alter them in any important respect are negligible), these implications may almost be regarded as imperatives.

It is a truism of education that the only thing well-motivated students are sure to learn is whatever their grades depend on, that the final examination defines the functioning objectives of any course. This applies to teacher evaluation and accountability as well. If teachers know the criteria on which decisions affecting their careers are based, they will meet the criteria if it is humanly possible to do so.

The research review reported in this chapter clearly identifies three ways in which classrooms of effective teachers of disadvantaged pupils in their first few years in school differ from those of ineffective teachers of the same kind of pupils. These differences are of such a nature that each of them can be reduced or removed by changes in the behavior of the teacher. How to maintain an orderly and supportive classroom climate, how to increase the amount of time devoted to learning activities, and how to improve the quality of learning activities—all three are determined largely by what the teacher does, and research provides detailed information about how teachers behave who do them successfully.

If teachers of such pupils were held accountable for their behavior in these ways, especially for maintaining the learning environment and for increasing the amount of learning time, and if evaluation of these qualities were used as the basis of selection, retention, merit pay, and so forth, the research strongly indicates that a substantial, if not dramatic, improvement in achievement, in attitudes toward school, and of disadvantaged pupils' self-images would result. The teaching profession should welcome a change from the present pressure to hold teachers accountable for outcomes (over which they have little control) to use of pupils' time (over which they have considerable control).

Teacher education, both at the preservice and the in-service level, should adopt as primary goals the development of the competencies needed to create and maintain the learning environment, to engage pupils in learning-related activities, and to implement the kind of instruction that research indicates is provided by effective teachers. There is an abundance of practical knowledge available about how to do these things; what has been missing in the past is a clear conviction on the part of teacher educators that these things are what teachers ought to be doing. Much effort has been wasted in training teachers to behave in the ways that the least effective ones do. A change of direction, so that beginning teachers will no longer need to unlearn so much, should produce a substantial, if not a dramatic, improvement in the achievement of pupils.

The implications of these findings for the future of research on the effectiveness of teachers do not promise immediate improvement in educating disadvantaged children, but they can be important for the future. No one should suppose that these findings account for more than a small part of the variance in teacher behavior that is relevant to teacher effectiveness. Classroom climate and the proportion of pupil time productively used are best regarded as enabling conditions for effective teaching; information about how to produce needed improvements in the quality of effective instruction is meager at best. More knowledge is needed before instruction can reach anything close to full efficiency.

It should be emphasized that Figure 1-1 includes only the most obvious, the virtually inescapable conclusions to be drawn from past research. In the 613 relationships reported there are many additional insights, particularly ones related to teaching other kinds of pupils. And in the 275 studies not summarized there is still more information.

The important conclusion for research in teacher effectiveness, however, is that future research should build on past findings and look for other ways to increase teacher effectiveness. Nobody really feels that the effective teachers presently in the schools, the ones identified in these studies, are effective enough; it is the state of the art of teaching itself that is in need of improvement. While the most urgent business of education is to improve the least effective teachers, improving the most effective ones is also important.

Nothing will be said here about needed changes in the strategy or tactics of research in teacher effectiveness. Process-product research, particularly when it meets the quality criteria used in this review (which it seldom does), can still yield much useful information, and the shift already under way to a focus on competencies rather than stylistic patterns of behavior should increase this yield. The tools needed to build a knowledge base for the effective education and evaluation of teachers are available.

NOTES

1. H. E. Kratz, "Characteristics of the Best Teachers as Recognized by Children," *Pedagogical Seminary* 3 (June 1896): 413-418.

2. Frank W. Hart, *Teachers and Teaching: By Ten Thousand High School Seniors* (New York: Macmillan Co., 1934), 278.

3. W. W. Charters and Douglas Waples, *The Commonwealth Teacher-Training Study* (Chicago: University of Chicago Press, 1929), 18.

4. Arvil S. Barr and Lester M. Emans, "What Qualities are Prerequisites to Success in Teaching?" *Nation's Schools* 6 (September 1930): 60-64.

5. Romiett Stevens, *The Question as a Measure of Efficiency in Instruction*, Contributions to Education No. 48 (New York: Teachers College Press, Columbia University, 1912).

6. Arvil S. Barr *et al.*, "The Validity of Certain Instruments Employed in the Measurement of Teaching Ability," in *The Measurement of Teaching Efficiency*, ed. Helen M. Walker (New York: Macmillan Co., 1935), 73-141.

7. Ned A. Flanders, *Teacher Influence, Pupil Attitudes, and Achievement*, Final Report, Cooperative Research Program Project No. 397 (Minneapolis, Minn: University of Minnesota, 1960).

8. N. L. Gage, ed., *Handbook of Research on Teaching* (Chicago: Rand McNally, 1963), 247-328.

9. Barak Rosenshine, *Teaching Behaviors and Student Achievement* (Slough, Eng.: National Foundation for Educational Research in England and Wales, 1971).

10. *Id.* and Norma Furst, "The Use of Direct Observation to Study Teaching," in *Second Handbook of Research on Teaching*, ed. Robert M. W. Travers (Chicago: Rand McNally, 1973), 156-157.

11. Virginia Koehler, "Projecting for the Future: Teacher Preparation and Research on Teaching," speech prepared for the faculty of the School of Education, University of Pittsburgh, December 1977.

2. Content, Time, and Direct Instruction

Barak V. Rosenshine

Research on the relationship between classroom instruction and gain in students' achievement might be seen as moving through three cycles. In the first cycle, research was on teacher personality and teacher characteristics. The second cycle looked at teacher-student interaction, and the third cycle focused more on student attention, the content that the student masters, and those settings that promote student attention. This chapter reviews research findings in the third cycle. Before considering that cycle, however, let us look at some of the work in the first and second cycles.

THE FIRST AND SECOND CYCLES

The first cycle, characterized by the work of Arvil S. Barr and his associates, focused on predictive variables such as teacher attitudes, interests, and personality, or on demographic variables such as specific knowledge or amount of training. The attempt was to determine which of these variables was consistently related to gain in students' achievement or to ratings of teachers by principals. In summarizing this research, Gage concluded that "these studies have yielded disappointing results: correlations that are nonsignificant, inconsistent from one study to the next, and usually lacking in psychological and educational meaning."[1] Similarly, Getzels and Jackson concluded that "despite . . . a half century of prodigious research effort, very little is known for certain about the relation between teacher personality and teaching effectiveness."[2] Such inconclusive results may have occurred because teacher personality and values, as measured by paper-and-pencil tests, did not always correspond with how a teacher actually taught in a classroom.

The second cycle began in the 1950s, particularly with the work of Ned Flanders, Donald Medley, and Harold Mitzel. The focus of this work was the systematic counting of specific teacher and student behaviors and relating the frequency of these behaviors to measures of gain in the achievement of students. The variables counted were primarily those of teacher-student interaction, although some studies also included ratings of specific teacher behaviors. Studies on teacher-student interaction are still being conducted.

In 1971, in the first review of the work in this cycle, Rosenshine and Furst[3] identified ten variables as having yielded the most consistent results: clarity of the teacher's presentation, enthusiasm of the teacher, variety of activities during the lesson, task-oriented and businesslike behaviors in the classroom, content covered by the class, the teacher's acknowledgement and encouragement of students' ideas during discussion, criticism of the student (negatively related to achievement), use of structuring comments at the start of and during a lesson, use of a variety of types of questions, and probing of students' responses by the teacher. The first five of these variables had the strongest support at that time. It is interesting to note what has been learned about these ten variables more recently.

Although observers' and students' ratings of the clarity of a teacher's presentation and ratings of the enthusiasm shown by the teacher remain potent predictors of student gains in achievement in college, these variables have not been significant correlates of gains in achievement in recent studies of instruction in the early grades (kindergarten through grade five). One likely cause is that the amount of discussion and verbal explanation by the teacher is relatively low in contemporary elementary classrooms. Today, students spend from 50 to 70 percent of their time working alone and only 10 to 15 percent of their time in teacher-led discussions. Thus, verbal variables such as clarity and enthusiasm have become less important in elementary classrooms. There has been relatively little new research on this aspect of teaching at the junior and senior high school levels.

Although frequency counts of the variety of activities occurring in a classroom were excellent predictors of gains and students' achievement in the earlier studies, the variety of activities occurring concurrently has correlated negatively with gains in achievement in subsequent ones. Although it would still seem important for students to have a variety of ways to learn the same material, classrooms in which a variety of activities are occurring simultaneously are usually more disorderly, and students are less attentive because a teacher is unable to monitor all activities. Students, as we shall see, are more task oriented when they are being supervised.

A determination of the amount of content covered in a classroom and ratings and counts of the extent to which classrooms are task oriented and academically focused have continued to yield excellent results in recent studies. Both variables are discussed in more detail below as they relate to research being carried on in the third cycle. Content covered emerges as one of the most important variables in our current thinking, with "student engaged time" serving as a proxy for content covered. As we shall see, current research shows that more content is covered and students are more attentive in classrooms that are task oriented and businesslike.

The results on acknowledgement and encouragement of student ideas during discussion remain similar to those in earlier studies: consistent positive but nonsignificant correlations. This may occur because verbal interaction is less frequently found in elementary classrooms today. Frequency counts of criticism of students by teachers continue to yield negative correlations with achievement. Frequency of criticism, however, particularly during discussions, is quite low. Large amounts of criticism appear to indicate difficulty in controlling students rather than attempts to demean students.

There is little to say about the remaining variables—use of structuring comments, use of a variety of types of questions, and probing of students' responses. Because such variables have not yielded particularly notable results with respect to relationships to achievement, they have not been studied systematically.

Thus, of the ten variables thought to be most promising for future research, the two that showed the best results in subsequent research are those relating to content covered and task orientation or academic focus. Variables such as the clarity of the teacher's presentation, enthusiasm, and acknowledgement of students' ideas appear to be less important in the primary grades but become more important in more verbal settings. Research in the second or interactive cycle is alive, well, and continuing. Studies completed since 1973, some of which are included in this volume and have been reviewed elsewhere as well,[4] are yielding encouraging results. Recent work has shifted from studying specific variables to looking at larger patterns, such as the size of the instructional group, effective patterns of responding to incorrect answers, effective patterns for managing students during seatwork, and optimal error rates in response to questions.

THE THIRD CYCLE

Research in the third cycle focuses on the student, particularly the content which the student covers or masters, the number of minutes a student is engaged in academically relevant tasks, and the settings which promote engagement. The work of David Berliner, Benjamin Bloom, Annegret Harnischfeger, and David Wiley[5] is prominent in this cycle. Whether a teacher is critical, or indirect, or enthusiastic still matters, but the new emphasis is on the time students spend engaged in mastering academic skills and the progress they have made toward mastering them.

Although content covered and minutes of student attention to academically relevant material are closely related, content covered is the more critical variable because it is closer to the outcome measures. As we shall see, it is easier to obtain data on academically engaged minutes, and most of the results reported below concern that variable. In this chapter, academically engaged minutes are used as a proxy for content covered.

Cautions

Two cautions should be noted. First, the research to be reported upon is limited to instruction in basic skills—reading and mathematics achievement—of students in grades one through five (ages six through ten) in the United States.[6] Although some will argue that this is a limited focus, the learning of basic skills is clearly a major purpose of schooling. The learning of basic skills, however, should *not* be equated with rote learning. The inferential and deductive skills necessary to answer comprehension questions in reading and problem-solving exercises in mathematics are far from rote learning. If such skills merely involved rote learning, it would have been relatively simple to bring all children to a high level of competence, and this has not been our experience. However, a focus on basic skills does not reflect a lessened concern with students' attitudes and feelings in the classroom, or a lessened concern with the teaching of heuristic methods. Rather, the investigators believe there is more to be gained by studying one area at a time.

A second concern is the need to proceed with caution in implementing these findings into teacher education programs or into evaluative checklists for teachers. Rather than quickly adopting another round of dicta on "teachers should," as we did in the late 1960s and early 1970s, we should preferably spend time thinking about and discussing the results, their implications, and possible alternatives.

Content Covered

Content covered, or "opportunity to learn," has been studied in many ways, including inspecting the content of textbooks used,[7] asking teachers to indicate the percentage of students who have had an opportunity to learn each item on a test,[8] counting the number of pages of the common textbook covered during a semester,[9] coding the content in a short presentation that was relevant to the test questions,[10] counting the number of words that the teacher attempted to teach,[11] counting the number of mathematics problems covered,[12] comparing the results of different curriculum programs on general and on curriculum-related posttests,[13] and coding the level of the workbook the students had completed just before they took a posttest.[14]

In all studies but one, significant relationships were found between content covered and gains in students' achievement.[15] Moreover, these correlations are usually larger than those obtained for variables of teacher behavior. As McDonald has noted, "If students have not been taught . . . some . . . content or procedure, they simply do not do well on those portions of the test relevant to that topic."[16]

The study of content covered has not been common practice in educational research. This is because different classrooms use different materials and texts and we have not developed a technology for studying content covered in such situations. Most of the studies cited above either used short common teaching units or relied upon teacher reports of content covered. Because of the difficulty in assessing content covered, researchers have turned to measures of the number of minutes students spend engaged in academically relevant tasks and use this measure as a proxy for content covered, as we shall see below.

Although the importance of content covered seems obvious, there are some unanswered questions. If content covered is so important, how can a student be allowed to enter grade two without having covered the content for reading and mathematics presented in grade one? How can we allow students to enter grade six when they have frequently covered only the content for reading and mathematics at the level of grade four? This is not to argue that students should be retained; rather, it argues for making provisions to enable all students to master the material for their grade. How this extra time will be found is an administrative problem because it seems unrealistic and unfair to expect classroom teachers to find extra time for a few children while simultaneously managing and teaching the rest of the class. The implication is that, if we want a student to be competent at a certain grade level, we have to ensure that he has mastered the work at the previous grade levels. As obvious as this seems, we are not doing it for all children.

Academically Engaged Minutes

The second major variable in this third cycle, student attention or engagement, is obviously necessary for learning. Despite the difficulties of measuring engagement and the crude and varied procedures used to gather these data, Bloom found clear and consistent results in the fifteen studies he reviewed. He found that the correlations of student attention with gain in achievement were about .40 when the student was the unit of analysis and about .52 when the class was the unit.[17] In another study, on different Follow Through classrooms, Stallings and Kaskowitz recorded what each child in the room was doing every fifteen minutes throughout the day.[18] The observers coded students as "attending" only when they were obviously working on activities in reading or mathematics. In that study, time spent attending to reading or mathematics activities yielded higher correlations (.30 to .60) with achievement gain than any of the other coded behaviors or interactions of teachers or students. Similarly, the use of textbooks, workbooks, or instructional materials yielded positive correlations with achievement, but *no* nonacademic activity correlated positively with achievement in reading or mathematics.

Stallings and Kaskowitz also presented the percentage of time students were attending to academic activities in each Follow Through program (Table 2-1). We see that in reading, children in the top three models in achievement were spending about 50 percent more time attending to academic reading activities than the children in the three models that ranked lowest in achievement gains. (The results on the non-Follow Through or control classrooms show that children were attending to reading and mathematics activities relatively frequently in those settings, and their achievement gain scores reflect this emphasis).

The amount of time *allocated* for covering or mastering content may be quite different from academically engaged minutes because allocated time can include time spent in preparation or transition or time spent on nonacademic activities. Thus, we find that, in studies that considered only allocated time, most of the results tended to be nonsignificant.[19] Despite the importance of academically engaged time, it should be emphasized that a teacher is not obliged to have all students engaged all of the time. The critical variable is the total number of academically engaged minutes per day.

Consider, for example, two teachers we studied in Urbana. Both were personable, warm, competent women in their early thirties. They were using the same materials (the McGraw-Hill Programmed Readers) with similar children (sons and daughters of college professors and graduate students). One teacher allotted thirty minutes per day for reading and ran a tightly structured classroom in which students were recorded as engaged 80 percent of the time. She maintained this high percentage by being very alert to the engagement of students and by using frequent means of social control, such as saying "Johnny, can I help you?" when a student was not working. The other teacher allotted sixty minutes to reading, but ran a more casual classroom and was less insistent on high engagement. On the average, the students in the class of the second teacher were academically engaged only 65 percent of the time. If one computes the number of engaged minutes, then the class of the first teacher

Table 2-1

Average percentage of engaged time and rank order for gain in achievement in grades one and three, by Follow Through program

Program	Grade one				Grade three			
	Reading		Mathematics		Reading		Mathematics	
	Percent engagement per day	Rank in gain	Percent engagement per day	Rank in gain	Percent engagement per day	Rank in gain	Percent engagement per day	Rank in gain
Oregon	54[a]	1[a]	27	5	58	2	27	1
Kansas	59	2	22	1	59	3	22	3
Non-Follow Through	50	3	18	3	48	1	22	2
Bank Street	40	6	16	4	38	7	20	4
High/Scope	40	5	20	8	46	—	16	—
Arizona	40	4	14	6	42	6	16	7
Far West	39	8	14	7	41	4	18	6
EDC	29	7	14	2	37	5	24	5

[a]The percentage of engaged time is that percent of time throughout the day that students were observed as engaged in reading or mathematics activities. The achievement rank is the rank order of the residual gain scores.

Note: Rank order correlations for percentage of engaged time and gain in achievement are: for grade one reading, .92; for grade one mathematics, .17; for grade three reading, .80; for grade three mathematics, .78.

Source: Jane A. Stallings and David H. Kaskowitz, Follow Through Classroom Evaluation, 1972-73 (Menlo Park, Calif.: Stanford Research Institute, 1974), Appendixes R-3, R-4, and O.

averaged twenty-four engaged minutes per day (80 percent of thirty minutes), whereas the class of the second teacher averaged thirty-nine engaged minutes because she allotted more time to reading. These differences were reflected in our results. During the ten weeks of our study, the students in the second classroom covered proportionately more books in the series of readers than did the equally bright children in the first classroom. Thus, a teacher is not obligated to maintain high engagement of students at all times; what is more critical is the total number of academically engaged minutes and the amount of content covered.

Unfortunately, it is not yet known how much content coverage or how many academically engaged minutes are necessary for an average student to make reasonable progress, or for a below-average student to cover the material for a year, or for a student who is reading three years below grade level to catch up. These are questions for further research. It seems quite clear, however, that the two variables of content covered and academically engaged minutes have yielded the highest and most consistent correlations with gain in achievement of any of the classroom variables studied to date. The message is clear: What is not taught and attended to in academic areas is not learned.

Descriptive Data on Academically Engaged Minutes

We need to collect more data on the number of academically engaged minutes that typically occur in reading and mathematics in public schools. Some relevant data are coming from Phase III of the Beginning Teacher Evaluation Study carried on at the Far West Laboratory for Educational Research and Development. The study had two parts. In the first part, students were observed in classrooms for five days between October and December, and in the second part they were observed for twelve days between January and May. The results for the two parts, shown in Table 2-2, were consistent. Note that these observations occurred across the entire day, so that all reading and mathematics activities, whether they took place in reading, mathematics, science, or social studies classes, are included in these figures.

A number of interpretations can be made of these new, needed, and welcome data. As mean scores, the data are fairly impressive. On the average, students are engaged for sixty-three to eighty-four minutes in relevant activities in reading and for twenty-six to thirty-one

Table 2-2

Average engaged and allocated minutes per day in reading, mathematics, and other academic subjects in grades two and five

Setting	Engaged minutes	Allocated minutes
Grade two		
Reading	63	85
Mathematics	26	37
Other academic	7	9
Grade five		
Reading	84	113
Mathematics	31	41
Other academic	16	21

Sources: Nikola N. Filby and Richard S. Marliave, *Descriptons of Distributions of ALT within and across Classes during the A-B Period,* Technical Note IV-1a (San Francisco: Far West Laboratory for Educational Research and Development); Charles W. Fisher, Nikola N. Filby, and Richard S. Marliave, *Descriptions of Distributions of ALT within and across Classes in the B-C Period,* Technical Note IV-1b (San Francisco: Far West Laboratory for Educational Research and Development, 1977).

minutes in mathematics. The overall engagement rate is from 70 to 78 percent. But there is still a lack of clear data on what activities the students are engaged in, that is, on how much time is spent studying words and texts and how much time is spent writing or listening to a teacher discuss the general topic of the story without studying words or the meaning of sentences.

Another way of looking at these data is to ask how many minutes in a school day a student spends engaged in *all* academic activities. Here the picture is less impressive. In the second grade, an average of 122 minutes (42 percent) are allocated to all academic subjects. The remainder of the time is spent in nonacademic activities (story time, breaks, lining up, taking seats, quieting down, collecting and distributing money or material, making arrangements for events, free time, music, art). In the total day in the second grade, 43 percent of the time is allocated for academic activities and 57 percent for nonacademic activities. If we take the engagement rate into account, the average student in the second grade is engaged in academic activities for about eighty-nine minutes. In the fifth grade, only 48 percent of the time is allocated to all academic activities, and there are 115 minutes of actual academically engaged time. Many of these nonacademic activities are clearly necessary. We need to think about how many of them can be diminished in view of the problems of dealing with twenty-five to thirty unique children at one time.

DIRECT INSTRUCTION

Direct instruction is a relatively new concept that has been developed independently by a number of researchers in recent years. Its definition is still loose, but it refers to those activities that are directly related to making progress in reading and mathematics and to the settings that promote such activities.

As will be seen from the studies reviewed below, direct instruction refers to academically focused, teacher-directed classrooms using sequenced and structured materials. It refers to teaching activities where goals are clear to students, time allocated for instruction is sufficient and continuous, coverage of content is extensive, the performance of students is monitored, questions are at a low cognitive level so that students can produce many correct responses, and feedback to students is immediate and academically oriented. In direct instruction the teacher controls instructional goals, chooses materials appropriate for the student's ability, and paces the instructional episode. Interaction is characterized as structured, but not authoritarian. Learning takes place in a convivial academic atmosphere. The goal is to move the students through a sequenced set of materials or tasks. Such materials are common across classrooms and have a relatively strong congruence with the tasks on achievement tests. Thus, we are limiting the term "direct instruction" to didactic ends, that is, to instruction toward rational, specific, analytic goals. The didactic exercises that characterize direct instruction are predominant in the materials for reading and mathematics that are currently in use as well as in achievement tests in those subjects.

The results of recent studies are grouped under five general topics: academic focus, grouping students for instruction, whether the teacher or the students select classroom activities, questioning, and management.

Academic Focus

Across a number of studies, the successful teachers were those who maintained a strong academic focus and spent less time in nonacademic activities. For example, in their study of one hundred first-grade and fifty third-grade Follow Through classrooms, Stallings and Kaskowitz found that time spent on activities involving reading or mathematics yielded positive, consistent, and usually significant correlations with gain in achievement, whereas activities involving group time, stories, arts and crafts, active play, or child selection of seating or work group always yielded negative correlations with gain in achievement. Similarly, use of texts, workbooks, or similar instructional materials yielded positive results, whereas use of toys, puzzles, and even academic games always yielded negative results.[20] Similarly, negative correlations with gain in achievement were found by Brophy and Evertson for the frequency of teachers' questions about family background or personal experience and for the frequency of student-initiated contacts involving personal concerns.[21]

In a study comparing the effects of formal and informal styles of teaching, Bennett and his colleagues found that students in formal classrooms showed the highest gain in achievement in reading and mathematics. The teachers in these classrooms reported that they emphasized regular homework assignments, gave weekly tests, marked and graded students' work, and expected students to be quiet.[22] In a study comparing schools that were similar in social and demographic characteristics but where students performed unusually well or unusually poorly on achievement tests, the teachers in the schools with the higher-achieving students were observed to be more task oriented in their classrooms than the teachers in the schools with the low-achieving students.[23] Brophy and Evertson characterized the successful teachers in their study as "determined that their students learn." The cognitively oriented, informal teacher in Bennett's study is another example of an academically focused teacher. "Academic focus" appears to be similar to the term "task oriented" that I used in my 1971 review.[24] This variable has had increased support in recent studies.

Throughout these studies there was no nonacademic activity that yielded positive correlations with achievement in reading and mathematics. This result is somewhat surprising because it has frequently been argued that some nonacademic activities contribute to academic gain by motivating students or by providing additional stimulation. Such indirect enhancement was not evident in any of these studies. The message is clear. What is not taught in academic areas is not learned.

As soon as the importance of a strong academic and cognitive focus is mentioned, we ask about the importance of an affective focus and about such variables as warmth, conviviality of interactions, and concern of the teacher for individual children. In general, classrooms that show high gains in achievement and a high number of academically engaged minutes are usually moderate to high with respect to having a warm classroom atmosphere. For example, in an ethnographic study by Tikunoff, Berliner, and Rist, the higher-achieving classrooms were observed to be convivial, cooperative, democratic, and warm, whereas in the lower-achieving classrooms there was more belittling and shaming of students and use of sarcasm.[25] Furthermore, competitiveness did not distinguish between higher and lower achievement. Other studies, such as that of Solomon and Kendall,[26] found that teachers' criticism of student behavior, shouting, scolding, ridicule, and sarcasm were consistently related negatively to gain in achievement.

In Phase III of the Beginning Teacher Evaluation Study, teachers who were high in academic focus, clarity, and task orientation also tended to be moderate to high on conviviality, warmth, and knowledge of individual students.[27] The worst situation, with respect both to students' engaged time and to gain in achievement, was found when teachers were high in affect but low in cognitive emphasis. Thus, for both academic engagement and gain in achievement it is best to be moderate to high on both academic emphasis and affective focus. But if one is going to be low on one of these, it is preferable to be low on the affective focus.

Studies that have looked at measures of student affect tend to support this finding. In the evaluation of Follow Through programs for children of low-income families, the measure of affect was the Coopersmith Self-esteem Inventory.[28] Assuming that this inventory is a valid measure, there was a high positive correlation between gain in achievement and self-esteem. That is, students in programs with the highest gains in achievement also had the highest scores for academic self-esteem.

These studies indicate that there is no need for teachers to be harsh and demeaning in order for their classes to be high in academically engaged time. Decent, humane, genuine interactions occur in many classrooms that are highly structured and teacher directed.

Direction of Activities

The studies by Soar, by Stallings and Kaskowitz, and by Solomon and Kendall showed that the teachers who most successfully promoted gains in achievement played the role of a strong leader.[29] They directed activities without giving their students choices; approached the subject matter in a direct, businesslike way; organized learning around questions they posed; and remained the center of attention. In contrast, the less successful teachers made the students the center of attention, organized learning around the students' own problems, and joined or participated in student activities.

The converse of teacher-centered instruction—students' choice of activities—yielded negative results. Classrooms organized so that students have a great deal of choice about the activities they will pursue are usually lower in academically engaged time and in achievement. For example, in the study by Soar free choice for students, limited choice for students, and free work groups were associated with lesser gain in achievement. In the study of Stallings and Kaskowitz, selection of seating and work groups by children similarly yielded consistently negative correlations with gain in achievement. These two studies were limited to children from low socioeconomic backgrounds. Solomon and Kendall, however, obtained the same results in their study of children in thirty fourth-grade suburban classrooms. In this study, classrooms in which students chose their own activities and followed their own interests, were responsible for class planning, and were not dependent on the teacher were also classrooms characterized by rowdiness, shouting, noise, and disorderliness. Permissiveness, spontaneity, and lack of control in classrooms were found to be negatively related not only to gain in achievement but also to positive growth in creativity, skills in inquiry, writing ability, and self-esteem. Similarly, a study by Good and Beckerman of student engagement in six sixth-grade classrooms with children of middle- and lower-class backgrounds found the students to be more engaged when the teacher assigned the work than when the students chose the work.[30]

These results do not mean that all attempts at informality were disastrous. Rather, extremes of autonomy and self-direction for students were usually associated with less task orientation and engagement and, consequently, with less gain on all measures. A possible explanation of these results is that, when students have many choices among a variety of activities occurring simultaneously, they are particularly susceptible to distraction and find it difficult to stay on task for a sustained period of time. Evidence for this explanation of distractability was obtained in a thoughtful ecological study by Kounin and Doyle,[31] who found that preschool children were quite attentive to construction tasks at their desks when the materials were arranged beforehand. But when the students had to leave their seats frequently to obtain materials, they were highly susceptible to distraction.

Grouping Students for Learning

The studies of primary-grade classrooms point to the need for adult monitoring and supervising of students' activities. Stallings and Kaskowitz found that time spent working with only one or two students was negatively related to gain in achievement for the class, whereas time spent working with small groups (three to seven students) or with large groups was consistently related positively to achievement. Similarly, classes that had a wide range of concurrent activities also had lower achievement scores, suggesting that teachers were unable to supervise such a variety of activities. Soar discovered that, when students worked in groups under adult supervision, there was a positive and often significant correlation between that grouping pattern and achievement. On the other hand, when small groups met without an adult, the correlations between that grouping pattern and achievement were negative and often significant.

In Phase III of the Beginning Teacher Evaluation Study, the results were equally dramatic.[32] When students were working with a teacher or another adult, they were usually engaged from 79 to 88 percent of the time. Indeed, in these situations most of the nonengaged time came from students who were waiting for instructions or who had finished their work early. When students were in a supervised situation, they were clearly off-task only 4 to 6 percent of the time. In the second setting, when students were working alone and pacing themselves, they were engaged only 68 to 73 percent of the time. They were clearly off-task about 16 percent of the time and spent another 10 percent of their time in transition between activities.

A simple inference may be made from these studies. Students spend more time off-task and in transition when they are working alone, whereas the use of large-group settings allows for more adult supervision. Although many educators prefer that teachers work with one or two children at a time, the reality is that when teachers were working with only one or two children they were unable to provide supervision for the remaining children, who, as a result, had less academically engaged time.

Verbal Interaction

New issues and problems are emerging in the area of questions and discussion. As will be noted below, discussion may not be as prevalent as it was once thought to be, and in the elementary grades verbal behavior (discussion, drill, recitation, and lecturing) appears to occur only about 20 to 30 percent of the time. The elementary teacher today is much more a manager of students, materials, and tasks than a discussion leader.

Factual Questions and Controlled Practice. The frequency of factual single-answer questions is positively related to gain in achievement in most of these studies. Stallings and Kaskowitz found that the frequency of academically focused and direct questions at the two lower levels of Bloom's taxonomy of educational objectives[33] resulted in increased acquisition of basic skills in arithmetic and reading. They identified a pattern of "factual question-student response-teacher feedback" as most functional. Using a sample of students from low-income families similar to those in the Stallings and Kaskowitz study, Soar also found that achievement usually correlated positively with factors that had high loadings from variables such as convergent questions, drill, or questions that have single answers. The results suggest that a pattern of "controlled practice" consisting of factual questions, students' academic responses, and academic feedback from adults appears to be functional.

Medley described two patterns of controlled practice.[34] The successful pattern (that is, a pattern that correlated positively with achievement) for children of low socioeconomic status was one with simple questions, a high percentage of correct answers, help when a student did not know the answer, and infrequent criticism. For students of high socioeconomic status, the successful pattern included harder questions, fewer (about 70 percent) correct answers, and calling on another student when a student did not know the answer. A pattern similar to the second of these patterns had a positive but nonsignificant relationship with achievement in the study by Solomon. Another similar pattern, labeled "recitation," was most successful in moderate amounts in Soar's study of fifth-grade classrooms with children of middle socioeconomic status. Thus, controlled practice appears to be generally functional.

An interesting corollary to the work on controlled practice is apparent from the current research at the Far West Laboratory on the error rate in children's work. The preliminary results show that students make more progress when they spend time on work where they have a low error rate. Time spent on material with which students' error rates were high or even moderate tended to be negatively related to gain in achievement. One possible interpretation of these results is that it pays to spend time reviewing and overlearning material so that students have clearly mastered one activity before moving on to the next. Challenging students with difficult or even moderately difficult material does not pay off as well.

Higher-Order Questions. Although teachers have been urged by teacher educators to ask higher-level cognitive questions, recent research does not support this emphasis. In the Stallings and Kaskowitz study, the frequency of open-ended questions (that is, questions requiring higher-level cognitive responses) was negatively related to gains in achievement. In Soar's study, factors with loadings from variables such as the frequency of divergent or open-ended questions usually correlated negatively with achievement.

In two well-designed experimental studies, teachers were semi-scripted in that they were provided with scripts containing the questions to be asked and the responses to be given.[35] Overall, both studies found that classes where students were asked more recall questions did slightly better on the recall tests, whereas all classes did equally well on tests that included higher-level questions no matter how many higher-level questions had been asked in class. In other words, asking different numbers of higher-level questions had no measurable effect on performance on essays or on tests containing higher-level questions.

Perhaps there is confusion over what is meant by higher-level cognitive questions. Questions that require a student to search the text and make inferences (for example, "What words tell you that Mary felt sad?") are frequently coded as "lower-order" because they have a single answer to be taken from the text, whereas questions of opinion (for example, "How do you think Mary felt?") are frequently coded as "higher-level" because they have more than one possible answer, although none of those answers is found in the text. Therefore, the inferential, lower-level questions, which require searching the texts, may be more representative of academically engaged time.

Many questions coded as "higher-level" may really be personal questions and questions about opinions. In the studies by Stallings and Kaskowitz, by Soar, and by Brophy and Evertson, open-ended questions, questions about personal experience, and questions about opinions were negatively correlated with achievement. Such results suggest that these questions are best categorized as outside the content to be covered and not representative of academically engaged time. Similarly, questions of opinion about a text (for example, "How do you think Mary felt?") may represent nonacademic questions.

If one inspects the comprehension questions that appear in the workbooks for basal readers,[36] one notes a general similarity between the types of questions that appear in those workbooks and the questions that appear on standardized reading tests. In this sense, the workbooks provide opportunities for students to "practice the test." From this point of view, it makes sense to expect that verbal activities that represent controlled practice would be positively related to gain in achievement, whereas the other types of verbal activities would be unrelated to such gains because they are too unlike the types of skills required for the test. Although verbal questions such as "What is a good title for this story?" or "How would you summarize this paragraph?" may be considered lower-level questions by many educators, it is these skills that are required on the tests. Questions coded as requiring interpretive or critical thinking simply do not appear on achievement tests.

Major Classroom Activities

Although many studies in the second cycle have focused on teacher-student interaction, descriptive research in the third cycle shows that students in elementary school classrooms spend most of their time working alone. This seatwork includes reading a book, completing an assignment in a workbook, writing a report, or using special cassette machines. In the study by the Far West Laboratory, students spent 55 to 70 percent of their time in seatwork or self-paced activities.[37] In other studies also involving students from age eight through eleven, students spent 50 to 60 percent of their time doing seatwork.[38] These seatwork activities were *not* trivial. In the Far West Laboratory study only 5 to 6 percent of the assigned tasks were coded as being below the level of the tests that will be used. In formal classrooms, where a single teacher is usually responsible for three reading groups, two-thirds of the students would be expected to be working alone at any one time.

In these same studies, students were recorded as spending from 11 to 30 percent of their time in verbal interaction with the teacher. These activities consisted of drill, recitation, or discussion. In general, then, students in grades one through five are spending about 66 percent of their time working alone and about 25 percent of their time in verbal interaction with a teacher. In learning to read and do mathematics, students proceed through a fairly common series of linear tasks. In doing these tasks, they are interacting with materials much more than they are interacting with a teacher.

The above suggests that management of students is a major problem for teachers. Although it is not difficult to manage a small group of students that a teacher is working with, the management of seatwork for the remaining students is a difficult and relatively unstudied task.

Two major questions that come from these descriptive data are: What is the optimal mixture of teacher-directed and self-paced activities? How can students be kept on-task during self-paced activities? We know little about the optimal mixture of time spent in working with the teacher. The mixture may be different for different subjects and grades. Nor do we have descriptive data on the activities that take place during seatwork. It may be that much of the seatwork during a reading lesson actually consists of writing.

The engagement rates when students work alone tend to run about 68 percent, as compared to 85 percent when they are working with a teacher or another adult. It would seem advantageous to learn how to increase this engagement rate. Researchers could probably learn a good deal from master teachers in this respect, but we have not yet done so. We need also to identify materials that tend to keep students engaged. Another problem arises because, when students work alone, most of the off-task time occurs as "wait time," that is, time when students are waiting for someone to correct their papers or to tell them what to do next. It is important to learn how to diminish this wait time.

THE RESEARCH DISCUSSED

A fairly clear and consistent pattern emerges from the studies that have been cited here. Time spent engaged in relevant content appears to be essential for achievement, and effective classroom teaching of basic skills, therefore, takes place in an environment characterized by an emphasis on academic achievement. Teaching behavior not directly aimed at furthering academic achievement of the kind measured by standardized achievement tests does not result in much academic gain. Teachers who make a difference in students' achievement are those who put students into contact with curriculum materials and find ways to keep them in contact. Although non-academic activities, nonacademic questions, and a concern with a student's opinions and personal life may have motivational value, such activities do not in themselves represent academically engaged time. In addition, as laudable as it may seem to offer choices to students and to have them work on their unique, individualized assignments, such activities are usually low in terms of academically engaged time. The more successful teacher is one who structures and selects the activities, whose students are academically engaged for many minutes each day, who tends to ask questions that have specific answers in a controlled-practice format, who places students in groups where they are supervised by the teacher, and who does all of this in a controlled but convivial classroom.

Value Questions

There is something grim about this picture of direct instruction: large groups, decision making by the teacher, limited choice of materials and activities by students, orderliness, factual questions, limited exploration of ideas, drill, and high percentages of correct answers. One immediate concern is about possible negative side effects.

Although there are a few exceptions, such as are found in the early Follow Through data reported by Stallings, the balance of the data until now does not show negative side effects. In the data reported for the two most recent Follow Through cohorts (for Cohorts III and IV, which entered school in the fall of 1971), the two models with the highest proportion of significant positive results on the Coopersmith Self-esteem Inventory were the Direct Instruction model (in Oregon) and the Behavior Analysis model (in Kansas). These were the two most structured direct instruction programs. Similarly, in the study of middle-class children by Solomon, the factor labeled "control and orderliness" was not only significantly related to gain in achievement but was also significantly related to gain in creativity, skills in inquiry, writing quality, and self-esteem. In Bennett's study, the students in the informal classrooms reported a better attitude toward school, but they also reported more anxiety than was found among students in other classrooms, a finding that matches Wright's report of lower achievement and higher anxiety about tests in informal classrooms.[39]

The image of the formal classroom as a humorless, cold, regimented, military-like workplace simply may not be accurate. Effective formal classrooms are not cold and critical. McDonald found that criticism was relatively rare in California's classrooms and that it was concentrated mainly in the less effective classrooms. Teachers in formal classrooms today are warm, concerned, flexible, and allow much more freedom of movement. But they are also task oriented and determined that children learn.

Didactic and Heuristic Instruction

The above discussion, particularly the points on individualization and student choice, remind us of the age-old controversy in education between a model of didactic, formal, controlled instruction, on the one hand, and heuristic, informal, inquiry-centered, and discovery-oriented instruction, on the other. The evidence reported here suggests that the formal model, with its behavior-analytic, detail-specific, teacher-directed, large-group, and narrow questioning approach is most effective for obtaining gains in reading and mathematics.

On the other hand, there is the more open model of instruction that focuses on inquiry, choice, individualized work, and time for exploration and discovery. Such approaches seem more suitable for achieving intuitive and creative goals. At any rate, using the open model to achieve analytic ends has not been effective.

There are schools that use both approaches, but separately.

Mornings in these schools are spent in structured approaches that concentrate on reading, writing, and mathematics. Afternoons are given to projects, exploration, "messing around," trips, and discussion. Thus, didactic methods are used for didactic ends, and more open methods are used for more open ends. Such an approach is quite prevalent in British junior high schools under the title "skills and frills."

QUESTIONS FOR RESEARCH

The research to date suggests a number of topics that might be studied in the areas of engaged minutes, content covered, individualization, seatwork, and verbal interaction. These topics are discussed below in the hope that others will see them as worthy of study.

There are only a few normative studies on academically engaged minutes, and there is a need for more studies covering a range of grade levels, subject areas, and types of students. Such descriptive studies would include data on engaged minutes for each subject area, engaged minutes for activities within a subject area (for example, reading, writing, and listening activities during reading), and engaged minutes in different contexts (for example, working alone, working on seatwork with teacher supervision). Such studies could also provide descriptions of engaged minutes in different types of classrooms such as formal and informal classrooms. An extension on these studies would be to follow Kounin's lead and try to determine the possible causes for different engagement in different settings.[40] Kounin's idea that signal continuity influences engagement might be applied and extended to elementary school settings.

Although it seems reasonable that a student who has mastered a third-grade text in reading or in mathematics can do work at the fourth-grade level, there has been little research on this topic. Particularly, we do not know which of the many third-grade texts will, if mastered, bring students to fourth-grade competence. Put another way, we do not know how much content needs to be covered or mastered for an average student to make average progress. Similarly, we do not know how many engaged minutes it takes for an average student to complete this work. Children who are reading two or three years below grade level need to spend more time on reading if they are to catch up, but two hours of academically engaged minutes in reading, per day, may be too difficult for them.

In addition, we might study whether all minutes of academically engaged time have equal value. It is possible that certain types and sequences of practice may be more effective than others; it is also possible that time spent on certain published materials is more effective than time spent on other materials. But it may also be that, if students work on materials that are of equivalent difficulty for them, their gains will be equivalent. These topics have not been adequately studied.

The topic of individualizing needs further study. Based on current research, allowing students choice of tasks or activities is negatively related to achievement gain. However, we do not know the value of allowing students other types of choices such as choice of time and sequence for doing prescribed activities, choice of behavior (for example, where to work, when to leave one's seat), and choice of how to think about the subject matter. There are some teachers who have formal, structured classrooms but also encourage and reward students for thinking independently.

The effects of allowing students choice of time and sequence for doing prescribed activities has been studied by Wang in classrooms that used Individually Prescribed Instruction (IPI).[41] Under these conditions, students who had prior experience working alone increased both their attention span and the number of units completed when they had choice over when to do their work. Similarly, in a correlational study of IPI classrooms, Leinhardt found that, although extensive choice was dysfunctional, giving students limited choice (for example, choosing what topic to study or when they needed special tutoring) was positively related to achievement gain.[42] Thus, there is a need for more research on the value of different types of student choice.

Although student choice of task or activities has yielded negative correlations, such results occurred in settings where students were working in different subject areas (for example, reading, science, dance) at the same time. Such a situation may be particularly difficult for a teacher to monitor. An alternative would be to allow students choices of activities *within* the same subject matter, thus allowing them access to more than one set of materials for mastering a skill. The value of this second type of student choice needs to be explored.

Seatwork is also a relatively unstudied area. One area for which descriptive research is sparse is the percentage of time students are engaged when they are in different seatwork contexts. The major contexts for seatwork might be: students working alone with and without teacher supervision and students working with others, with and without teacher supervision. Descriptive studies might follow the suggestions of Kounin and attempt to develop explanations for differing engagement in different contexts.[43]

But the major problem is learning how to manage the engagement of students when they are working alone. As noted above, students spend from 55 to 70 percent of their time working alone. One research approach would be first to identify those teachers who were particularly successful and unsuccessful at this task and then to do intensive study of the teachers' classroom procedures. Some of the questions to study might include: How do these teachers prepare students for their tasks? How do they structure the distribution of materials and the transition from one activity to another? Do successful teachers make rounds or do they work at their desks with an eye out for students? How do they respond to students' requests for help and clarification?

There is relatively little research on the management of seatwork. In separate studies, both Brophy and Evertson and Good and Grouws found that the number of times teachers talked to students about procedures was negatively related to achievement gain, suggesting that effective teachers organized activities so that it was not necessary to talk about procedures. Both investigations also found that teacher-initiated contacts during seatwork were negatively related to achievement, whereas student-initiated private contacts were positively related to achievement.

Many teachers find it difficult to work with a small group of children and to manage seatwork of the other children at the same time. Some teachers have solved this problem by only working with students in a large-group setting. One hopes that other, reasonable, and affective alternatives might be found. A number of investigators are conducting experimental studies aimed at increasing engagement during seatwork, and more experimental studies should be encouraged.

Some of the readers, books, workboxes, and workbooks that students use during seatwork are probably more engaging than others, but we know little about these engaging characteristics. Developing or identifying engaging materials is another topic for study.

Another emerging question is the value of time spent on seatwork compared to time spent in discussion. Some studies have found greater value for teacher-led discussion, whereas others have found value for teacher-supervised seatwork for the whole class. There is a strong similarity between the controlled practice pattern used in discussion and the questions that appear in workbooks. Similar questions are asked in each case, but we do not know when it is more efficient to conduct this practice verbally and when it is more efficient to let the workbooks do it. One type may be more efficient than the other for different types of students. One problem with teacher-led controlled practice is that all students may not participate, yet some students may gain from the responses of the more able students. It is not clear when discussion and when supervised seatwork yields more engaged time.

IN SUMMARY

In this chapter, research on content covered, academically engaged minutes, and direct instruction has been discussed. This approach is a shift from the past practice of looking at teacher variables such as warmth, criticism, clarity, amount of teacher talk, and enthusiasm. There are no lists of essential behaviors for teachers (although there are suggestions); nor is it claimed that any one type of teaching style is inherently superior. Thus, we can recognize the appropriateness of informal classrooms that are high in academically engaged minutes, as well as the inappropriateness of disorderly, formal classrooms.[44]

The research to date also suggests that the following instructional variables are usually associated with content covered, academically engaged minutes, and achievement gain: teachers maintaining a strong academic focus with encouragement and concern for the academic progress of each student; teacher, rather than student, selection of activities; grouping of students into small and large groups for instruction; and using factual questions and controlled practice in teacher-led groups. In addition, the frequency of nonacademic activities such as arts and crafts, reading stories to a group, or questions to students about their personal experience usually are negatively related to achievement gains. This overall pattern might be labeled "direct instruction."

The primary goal of a teacher in terms of reading and mathematics achievement is to obtain sufficient coverage of content and a sufficient number of academically engaged minutes. But a teacher has options. One would be to run a structured, orderly, teacher-directed classroom with an academic focus and with frequent monitoring and supervision of the students. The research suggests that such classrooms are high in academic engagement per minute and can also be warm and encouraging. A teacher could also, however, choose a more flexible setting in which there is more individual work or more student choice. Because students in such settings tend to be lower in terms of academic engagement per minute, a teacher should use such settings only if allotted time can be increased. In all cases, teachers should examine their teaching to determine how successful their current procedures are for obtaining academically engaged minutes. Teachers whose unique blend of procedures is already obtaining sufficient academically engaged minutes need not change their procedures.

NOTES

1. N. L. Gage, "Paradigms for Research on Teaching," in *Handbook of Research on Teaching*, ed. N. L. Gage (Chicago: Rand McNally, 1963), 118.

2. Jacob W. Getzels and Philip W. Jackson, "The Teacher's Personality and Characteristics," in *Handbook of Research on Teaching*, ed. Gage, 574.

3. Barak Rosenshine and Norma F. Furst, "Research on Teacher Performance Criteria," in *Research in Teacher Education: A Symposium*, ed. B. Othanel Smith (Englewood Cliffs, N.J.: Prentice-Hall, 1971), 37-72; id., "The Use of Direct Observation To Study Teaching," in *Second Handbook of Research on Teaching*, ed. Robert M. W. Travers (Chicago: Rand McNally, 1973), 122-183.

4. Donald Medley, *Teacher Competence and Teacher Effectiveness* (Washington, D.C.: American Association of Colleges for Teacher Education, 1977).

5. See, for example, John B. Carroll, "A Model of School Learning," *Teachers College Record* 64 (1963): 723-732; Benjamin S. Bloom, *Human Characteristics and School Learning* (New York: McGraw-Hill, 1976); Annegret Harnischfeger and David Wiley, "The Teaching-Learning Process in Elementary Schools: A Synoptic View," *Curriculum Inquiry* 6 (1976): 6-43; David C. Berliner *et al.*, *Proposal for Phase III of the Beginning Teacher Evaluation Study* (San Francisco: Far West Laboratory for Educational Research and Development, 1976).

6. Harry S. Broudy, "Didactics, Heuristics, and Philetics," *Educational Theory* 22 (1972): 251-261.

7. Douglas A. Pidgeon, *Expectation and Pupil Performance* (Slough, Eng.: National Foundation for Educational Research in England and Wales, 1970).

8. Torsten Husén, *International Study of Achievement in Mathematics: Comparison of Twelve Countries*, Volumes I and II (New York: John Wiley and Sons, 1967); L. C. Comber and John P. Keeves, *Science Education in Nineteen Countries* (New York: John Wiley and Sons, 1973); Sunnyuh Shin Chang and James P. Raths, "The School's Contribution to the Cumulating Deficit," *Journal of Educational Research* 64 (1971): 272-276.

9. Thomas L. Good, Douglas A. Grouws, and Terrill Beckerman, "Curriculum Pacing: Some Empirical Data in Mathematics," *Journal of Curriculum Studies* 10 (1978): 75-82.

10. Beverly J. Armento, "Teacher Verbal Cognitive Behaviors Related to Student Achievement on a Social Science Concept Test," unpub. diss., Indiana University, 1977; Barak Rosenshine, *Teaching Behaviors and Student Achievement* (Slough, Eng .: National Foundation for Educational Research in England and Wales, 1971); Robert E. Shutes, "Verbal Behaviors and Instructional Effectiveness," unpub. diss., Stanford University, 1969.

11. W. Victor Beez, "Influence of Biased Psychological Reports on Teacher Behavior and Pupil Performance," *Proceedings of the Seventy-sixth Annual Convention of the American Psychological Association* (1968), 605-606; Ronald M. Carter, "Locus of Control and Teacher Expectancy as Related to Achievement of Young School Children," unpub. diss., Indiana University, 1969; William E. Brown, "The Influence of Student Information on the Formulation of Teacher Expectancy," unpub. diss., Indiana University, 1969); Rebecca C. Barr, "Instructional Pace Differences and Their Effect on Reading Acquisition," *Reading Research Quarterly* 9 (1973-74): 526-554.

12. Frederick J. McDonald, *Research on Teaching and Its Implications for Policy Making: Report on Phase II of the Beginning Teacher Evaluation Study* (Princeton, N.J.: Educational Testing Service, 1976).

13. Decker F. Walker and Jon Schaffarzick, "Comparing Curricula," *Review of Educational Research* 44 (1974): 83-111.

14. Barak Rosenshine, "Classroom Instruction," in *The Psychology of Teaching Methods*, Seventy-fifth Yearbook of the National Society for the Study of Education, Part I, ed. N. L. Gage (Chicago: University of Chicago Press, 1976), 335-371.

15. Brown, "Influence of Student Information on the Formulation of Teacher Expectancy."

16. McDonald, *Research on Teaching and Its Implications for Policy Making*, 27.

17. Bloom, *Human Characteristics and School Learning*.

18. Jane A. Stallings and David H. Kaskowitz, *Follow Through Classroom Observation Evaluation, 1972-73* (Menlo Park, Calif.: Stanford Research Institute, 1974).

19. N. M. Smith, "Time Allotments and Achievement in Social Studies," unpub. paper, John F. Kennedy Institute for Rehabilitation, Johns Hopkins University, Baltimore, 1976; Wayne W. Welch and Robert G. Bridgham, "Physics

Achievement Gains as a Function of Teaching Duration," *School Science and Mathematics* 68 (1968): 449-454; John T. Guthrie, Victor Martuza, and Mary Seifert, *Impacts of Instructional Time in Reading* (Newark, Del.: International Reading Association, 1976).

20. Stallings and Kaskowitz, *Follow Through Classroom Observation Evaluation.*

21. Jere E. Brophy and Carolyn M. Evertson, *Process-Product Correlations in the Texas Teacher Effectiveness Study: Final Report* (Austin, Tex.: University of Texas, 1974).

22. Neville Bennett *et al., Teaching Styles and Pupil Progress* (Cambridge, Mass.: Harvard University Press, 1976).

23. California State Department of Education, *California School Effectiveness Study: The First Year, 1974-1975* (Sacramento, Calif.: California State Department of Education, 1977).

24. Rosenshine, *Teaching Behaviors and Student Achievement.*

25. William J. Tikunoff, David C. Berliner, and Ray C. Rist, *An Ethnographic Study of the Forty Classrooms of the Beginning Teacher Evaluation Study Known Sample,* Technical Report No. 75-10-5 (San Francisco: Far West Laboratory for Educational Research and Development, 1975).

26. Daniel Solomon and Arthur J. Kendall, *Individual Characteristics and Children's Performance in Varied Educational Settings* (Rockville, Md.: Montgomery County Public Schools, 1976).

27. Nikola N. Filby and Leonard S. Cahen, *Teaching Behavior and Academic Learning Time in the A-B Period,* Technical Note V-1b (San Francisco: Far West Laboratory for Educational Research and Development, 1977).

28. Abt Associates, *Education as Experimentation: A Planned Variation Model,* Volumes III and IV (Cambridge, Mass.: Abt Associates, 1977).

29. Robert S. Soar, *Follow Through Classroom Process Measurement and Pupil Growth (1970-71): Final Report* (Gainesville, Fla.: College of Education, University of Florida, 1973); Stallings and Kaskowitz, *Follow Through Classroom Observation Evaluation, 1972-73;* Solomon and Kendall, *Individual Characteristics and Children's Performance in Varied Educational Settings.*

30. Thomas L. Good and Terrill Beckerman, "Time on Task: A Naturalistic Study in Sixth-grade Classrooms," *Elementary School Journal* 78 (1978): 192-201.

31. Jacob S. Kounin and P. H. Doyle, "Degree of Continuity of a Lesson's Signal System and Task Involvement of Children," *Journal of Educational Psychology* 67 (1975): 159-164.

32. Nikola N. Filby and Richard S. Marliave, *Descriptions of Distributions of ALT within and across Classes during the A-B Period,* Technical Note IV-1a (San Francisco: Far West Laboratory for Educational Research and Development, 1977); Charles W. Fisher, Nikola N. Filby, and Richard S. Marliave, *Descriptions of Distributions of ALT within and across Classes during the B-C Period,* Technical Note IV-1b (San Francisco: Far West Laboratory for Educational Research and Development, 1977).

33. Benjamin S. Bloom, *Taxonomy of Educational Objectives: The Classification of Educational Goals. Handbook 1: Cognitive Domain* (New York: David McKay Co., 1956).

34. Medley, *Teacher Competence and Teacher Effectiveness.*

35. Meredith D. Gall *et al.*, *The Effects of Teacher Use of Questioning Techniques on Student Achievement and Attitude* (San Francisco: Far West Laboratory for Educational Research and Development, 1975); Stanford Program on Teacher Effectiveness, *A Factorially Designed Experiment on Teacher Structuring, Soliciting, and Reacting* (Stanford, Calif.: Stanford Center for Research and Development in Teaching, 1976).

36. Bonnie B. Armbruster, Robert S. Stevens, and Barak Rosenshine, *Comprehension Emphases in Basal Readers and in Standardized Tests* (Urbana, Ill.: Reading Center, College of Education, University of Illinois, 1977).

37. Filby and Marliave, *Descriptions of Distributions of ALT within and across Classes during the A-B Period.*

38. McDonald, *Research on Teaching and Its Implications for Policy Making;* M. J. Angus, K. W. Evans, and B. Parkin, *An Observational Study of Selected Pupil and Teacher Behavior in Open Plan and Conventional Design Classroom,* Technical Report No. 4, Australian Open Area Schools Project (West Perth: Education Department of Western Australia, 1975); Good and Beckerman, "Time on Task: A Naturalistic Study in Sixth-grade Classrooms."

39. Robert J. Wright, "The Affective and Cognitive Consequences of an Open Education Elementary School," *American Educational Research Journal* 12 (1975): 449-468.

40. Kounin and Doyle, "Degree of Continuity of a Lesson's Signal System and Task Involvement of Children"; Jacob S. Kounin and Paul V. Gump, "Signal Systems of Lesson Settings and the Task-related Behavior of Preschool Children," *Journal of Educational Psychology* 66 (1974): 554-562.

41. Margaret C. Wang, *Maximizing the Effective Use of School Time by Teachers and Students* (Pittsburgh, Pa.: Learning Research and Development Center, University of Pittsburgh, 1976).

42. Gaea Leinhardt, *Evaluation of Educational Progress in Individualized Instruction: Third Year Report* (Pittsburgh, Pa.: Learning Research and Development Center, University of Pittsburgh, 1975).

43. Kounin and Gump, "Signal Systems of Lesson Settings and the Task-related Behavior of Preschool Children."

44. Hermine H. Marshall, *Dimensions of Classroom Structure and Functioning Project: Summary of Final Report* (Berkeley, Calif.: School of Education, University of California, 1976), mimeo.

3. Direct Instruction Reconsidered

Penelope L. Peterson

Two decades ago, Richard Anderson reviewed the research studies comparing two basic teaching styles: teacher-centered (directive) and learner-centered (nondirective). In a summary of his research he reported that, of thirty-two studies reviewed, eleven indicated greater learning when learner-centered methods were used, eight indicated greater learning when teacher-centered methods were used, and thirteen indicated that learning was the same regardless of the method used. He concluded:

Much of the research on teaching methods in the last twenty years seems bent on discovering whether "The meek shall inherit the earth," or whether, on the hand, "Nice guys lose." . . . Teacher-centered and learner-centered methods have been repetitiously investigated not because they were well conceived ideas as to *how* one would lead to superior learning, but merely to find out *if* one style was superior to the other. We were not fortunate enough to find that one method is consistently better than or even consistently different from the other; thus, we are now forced to explore new avenues.[1]

The work on this chapter was supported by the Wisconsin Research and Development Center for Individualized Schooling, which is supported in part as a research and development center by funds from the National Institute of Education, Department of Health, Education, and Welfare (Grant No. OB-NIE-G-78-0217).

Now, nearly twenty years after Anderson's review, we seem to be traversing the same old avenue again, only this time the teacher-centered or directive method is called "direct instruction" and the other method is referred to as an "open," "indirect," or "non-traditional" approach.[2] Also, this time there appear to be some well-conceived ideas as to *how* direct instruction will lead to superior learning. As Barak Rosenshine points out in Chapter 2, researchers have moved from a primary concern with teacher behaviors—a concern that began in 1958 with the work of Ned Flanders and Donald Medley—to a focus on student attention or engagement and content covered or "opportunity to learn." Student attention, student engagement, and content covered seem to be increased by certain teaching activities and settings that Rosenshine terms "direct instruction." According to Rosenshine, direct instruction has the following dimensions: an academic focus, a teacher-centered focus, little student choice of activity, use of large groups rather than small groups for instruction, and use of factual questions and controlled practice in instruction.

Recent reviews of research on teaching strongly suggest that direct instruction is the most effective way of teaching.[3] The reviews consider only several of the many studies comparing open and traditional teaching, however, and a closer and more exhaustive survey of the literature suggests that such a conclusion may be simplistic. Direct instruction may be effective for attaining some educational outcomes or objectives, but not for attaining others. Also, direct instruction may be effective for some kinds of students, but not for others. Although Rosenshine has alluded to the idea that different teaching approaches may be effective for different ends and for different types of students, he leaves the reader with the overriding impression that direct instruction is best.[4]

This chapter reviews the research on the effectiveness of direct instruction and related teaching variables.[5] The intent is not to answer whether direct instruction is more effective than more indirect or open ways of teaching. Rather, it is to address other questions: For what educational outcomes is direct instruction most effective and for what kinds of students? For what educational outcomes are indirect or open ways of teaching most effective and for what kinds of students? I review studies that compare direct instruction with more indirect, open, or nontraditional approaches and consider various cognitive outcomes of instruction as well as various affective outcomes. I also discuss the effect of student characteristics on outcomes from both approaches. Most of the research reviewed here was conducted at the elementary school level, but some studies were conducted at the middle school or junior high school levels.

COMPARISONS OF DIRECT AND OPEN INSTRUCTION

In a recent review, Robert Horwitz located nearly two hundred studies that compared educational outcomes of open-classroom teaching with traditional teaching.[6] In these studies, open-classroom teaching was generally referred to as "a style of teaching involving flexibility of space, student choice of activity, richness of learning materials, integration of curriculum areas, and more individual or small-group than large-group instruction."[7] This open style was compared with traditional teaching. Although traditional teaching may not be completely synonymous with "direct instruction" as described by Rosenshine, it is clear that traditional teaching is more direct than open teaching. Furthermore, the characteristics of open teaching described above are the opposite of the characteristics of direct instruction given by Rosenshine.

Horwitz used a "box score" or "voting method" to integrate findings across research studies. For each study he simply tallied whether the results favored open teaching, traditional teaching, or indicated no significant differences. If the results were ambiguous, he counted the study as showing mixed results. After all studies had been reviewed, he tallied the number of studies falling into each of the four categories and then attempted to draw conclusions from the box score results. Typically, the procedure for drawing conclusions from box score results is as follows: If there is a plurality of studies in any one of the categories with fewer studies in other categories, than the category with the plurality is declared the winner. It is assumed that the winning category will provide the best estimate of the direction of the true relationship between the independent and the dependent variable—in this case, the teaching approach and the educational outcome.

One major problem with Horwitz's procedure is that, by basing the tally on the statistical significance of the results rather than on the direction of the results regardless of statistical significance, Horwitz maximized the risk of Type II errors. Gage has suggested that, in view of the small sample sizes in most studies of teaching, "it seems evident that most of the single studies should not be expected to yield statistically significant results."[9] Thus, by relying on statistical significance, Horwitz increased the probability of concluding that no difference existed between direct and open instructional approaches when, in fact, a true difference may have existed.

A second problem with Horwitz's procedure is a deficiency of the box score or voting method in general. The box score or voting method ignores good descriptive information in the studies. As Glass has pointed out: "To know that televised instruction beats traditional classroom instruction in 25 to 30 studies—if, in fact, it does—is not to know whether TV wins by a nose or in a walkaway."[10] Thus, Glass recommends calculating the strength of the experimental effect in each study because it gives the reader an indication of the importance of the relationship rather than just the significance or the nonsignificance. He suggests using "effect size" as a measure of the strength or importance of an effect. Effect size is calculated by subtracting the mean on the outcome variable in the control group from the mean on the same variable in the experimental group and dividing the result by the standard deviation of the control group.[11] This gives an indication of the size of the difference in effect between the two groups in terms of the standard deviation. Effects sizes can then be averaged across studies, and one can determine whether a particular approach makes a greater difference (for example, one standard deviation or more) or much less difference (for example, .5 standard deviation or less).

I attempted to calculate effect size for the studies located by Horwitz and for several additional studies that I found. I reviewed only those studies that compared educational outcomes for open approaches and traditional approaches. Effect size was calculated by subtracting the mean on the outcome in the traditional approach and dividing the result by the standard deviation of the traditional approach. Thus, positive effect sizes were those that favored the open approach, and negative effect sizes were those that favored the traditional approach.

Unfortunately, most of the studies did not contain enough information to permit calculating effect size. Many of the studies were unpublished dissertations, and the dissertation abstracts contained insufficient information. Since the review does not include many unpublished studies, one can only speculate how the results would differ if all unpublished studies were included. In a comparison of the results of published studies and unpublished studies in the field of psychotherapy, Glass reported that published studies showed a slightly larger effect size than unpublished studies: "studies published in books showed an average effect size of $.8\sigma_x$; studies from journals had a mean effect size of $.7\sigma_x$; thesis studies averaged $.6\sigma_x$; and unpublished studies averaged $.5\sigma_x$."[12] One might infer from the above results that, if dissertations and other unpublished studies were included in the present review, the average effect size across studies may be slightly reduced.

A total of forty-five studies did, however, contain sufficient information to permit calculating effect size. After reviewing all of the studies, I calculated the mean and median effect sizes across those studies for twelve different educational outcomes. These results and the results of Horwitz's review are presented in Table 3-1. In the remainder of the chapter, I discuss the results according to the type of educational outcome measured.

COGNITIVE OUTCOMES

Cognitive outcomes included composite achievement, achievement in mathematics, achievement in reading, creativity, and problem solving. Horwitz reviewed 102 studies that investigated composite achievement on standardized tests and found that the plurality of studies indicated no significant difference between open and traditional approaches. When effect sizes were calculated for twenty-five of these studies, they were found to average $-.12$, with the lowest effect size being $-.78$ and the highest effect size being $.41$. Effect sizes were also calculated for studies that provided separate data on achievement in mathematics and reading. The average and range of effect size for reading achievement were similar to those for composite achievement. The data on effect size suggest that, although on the average students tended to achieve more with traditional teaching than with open-classroom teaching, the average effect size was quite small. The difference between the two approaches in terms of students' achievement was about one-tenth of a standard deviation.

Table 3-1

Summary of studies comparing open and traditional teaching approaches

Educational outcomes	Peterson review				Horwitz review[b]				
	Number of studies	Size of effect[a]			Number of studies	Percentage of studies showing—			
		Mean	Median	Range		Open is better	Traditional is better	Mixed results	No difference
Cognitive									
Achievement-composite	25	−.12	−.20	−.78 to +.41	102	14	12	28	46
Achievement-mathematics	18	−.14	−.04	−1.01 to +.58	—	—	—	—	—
Achievement-reading	20	−.13	−.22	−.72 to +.44	—	—	—	—	—
Creativity	11	.18	.32	−.23 to +.50	33	36	0	30	33
Problem solving	1	.98	.98	—	—	—	—	—	—
Affective									
Self-concept	14	.16	.16	−.14 to +1.45	61	25	3	25	47
Attitude toward school	15	.12	.21	−.43 to +.48	57	40	4	25	32
Attitude toward teacher	2	.42	.42	−.29 to +.56	—	—	—	—	—
Curiosity	3	.14	.08	−.17 to +.52	14	43	0	36	21
Locus of control	5	.03	−.14	−.34 to +.70	24	25	4	17	54
Anxiety	5	.07	.41	−.63 to +.69	17	18	29	6	47
Independence	3	.30	.29	+.07 to +.55	23	78	4	9	9

[a] A positive effect size favors the open approach; a negative effect size favors the traditional approach.

[b] From Robert A. Horwitz, "Effects of the 'Open Classroom,'" *Educational Environments and Effects: Evaluation, Policy, and Productivity*, ed. Herbert J. Walberg, (Berkeley, Calif.: McCutchan Publishing Corporation, 1979), chap. 14.

As for creativity, however, the results indicate that students in open approaches tend to be more creative than those in traditional approaches. Creativity was typically assessed with paper-and-pencil tests, and answers were scored for fluency, flexibility, originality, and elaboration. Horwitz found that in a plurality of studies (36 percent), creativity was higher in open approaches than in traditional ones. I found that the average effect size for creativity was .18. In other words, students in open approaches had creativity scores that were, on the average, a fifth of a standard deviation higher than the creativity scores of students in traditional classrooms. In an additional study, which looked at students' ability to solve problems as measured by Raven's Progressive Matrices, it was found that students in open approaches scored approximately one standard deviation higher than students in more traditional approaches. This finding should, however, be regarded as tentative since it is based on only one study.

When taken together, the findings for cognitive outcomes of teaching suggest that the effects of open and more direct or traditional approaches do depend on the type of cognitive outcome. Although the effects in all cases are quite small, they suggest that, with traditional teaching, students tend to perform slightly better on achievement tests, but they do worse on tests of more abstract thinking, such as creativity and problem solving. Conversely, with open teaching, students may perform worse on achievement tests, but they tend to do better when it is necessary to be creative and to solve problems.

AFFECTIVE OUTCOMES

Affective outcomes included self-concept, attitude toward school, attitude toward teacher, curiosity, locus of control, anxiety, and independence. Self-concept, attitude, locus of control, and anxiety were assessed using self-report, paper-and-pencil measures. In some cases, curiosity and independence were assessed with paper-and-pencil measures and in other cases behavioral ratings were used.

The clearest differences between open and traditional approaches appeared for attitude toward school, attitude toward teacher, independence, and curiosity. Horwitz reviewed fifty-seven studies that investigated attitude toward school and found that a plurality (40 percent) favored open instruction. I found that the average effect size for attitude toward school was small—only about .12. A stronger effect appeared for attitude toward teacher. Although only two studies were reviewed, the average effect size was .42. Horwitz found that of twenty-three studies that investigated independence, the vast majority (78 percent) favored the open approach. In other words, students where open approaches were used were more independent than students where traditional approaches were used. The average effect size for three studies was .30, or approximately one-third of a standard deviation. When curiosity was the educational outcome, Horwitz again found that the plurality of studies (43 percent) favored open approaches. Students were more curious in open approaches than in traditional approaches. The average effect size was .14 across three studies.

The research on self-concept, locus of control, and anxiety indicated little difference on these outcomes between open and traditional approaches. On all three outcomes, Horwitz found that the plurality of the studies showed no significant difference between the approaches. For locus of control and anxiety, the average effect size approached zero. The average effect size was larger for self-concept (.16), but was still small.

What the research suggests, therefore, is that open approaches surpass traditional ones in improving students' attitude toward school and toward their teacher and in promoting students' independence and curiosity, but the size of the effect is small. On the other hand. the research on self-concept, locus of control, and anxiety indicates that there is little or no difference between open and traditional approaches on these affective outcomes.

THE EFFECT OF STUDENT CHARACTERISTICS

Seven studies investigated the effect of student characteristics on educational outcome in open and traditional approaches. The results of these studies suggest that the effectiveness of the approach depends on the type of student being taught.

Several studies examined the effect of students' ability on achievement and creativity in open and traditional approaches. Ward and Barcher found that, although the achievement of low-ability students did not differ in open and traditional approaches, the achievement of high-ability students was significantly greater in traditional approaches than in open approaches.[13] Similarly, Bennett found that students with high prior achievement achieved more in traditional approaches than in open approaches, but boys who had low prior achievement did better in open than in traditional approaches.[14] In contrast, Grapko reported that high-ability students did not differ in achievement in open and traditional approaches, but low-ability students did significantly better in traditional approaches.[15] Similarly, Solomon and Kendall found that low-ability students achieved more in traditional approaches. They also found that the achievement of high-ability students depended on their level of compliance or conformity. High-ability students who were low on conformity did better in traditional approaches than in open ones. High-ability students who were moderate or high in their levels of conformity achieved more in open than in traditional approaches.[16]

When creativity was the educational outcome, Ward and Barcher reported that low-ability students did not differ in their creativity in open and traditional classes, but high-ability students were significantly more creative in traditional classes than in open classes.[17] In contrast, Solomon and Kendall found that low-ability students were more creative in traditional approaches, and high-ability students were more creative in open approaches.[18]

The remaining studies examined the effect of student personality and motivation on achievement and attitude in open and traditional approaches. Bennett found that motivated, sociable students who had positive self-concepts achieved more in traditional approaches than in open approaches. Unmotivated, unsociable, nonconforming students who had negative self-concepts achieved more in approaches that were a combination of open and traditional.[19] Papay and his colleagues investigated students' trait anxiety and found that low-anxious students performed better on a mathematics test where a traditional teaching approach was used than where an open approach was used; high-anxious students performed better where an open approach was used than where a traditional approach was used.[20]

Two studies investigated the effect of locus of control on outcomes in open and traditional approaches and reported similar findings. The results reported in the previous section indicated that, when locus of control was considered as an outcome, students in open and traditional approaches did not differ on locus of control. But Wright and DuCette found that students who had an internal locus of control (that is, when they felt that they had personal control over their successes and failures) achieved more in open approaches than in traditional ones. Students who had an external locus of control (that is, when they felt that their successes and failures were due to fate, luck, or other forces outside their control) achieved as well in traditional as in open approaches.[21] Arlin reported similar findings when attitude toward school and attitude toward teacher were the educational outcomes. Internals had more positive attitudes in an open approach than in a traditional approach; externals did not differ in their attitudes in open and traditional approaches.[22] These findings can be explained in terms of the type of student one would expect to do well in an open approach. Since an open approach typically encourages students to take more responsibility for their own learning than a traditional approach, one would expect that a student who has an internal locus of control would be particularly suited to an open approach.

In sum, the findings are inconsistent as to the effect of students' ability on achievement and creativity in open and traditional approaches, and no definitive conclusions can be drawn. But the findings on students' locus of control are provocative and suggest that the effectiveness of the open approach in promoting student achievement and attitude may depend on the individual student's own sense of personal control over his or her actions.

IMPLICATIONS

Rosenshine admits that the picture of direct instruction seems grim: "large groups, decision making by the teacher, limited choice of materials and activities by students, orderliness, factual questions, limited exploration of ideas, drill, and high percentages of correct answers."[23] To me, the picture of direct instruction seems not only grim but unidimensional as well. It assumes that the only important educational objective is to increase measurable student achievement and that all students learn in the same way and thus should be taught in the same way. Yet most educators agree that a broad range of educational goals is important, including increasing students' creativity, independence, curiosity, self-concept, and attitude toward school and learning. Furthermore, a recent survey indicates that taxpayers support a wide variety of social and humanistic goals—not just the so-called basics—for public education and are willing to support higher taxes to help meet these goals.[24]

In this review of the research, we have seen that, although a more direct or traditional teaching approach may be slightly better, on the average, than an open approach for increasing students' achievement, an open approach appears to be better than a more direct approach for increasing students' creativity, independence, curiosity, and favorable attitudes toward school and learning. In addition, the research suggests that some kinds of students may do better in an open approach and others may do better in a more direct approach. The implication is that, if educators want to achieve a wide range of educational objectives and if they want to meet the needs of all students, then neither direct instruction alone nor open-classroom teaching alone is sufficient.

Educators should provide opportunities for students to be exposed to both teaching approaches. One solution would be to reserve part of the school day for direct instruction in reading and mathematics and the remainder of the school day for a more open approach to learning.[25] Another solution now being used in some school districts is to allow parents to select the type of school and classroom best suited to their child's needs for a particular school year. Some students might need a more open approach to become interested in reading while others might need a more structured approach to learn reading. Some students might not need to improve their reading skills, but, rather, they may need to learn to be more independent and curious. The picture thus becomes multidimensional—children learning the basic skills but also learning to be happy, creative, curious, and independent persons in the way they learn best.

NOTES

1. Richard C. Anderson, "Learning in Discussions: A Resume of the Authoritarian-Democratic Studies," *Harvard Educational Review* 29 (1959): 201-215, esp. 211-212.

2. See Chapter 2.

3. See, for example, Barak V. Rosenshine, "Classroom Instruction," in *The Psychology of Teaching Methods*, Seventy-fifth Yearbook of the National Society for the Study of Education, Part I, ed. N. L. Gage (Chicago: University

of Chicago Press, 1976), 335-371; see also Chapter 2 in this volume and N. L. Gage, *The Scientific Basis of the Art of Teaching* (New York: Teachers College Press, 1978), 31-35.

4. See Chapter 2. See also Barak V. Rosenshine, "Review of *Teaching Styles and Pupil Progress* by Neville Bennett," *American Educational Research Journal* 15 (1978): 163-169.

5. I thank Dawn Durst who helped search the literature for this chapter.

6. Robert A. Horwitz, "Effects of the 'Open Classroom,'" in *Educational Environments and Effects: Evaluation, Policy, and Productivity*, ed. Herbert J. Walberg (Berkeley, Calif: McCutchan Publishing Corporation, 1979), chap. 14.

7. *Ibid.*, 7.

8. Richard J. Light and Paul V. Smith, "Accumulating Evidence: Procedures for Resolving Contradictions among Different Research Studies," *Harvard Educational Review* 4 (1971): 429-471.

9. Gage, *The Scientific Basis of the Art of Teaching*, 27.

10. Gene V Glass, "Integrating Findings: The Meta-analysis of Research," in *Review of Research in Education*, Volume V, ed. Lee S. Shulman (Itasca, Ill: F. E. Peacock Publishers, 1977), 359.

11. *Ibid.*, 366.

12. Gene V Glass, "Primary, Secondary, and Meta-analysis of Research," presidential address presented at the meeting of the American Educational Research Association, San Francisco, April 1976, page 42.

13. William D. Ward and Peter R. Barcher, "Reading Achievement and Creativity as Related to Open Classroom Experience," *Journal of Educational Psychology* 67 (1975): 683-691.

14. Neville Bennett, *Teaching Styles and Pupil Progress* (Cambridge, Mass: Harvard University Press, 1976), 80-97.

15. Michael P. Grapko, *A Comparison of Open Space and Traditional Classroom Structures According to Independence Measures in Children, Teachers' Awareness of Children's Personality Variables, and Children's Academic Progress*, Final Report (Toronto: Ontario Department of Education, 1972). ERIC: ED 088 180.

16. Daniel Solomon and Arthur J. Kendall, "Individual Characteristics and Children's Performance in 'Open' and 'Traditional' Classroom Settings," *Journal of Educational Psychology* 68 (1976): 613-625.

17. Ward and Barcher, "Reading Achievement and Creativity as Related to Open Classroom Experience."

18. Solomon and Kendall, "Individual Characteristics and Children's Performance in 'Open' and 'Traditional' Classroom Settings."

19. Bennett, *Teaching Styles and Pupil Progress*, 132-140.

20. James P. Papay *et al.*, "Effects of Trait and State Anxiety on the Performance of Elementary School Children in Traditional and Multiage Classrooms," *Journal of Educational Psychology* 67 (1975): 840-846.

21. Robert J. Wright and Joseph P. DuCette, *Locus of Control and Academic Achievement in Traditional and Non-Traditional Educational Settings*, Unpub. MS, Beaver College, Glenside, Pa., 1976. ERIC: ED 123 203.

22. Marshall Arlin, "The Interaction of Locus of Control, Classroom Structure, and Pupil Satisfaction," *Psychology in the Schools* 12 (1975): 279-286.

23. See Chapter 2.

24. Jeff Browne, "Poll Finds Public Prefers Broad Education Goals," *Milwaukee Journal* July 23, 1978, 9.

25. Rosenshine, "Review of *Teaching Styles and Pupil Progress* by Neville Bennett."

4. College Teaching

James A. Kulik and *Chen-Lin C. Kulik*

The scientific study of learning is now nearly a century old. It has been almost a hundred years since Hermann Ebbinghaus first plotted his progress in learning lists of nonsense syllables, over seventy-five years since Edward L. Thorndike taught cats to escape from puzzle boxes and Ivan Pavlov conditioned dogs to salivate at the sound of a buzzer, and more than fifty years since John B. Watson taught Little Albert to fear a rat. While time has by no means revealed all of the secrets of learning, it has at least indicated the complexity of the subject.

Most educators are reluctant to apply what is learned in laboratory experiments to teaching and learning in colleges. For one thing, laws that describe animal behavior in laboratories may not apply to adult behavior in complex environments. Also, in the minds of many educators college learning even differs from other kinds of school learning in that it takes place in a uniquely free environment. Students have unparalleled freedom to choose among fields, courses, sections, and teachers, and within courses they decide when, how, and how much to study. College students, besides, represent that select group of students who have mastered the basic skills taught at lower levels and are prepared to learn how to make subtle discriminations, use complex concepts and symbols, form independent judgments, and produce original works. These tasks are more complex, and the laws describing learning in other settings may not apply.

If one considers characteristics unique to college learning, it is reasonable to expect that effective college teaching has its own set of characteristics and its own effects on students. It is important to review research on teaching and learning carried out in college classrooms. This chapter provides an overview of fifty years of research on alternatives to the lecture method of teaching before it turns to recent innovations in college teaching that are intended to restructure the student's approach to study and provides some general characteristics of college teaching that make a difference for college learning.

ALTERNATIVES TO THE LECTURE METHOD

There is a long history of research on the laws that determine the effectiveness of college teaching. Empirical studies go back at least to 1923 when Jones investigated learning in lecture classes.[1] Throughout fifty years of research, the lecture method remained the most frequently used approach in college teaching, and so it is not surprising that researchers have used it as the yardstick for measuring other teaching methods. They have asked a number of basic questions: What happens to student learning when a teacher replaces lectures with group discussions in college courses? What is the effect of replacing live lectures with filmed presentations? Is it damaging to have students simply read textbooks instead of attending lectures?

Many researchers compared student performance in college courses taught by lectures and by discussion. Dubin and Taveggia tabulated results from eighty-eight comparisons carried out in thirty-six separate studies.[2] McKeachie[3] and Costin[4] each listed twenty studies comparing achievement in the two kinds of courses, and Bligh,[5] Olmstead,[6] and the Galls[7] drew conclusions about the effectiveness of teaching by lecture versus teaching by discussion.

These reviewers agree on some basic conclusions. First, they point out that teaching by discussion is neither more nor less effective than teaching by lecture when the criterion of effectiveness is learning of factual information. In the eighty-eight comparisons of lecture and discussion methods located by Dubin and Taveggia, for example, the criterion of achievement was performance on a final examination, usually an objective test. In 51 percent of the comparisons, students learned more from lectures, and in 49 percent of the comparisons, they learned more from discussions. Other reviewers describe the same standoff. In McKeachie's twenty-two comparisons from twenty studies, the results were inconsistent from study to study. Thirteen comparisons favored lecturing, seven favored discussions, and two suggested equal use of both methods. McKeachie reported that results of only two of the twenty-two comparisons reached conventional levels of significance. Costin found significant differences in seven of his twenty studies. Learning was greater for lecture classes in two studies; it was greater for discussion classes in five. The other reviewers reached similar conclusions about the effectiveness of lectures and discussions in the teaching of factual information.

The reviewers also agree that teaching by discussion is more effective than teaching by lecture for more ambitious cognitive objectives, such as developing problem-solving ability. Both McKeachie and Costin considered this sort of outcome separately from acquisition of factual content. McKeachie found six studies that compared higher retention and thinking of groups taught by either lecture or discussion. In all six instances, retention or problem solving was somewhat greater for students in the discussion groups, and in three of the instances, differences between groups were large enough to be statistically significant. In five of the studies reviewed by Costin, higher-level cognitive outcomes were measured separately from acquisition of factual information. In each of the studies, the methods produced equivalent results on measures of acquisition of information, but discussion methods were superior in developing higher-level skills. Bligh, Olmstead, and the Galls also concluded that discussion methods are more effective in stimulating thought and in teaching problem-solving skills.

McKeachie, Bligh, and Costin reviewed research on the relative effectiveness of discussion versus lecturing in terms of changing attitudes and found a third area of agreement. Attitudes included interest in the subject, scientific attitudes, general curiosity, democratic attitudes, and so on. McKeachie and Bligh report that the preponderance of comparisons favors teaching by discussion. Costin, however, feels that evidence showing that the discussion method has greater effects on attitude is slight.

Where the reviewers disagree somewhat is in their conclusions about student satisfaction with teaching by lecture versus teaching by discussion. Olmstead reports greater satisfaction in most instances where the discussion method is used, and Costin finds no consistent differences in student satisfaction associated with either of the teaching methods.

Instructional Media

A number of educators predicted that television would radically change the nature of college teaching. These educators recognized some possible drawbacks of television (for example, it reduced the likelihood of student-teacher interaction), but they also saw some strengths. Television could provide drama that few lecturers could create, and it could overcome restrictions of time and place to give students a close-up view of distant persons, places, things, and events. Since videotapes are reusable, they can also be produced with greater care than often went into lectures, and poor-quality videotapes can be withdrawn or remade.

Because of this potential, numerous reasonably well-controlled studies of teaching by television were carried out in the 1950s. Chu and Schramm reported on an analysis of over four hundred comparisons made before 1966 of televised and conventional teaching.[8] In most of the studies there were no significant differences in achievement of students taught by either method. In 15 percent of the studies, however, televised instruction was superior to conventional teaching, while in 12 percent of the cases it was inferior. When Chu and Schramm limited their tabulations to studies of college-level instruction, their results were a bit less favorable to instructional television. In 11 percent of the comparisons instructional television was more effective than traditional instruction, and in 14 percent of the cases it was less effective. In most of the comparisons, however, there were again no differences between the two approaches to teaching. In a more detailed review of research on the effectiveness of instructional television at the college level, Dubin and Hedley also found very little difference between televised and conventional teaching.[9]

More recent research results do little to alter the picture. Kulik and Jaksa report on ten studies carried out in the last decade on the effectiveness of television as an alternative to traditional college teaching.[10] In seven of the ten studies, there were no significant differences in the achievement of students taught by television and conventional face-to-face instruction. Two studies found significantly greater gains on the part of students taught by television, and one study reported significantly greater gains on the part of students taught by conventional methods.

Programmed Instruction

Then, in the 1960s teaching machines stimulated both controversy and research, and programmed instruction promised to revolutionize education. Although the excitement has died down in recent years and the volume of research has decreased, this instructional approach has left its mark on nearly every educational innovation that has followed it.

The research on programmed instruction has been reviewed often. Schramm tabulated thirty-six reports comparing programmed with conventional classroom instruction.[11] Eighteen of the studies reported no significant difference when the groups were measured on the same criterion test, seventeen studies showed a significant superiority for students learning from programs, and one study showed a superiority for students in conventional classes. A number of the studies reviewed by Schramm mentioned a time advantage for the students studying programmed material.

Nash, Muczyk, and Vettori were able to locate over a hundred comparisons of end-of-training performance by learners taught by programmed and conventional methods of instruction.[12] In 36 percent of the studies, groups learning from programmed instruction performed significantly better, in 13 percent of the studies performance was significantly poorer, and in the remaining cases there were no significant differences between the methods. Nash and his colleagues also located thirty-three studies involving a retention measure of performance. Differences between teaching methods were somewhat less pronounced with this criterion of effectiveness. Programmed instruction, however, resulted in a saving in student time in almost all courses where it was investigated. On the average, students in sections taught by programmed instruction spent one-third less time on their courses than students in sections taught by conventional methods.

Since reports reviewed by Schramm and by Nash and his colleagues cover a variety of populations and settings, they provide a poor basis for drawing conclusions about the effectiveness of programmed instruction as an alternative to traditional college teaching. Kulik and Jaksa, however, located a total of nine studies that compared the effectiveness of programmed instruction and conventional instruction in college teaching.[13] In three of the nine courses, achievement was significantly higher in the groups using programmed instruction, as indicated by performance on a final examination. In the remaining six courses, there was no significant difference. There was also evidence that programmed instruction reduced the time required for students to complete course work. Data on this point were available from three of the college courses. In one course, programmed and conventional instruction made equal time demands on students. In two other courses, there was a saving of time with programmed instruction.

Computer-Based Teaching

The most recent hope for an instructional revolution, which came in the 1970s, was based on the computer. It has been used for drill and practice, problem solving, simulation, and tutoring, and in other ways for the direct instruction of students. Both historically and conceptually, the use of computers in teaching is closely related to work in programmed instruction.

There are good recent reviews of research on teaching with computers. Edwards and her colleagues located twenty studies of student achievement in traditional classes and in classes using computer-based teaching as a substitute, in whole or in part, for traditional instruction.[14] In nine of the studies, computer-based teaching led to greater student achievement, and in the remaining studies, there were few or no differences or mixed results for the two teaching methods. In all studies investigating time required for learning, however, it took less time for students to learn with computer-based teaching. Finally, there was some evidence that students learning through computers may not retain as much as students traditionally taught. Two studies showed that students who learned through traditional methods retained more of what they learned than students who learned through computer interactions, and one study showed retention to be equal for the two approaches. While relatively few of the studies reviewed by Edwards and her colleagues were actually carried out in college classrooms, results from the college-level studies were consistent with the general findings.

Jamison and his colleagues felt that no simple and uniform conclusions could be drawn about the effectiveness of computer-based instruction.[15] At the elementary school level, they felt that computer-assisted instruction is apparently effective as a supplement to regular instruction. At the secondary school and college levels, they concluded that computer-based teaching is about as effective as traditional instruction when it is used as a replacement. They also felt that it might result in a substantial saving of student time in some cases.

Kulik and Jaksa reviewed five studies at the college level that compared end-of-course achievement of students in computer-based and traditionally taught classes.[16] Computer-based instruction produced superior performance in a final examination in two of the courses. In the other three studies there was no significant difference between methods. As with programmed instruction, computer-based teaching seemed to lead to substantial savings in student time. Use of a computer resulted in a 40 percent saving of student time in one course and a 33 percent saving of time in another course.

Summary on Alternatives to Lectures

Fifty years of research have produced an enormous number of studies of alternatives to the lecture. These methods differ dramatically in such presumably important characteristics as degree of organization of the material to be learned, learner activity, availability and timing of feedback, and in many other seemingly important ways. And yet, in terms of outcomes, they seem remarkably similar. Few studies have reported large (or even significant) differences in outcomes of demonstrably different approaches to college teaching.

Why have researchers failed to find consistent outcome differences for different teaching methods? There are several possible explanations. First of all, most college courses have two parts: classroom hours and individual study hours. In most college courses students divide their time between classroom instruction and individual study. Research studies reviewed so far have focused on the time students spend in classrooms. Researchers have replaced lecture hours with group discussions, films, exercises at a teaching machine or in a programmed workbook, or exercises at a computer terminal, but these activities do not directly affect individual study time in college courses.

It is possible that individual study has a greater influence than classroom instruction on student achievement in college courses. Although this possibility is unsettling, it gets some support from major investigations of independent study in college carried out in the late 1950s and the 1960s. In large-scale studies at Antioch College and the University of Colorado, investigators found that they could reduce by two-thirds or more the amount of time students spent in classrooms without affecting the students' end-of-course achievement.[17] In the late 1960s Dubin and Taveggia went further, demonstrating that such typical classroom activities as lectures and discussions might be eliminated completely from college teaching without altering student achievement.[18] Pooling data from numerous studies of college teaching conducted between 1924 and 1965, they showed that students learned as much from unsupervised independent study as they did from more conventional approaches to college teaching.

In the 1960s, therefore, a number of college teachers changed their focus from the presentation of classroom instruction to the development of techniques for influencing how, when, how much, and what students studied on their own time. By shifting their focus from group to individual aspects of teaching, these educators hoped to make college teaching more effective. Their work on individualized instruction stimulated an unprecedented amount of research on college teaching.

Other reviewers have cited an additional explanation for the failure to find strong differences among demonstrably different approaches to college teaching. In studies reviewed so far, variables are defined globally and imprecisely. Teaching by "lecture" or "discussion" methods can mean a variety of things. There is considerable variation among lectures and lecturers, among discussions and discussion leaders. Some commentators have severely criticized the practice of comparing global approaches to teaching. If sufficiently analytic research were carried out, these critics suggest, more consistent findings would emerge.

INDIVIDUALIZED INSTRUCTION

Individualized instruction is teaching adapted to the background and aptitude of individual learners. Most systems of individualized instruction are mastery oriented and self-paced, and they rely heavily on instructional materials. Not only do individualized systems of instruction change the use of classroom time, but materials and procedures in individualized teaching are also designed to influence how, when, how much, and what students study on their own time. Individualized systems of instruction represent, therefore, a distinct alternative to conventional forms of college teaching.

Since the 1960s there have been three highly influential approaches to individualized instruction at the college level: Postlethwaite's Audio-Tutorial Method,[19] Bloom's Mastery Learning,[20] and Keller's Personalized System of Instruction (PSI).[21] While all of these methods have adherents, it is Keller's plan that has generated the most research at the college level, and it is the focus of our discussion of individualized approaches to college teaching.

Basic Features of PSI

First used at the University of Brasilia in 1964, PSI was originally developed by psychologists Fred Keller, J. Gilmour Sherman, Carolina Martuscelli Bori, and Rodolfo Azzi. The PSI system devised by Keller and his colleagues has five defining features. The courses are individually paced, mastery oriented, and student proctored. There are printed study guides for communication of information, and a few lectures are included to stimulate and motivate the students.

Course work is divided into topics or units, typically between ten and twenty. At the start of a course, the student receives a printed study guide to direct work on the first unit. The student may work anywhere, including the classroom, to achieve the objectives outlined in the study guide. The student can come to class during regular class hours to receive individual help or, after adequate preparation, simply take a quiz on the unit.

The quiz is evaluated immediately by a proctor, usually an undergraduate student who has studied course material in the previous semester. There is no penalty for failure to pass a first, second, or later quiz on a unit in a PSI course, but the student must pass the quiz, thereby demonstrating mastery, before going on to the next unit. A student thus moves through a PSI course at his or her own pace. Some students meet all course requirements before the term is half finished; others require a full term or even longer.

Research on PSI

Research has produced impressive evidence on the effectiveness of PSI as a total system. More than fifty researchers have carried out studies comparing the educational outcomes in PSI and conventional courses, and a number of people have reviewed the comparative studies.[22] All reviewers have concluded that personalized instruction usually leads to higher levels of achievement and more favorable student attitudes. The sections that follow contain conclusions based on review of all the studies located by different reviewers.

End-of-Course Achievement. The reviewers cite a total of fifty-two reasonably well-controlled and adequately described studies comparing final examination scores in PSI and conventional courses. These are studies in which there is no evidence of nonequivalent comparison groups, differential attrition from comparison groups, or differential prior exposure to examination items by one of the comparison groups. In fifty-one of these studies, performance of PSI students was superior to performance of students in the conventional course, and in forty-seven of the studies the difference between the two kinds of courses was statistically significant. Forty-two of the fifty-two studies reported average final examination scores for PSI and conventional courses. Figure 4-1 gives distributions of average examination scores in the two kinds of classes. In the typical PSI course, the average final examination score was 74 percent; in the typical conventional course, the average final examination score was 66 percent.

Five of the fifty-two studies described performance of students both on multiple-choice tests and on integrative essay tests in both PSI and conventional courses. In each of the five studies, PSI had a pronounced effect both on performance on recognition tests and on tests calling for integrative responses. The superior effectiveness of PSI was somewhat clearer, however, on essay and integrative questions. In one study, for example, five percentage points separated group means of PSI and conventional classes on recognition items

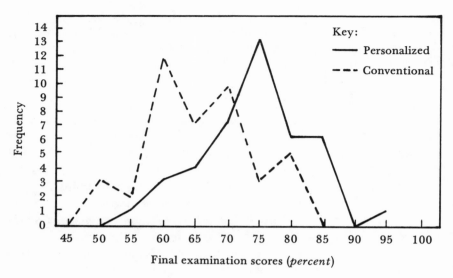

Figure 4-1

Distribution of average final examination scores

in 42 PSI and conventional classes

(PSI mean = 72 percent; conventional mean = 67 percent), but ten percentage points separated group means of PSI and conventional classes on recall and application items (PSI mean = 68 percent; conventional mean = 58 percent).[23] Figure 4-2 is a composite figure, based on the three studies with relevant data, showing performance of PSI and conventional groups on objective and essay items on final examinations.

A number of investigators have looked at examination scores of high- and low-aptitude students within PSI and conventional classes. In some studies PSI had its strongest effect on high-aptitude students,[24] in some classes it had its strongest effect on low-aptitude students,[25] and, in some cases, effects seemed equally strong on high- and low-aptitude students.[26] This last finding appears to be the most nearly typical. Figure 4-3 is a composite based on results from nine studies of the performance of high- and low-aptitude students in PSI and conventional classes. The average correlation between aptitude and achievement is PSI classes was .51; the average correlation for conventional classes was .52.

Retention and Transfer. As important as final examinations are,

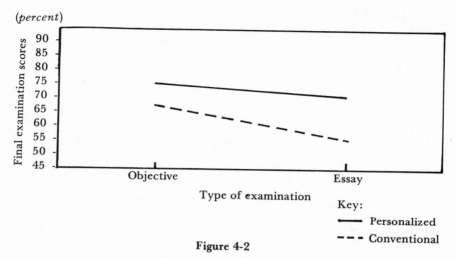

Figure 4-2

**Average scores on objective and essay final examinations
in PSI and conventional classes**

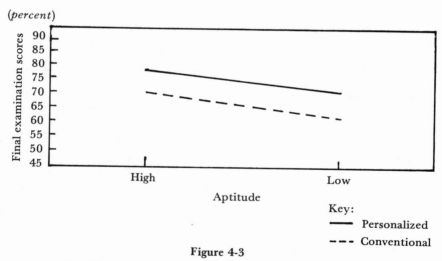

Figure 4-3

**Average final examination scores of low- and high-aptitude groups
in PSI and conventional classes**

they have their limitations. They do not test for long-range retention of facts, principles, and concepts, and they seldom test students for ability to make major applications of concepts in new situations. Studies of retention and transfer, therefore, are important supplements to studies of end-of-course achievement.

With the help of Beverly Smith, we were able to locate nine studies of long-range retention of PSI course content.[27] These studies reported on retention over intervals ranging from three weeks to fifteen months after the completion of a course. In each of the studies, the PSI students performed better on a follow-up examination than students from lecture courses, and in each study the difference between groups reached statistical significance. In most of the studies, differences at the time of follow-up were somewhat greater than differences at the time of final examinations. Figure 4-4 is a composite of results from these nine studies.

Transfer studies shed more light on the nature of student learning in PSI classes. In a transfer study, groups of students learn course material by experimental and control methods. Effectiveness of the methods is measured by comparing performance of the two groups on a subsequent standard learning task. Suppose that one group of

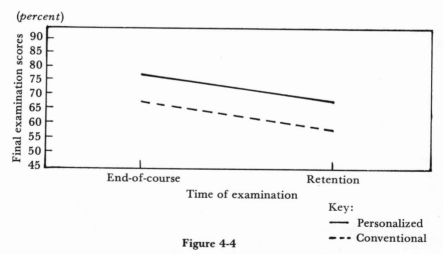

Figure 4-4

**Average scores on end-of-course and retention examinations
in PSI and conventional classes**

students takes Mathematics 1 in a personalized format and a second comparable group takes the same course in a conventional format. How will the groups do in a common Mathematics 2 course? We located five comparisons of transfer effects, and in each of these comparisons PSI students outperformed other students in a follow-up course—even though the follow-up courses were taught by conventional methods by other teachers.[28]

Retention and transfer studies suggest that PSI promotes something more than rote memorization. Facts, information, and concepts are quickly forgotten if they are not organized and interrelated in memory. The long-range retention of PSI learners suggests organized learning. In addition, transfer studies show that PSI students learn general skills that transfer to new situations. It seems likely, therefore, that PSI can be helpful to teachers not only in communicating facts to students, but also in achieving more ambitious instructional goals.

Time to Complete Learning. In addition to knowing that PSI is an effective teaching method, it is important to know whether it makes reasonable time demands on students. Early self-report studies suggested that students put more time and effort into PSI courses. At the College of Engineering at the University of Texas at Austin, for example, nearly 90 percent of the students in PSI courses felt that work requirements were greater than they were in lecture courses in the same areas; the remaining students felt that about the same amount of effort was required.[29] No one felt that the amount of time required in PSI sections was less. Other investigators who collected student self-reports at the end of courses confirmed these findings.

Recent studies, using an improved methodology, have reported different results. Researchers at the University of Utah, for example, performed a careful observational study.[30] They deposited in a special study center all the materials for a course in beginning psychology, and then they monitored the amount of study time spent by students enrolled in PSI and lecture sections of the course. For each student they noted time of entry, course material requested, and time of exit from the study center. The average study time of students in the PSI section was 45.5 hours. Time requirements for lecture students were nearly equal: 19 hours for lecture attendance and 30.2 hours of study time. Other investigators have since confirmed these findings. Whenever students have reported study times frequently during a course rather than once at the end of a semester, they report overall time requirements for PSI courses that are consistent with time requirements for conventional ones.

Student Satisfaction. Most investigators have found that students react favorably to PSI courses, but they have documented their findings in different ways. First, some investigators have collected open-ended course evaluations from students. Judging from published reports, only one or two students in a typical class of fifty react negatively to the PSI format. Other investigators have asked students to compare their PSI courses to the typical course that they have taken in college. In representative studies at the College of Engineering at the University of Texas at Austin, about 70 percent of the PSI students consider the method better than the lecture approach, about 20 percent consider the two methods about equal, and about 10 percent prefer the lecture method. Finally, a number of investigators have compared the student ratings from PSI courses to ratings from conventionally taught courses. In eight out of nine cases, PSI ratings are higher than those from lecture courses.[31]

PSI in Review

In the past ten years, educational research has established that Keller's Personalized System of Instruction is effective in promoting student achievement. Its educational record stands in stark contrast to that of earlier alternatives to the lecture method of teaching, for its use has consistently improved student performance on final examinations in college courses. Its superiority has been apparent on both objective tests and integrative essay tests, and with both high- and low-aptitude students. In addition, PSI has produced superior long-range recall of course content, and it has proved to be a highly attractive learning method to college students. Finally, while producing consistently superior student learning, Keller's system has not increased the time students spend on college courses.

COMPONENTS OF EFFECTIVE COLLEGE TEACHING

When researchers establish that one approach to teaching is more effective than others, they have the beginnings of a science of instruction. A next step is to find out what makes a certain approach superior. Researchers have carried out many analytic studies designed to isolate effective features in college teaching in the past fifty years. They have studied, for example, the instructional effects of different class sizes, of student-centered versus instructor-centered discussions, of variations in teacher humor, and so on. Manipulations of such features of classroom instruction have seldom produced strong or consistent effects on student achievement. Manipulations that affect how, when, how much, and what students study individually, on the other hand, have produced more consistent results.

Frequent Quizzing

In many conventional courses, teachers evaluate student performance by giving one or two one-hour quizzes during a term and then administering a final examination. In other college courses, teachers give weekly quizzes and then a final examination. Scores on final examinations are almost invariably better in courses with frequent quizzes,[32] and so it appears that frequent quizzing leads to improved student performance in college classes.

There are at least two possible explanations. First, with more frequent quizzes students can receive more feedback about performance. They are usually asked more quiz questions and spend more time listening to class discussions of quiz answers. The studies by Dustin and by Keys, however, controlled for sheer amount of feedback and still found that frequent quizzes had a beneficial effect on students' performance. In these studies, teachers did not discuss examinations in class and gave experimental and control groups exactly the same examination questions. Dustin has suggested therefore that frequency of quizzing also affects students' performance by influencing study behavior, either the amount students study or their distribution of study time.

Research on individualized instruction also demonstrates the importance of frequent quizzing in college teaching. In a typical PSI course, for example, students take quizzes frequently, perhaps fifteen to eighteen in the course of a term. In a few experimental studies, however, investigators have lengthened units in PSI courses so that students were required to show mastery on quizzes for only four or five long units. Some studies have found significantly poorer performance on final examinations when there were fewer quizzes.[33] PSI researchers have also investigated other effects of number of quizzes in individualized classes. For example, in one study it was found that students needed more calendar days but not more total hours to complete PSI courses when number of quizzes was increased,[34] while another investigator found no difference in student ratings between comparison groups taught with few or many quizzes.[35]

Immediate Feedback

In addition to establishing that frequent quizzing improves student performance in college classes, Pressey's study showed that quizzes influence student learning most when students receive immediate feedback on the accuracy of their answers.[36] In Pressey's study, final examination scores of students who received such feedback on quizzes were typically several points higher than scores of students for whom feedback was delayed. A number of researchers have since confirmed Pressey's findings.

Calhoun, for example, studied the effect of immediate feedback in individualized courses. In his study, four of six groups received immediate feedback on quiz performance from a proctor. For the remaining two groups, feedback was delayed until the next class and came either from a proctor or in written form. Calhoun found that achievement was higher whenever feedback was immediate. Achievement was significantly lower in the two conditions where feedback was delayed.[37]

Other studies support Calhoun's finding.[38] In these studies, the investigators compared conventional PSI groups to groups that received delayed written feedback on quiz performance. Farmer and his associates reported poor performance on final examinations for students who received delayed quiz evaluations throughout the course. In Johnson and Sulzer-Azaroff's study, there was a high withdrawal rate from a group that received delayed evaluations. These studies are less definitive than Calhoun's, however, since two factors are confounded in them: immediate versus delayed feedback and proctor-mediated versus written evaluation. Whenever feedback was delayed in these studies, it was given in written form; whenever it was immediate, it was provided by a proctor.

Studies by other investigators strongly suggest that it is the timing of feedback, not the form, that is the critical factor in producing the experimental effects in these experiments. We, in this case with the help of Peter Jaksa, have reviewed five studies that compared effectiveness of feedback given by a proctor with effectiveness of feedback given without proctor interaction. Proctorial interactions did not raise student achievement in any of these studies. In two of the studies, in fact, student achievement was somewhat better with less proctoring. Other studies reviewed show equivalent end-of-course achievement for students whose quizzes were self-scored and for students whose quizzes were proctor-scored.[39] How students receive feedback seems less important than that they receive it immediately.

A number of verbal learning studies carried out in conventional classrooms during the past decade seem to challenge the principle that learning is improved when feedback promptly follows one's behavior. These studies report an effect labeled the Delay-Retention Effect (DRE): with meaningful multiple-choice tests, learners who receive immediate feedback retain less than learners for whom feedback is presented after a period of delay. It has been shown, however, that this effect occurs only when testing material far exceeds the learner's level of ability or when test answers are so readily available that learners copy them without trying to reach their own solutions.[40] Studies of DRE do not challenge the superiority of immediate feedback under testing conditions that usually prevail in classrooms.

Required Remediation

A number of investigators have also demonstrated that student achievement is further enhanced when students are required to re-study and repeat quizzes if they do not reach a defined level of mastery. Pressey provided an early demonstration of the importance of requiring remediation of poor performance in college courses.[41] Since Pressey's study, numerous other investigators have produced data on the importance of required remediation in college teaching.

We, again with Jaksa, have reviewed seven studies in which investigators compared the performance of two groups of students taught with differing remediation requirements.[42] In these seven investigations, further study and retesting were required of students in an experimental group whenever unit-quiz performance failed to reach a predefined level of excellence (usually 90 percent). In another group, remediation was not required when students failed to reach this level. In each of the nine comparisons cited in the seven studies, the group that required remediation did better on a final examination than the group for which remediation was not required. In five of the nine comparisons, differences were great enough to be considered statistically reliable.

In addition to showing that required remediation usually leads to higher performance on final examinations, we reviewed evidence that suggests that a remediation requirement has little effect on the proportion of students who complete courses. A remediation require- ment also seems not to affect the overall satisfaction of students with their college courses.

Effective Components of College Teaching in Review

Research studies suggest that college teachers can often improve their effectiveness by focusing on conditions of learning in their courses. Three conditions seem especially important. Students are most likely to achieve course goals when they move through course material step by step, with examination of proficiency at each step; when they receive immediate feedback on each examination; and when they must restudy material each time an examination shows that they have not achieved proficiency. Manipulation of other aspects of teaching may also make a difference for student learning. At this point, however, research results on other components of college teaching are either too inconsistent or too sketchy to warrant further confident conclusions.

Why do these features make a difference? While the research evidence is not all in, some speculation is possible. In college courses with many quizzes, students study differently.[43] They may not study more, but, instead of cramming for one or two major examinations, they distribute their study time over a term in preparing for many small quizzes. On college learning, just as in many other learning situations, distributed practice may be superior to massed practice. In addition, when students receive immediate feedback on their examinations, they have a chance to correct misunderstandings before errors are consolidated and interfere with new learning. Finally, a remediation requirement ensures that these errors are corrected, and that, at some point, each student has a chance to respond correctly to each important kind of question asked in a college class.

Research on college teaching methods has a long history, much of it based on false leads, frustrations, and inconsistent findings.

Dubin and Taveggia summarized forty years of this history in *The Teaching-Learning Paradox*. On the basis of their statistical integration of results reported in the major reviews of research on college teaching, they "reported the results of a reanalysis of the data from 91 comparative studies of college teaching technologies conducted between 1924 and 1965." And they concluded that the data "demonstrate clearly and unequivocally that there is no measurable difference among truly distinctive methods of college instruction when evaluated by student performance on final examinations."[44]

In the past ten years, however, evidence has accumulated that individualized teaching methods can make a difference in the outcomes of college teaching. In numerous comparisons, for example, Keller's individualized approach to instruction has produced better results than conventional college teaching. Measures in these studies included end-of-course performance, retention and transfer, and student satisfaction. By any of these measures, the Keller plan is more effective than conventional approaches to college teaching.

Why have so many attempts to improve college teaching failed over the past half century? One possible explanation is their focus on classroom instruction rather than on individual study by students. Almost all college courses are divided into these two parts: classroom instruction and individual study by students on their own time. Most of the teaching innovations of the past fifty years have focused on classroom hours. Researchers have studied instructional effects of various replacements for the lecture: discussions, computer exercises, films, television, and so on. While such innovations change student behavior in the classroom, they apparently have little effect on what students do after class. Lecture students and students in more innovative college classrooms read assigned materials, review their notes, write term papers, talk to fellow students, cram for midterm and final examinations, and so on.

Individualized instruction, on the other hand, focuses on students' individual study time and neglects (and sometimes even eliminates) group activities in the classroom. Individualized systems of college teaching are designed to influence how, how much, when, and what students study on their own. Three features of individualized college teaching appear to have especially clear effects on student study: the number of times students are examined on their proficiency, the timing of the feedback after each examination, and the degree to which students are required to correct any deficiencies revealed in the examination. In research carried out in both conventional and individualized college courses, frequent quizzing, immediate feedback, and a remediation requirement have consistently increased the effectiveness of college courses.

NOTES

1. Harold E. Jones, "Experimental Studies of College Teaching," *Archives of Psychology*, 68 (1923): entire issue.

2. Robert Dubin and Thomas C. Taveggia, *The Teaching-Learning Paradox* (Eugene, Ore.: Center for the Advanced Study of Educational Administration, University of Oregon, 1968).

3. Wilbert J. McKeachie, *Research on College Teaching: A Review*, ERIC Clearinghouse on Higher Education Report No. 6 (Washington, D.C.: George Washington University, 1970).

4. Frank Costin, "Lecturing versus Other Methods of Teaching," *British Journal of Teaching* 3 (1972): 4-30.

5. D. A. Bligh, *What's the Use of Lectures?* (Middlesex, Eng.: Penguin Books, 1972).

6. J. A. Olmstead, *Small-Group Instruction: Theory and Practice* (Alexandria, Va.: Human Resources Research Organization, 1974).

7. Meredith D. Gall and Joyce P. Gall, "The Discussion Method," in *The Psychology of Teaching Methods*, Seventy-fifth Yearbook of the National Society for the Study of Education, Part I, ed. Nathaniel L. Gage (Chicago: University of Chicago Press, 1976), 166-216.

8. Godwin C. Chu and Wilbur Schramm, *Learning from Television: What the Research Says* (Washington, D.C.: National Association of Educational Broadcasters, 1967).

9. Robert Dubin and R. Alan Hedley, *The Medium May Be Related to the Message: College Instruction by TV* (Eugene, Ore.: Center for the Advanced Study of Educational Administration, University of Oregon, 1969).

10. James A. Kulik and Peter Jaksa, "A Review of Research on PSI and Other Educational Technologies in College Teaching," *Educational Technology* 17 (1977): 12-19.

11. Wilbur Schramm, *The Research on Programmed Instruction: An Annotated Bibliography*, U.S. Office of Education Publication No. OE-34034 (Washington, D.C.: U.S. Government Printing Office, 1964).

12. Allan N. Nash, Jan P. Muczyk, and Frank L. Vettori, "The Relative Practical Effectiveness of Programmed Instruction," *Personnel Psychology* 24 (1971): 397-418.

13. Kulik and Jaksa, "Review of Research on PSI and Other Educational Technologies."

14. Judith Edwards *et al.*, "How Effective Is CAI?: A Review of the Research," *Educational Leadership* 33 (1975): 147-153.

15. Dean Jamison, Patrick Suppes, and Stuart Wells, "The Effectiveness of Alternative Instructional Media: A Survey," *Review of Educational Research* 44 (1974): 1-67.

16. Kulik and Jaksa, "A Review of Research on PSI and Other Educational Technologies."

17. Ruth Churchill and Samuel Baskin, *Experiments on Independent Study* (Yellow Springs, Ohio: Antioch College, 1958); Howard E. Gruber and Morris Weitman, *Self-directed Study: Experiments in Higher Education,* Behavior Research Laboratory Report No. 19 (Boulder: University of Colorado, 1962).

18. Dubin and Taveggia, *Teaching-Learning Paradox.*

19. S. N. Postlethwaite, K. Novak, and H. T. Murray, Jr., *An Integrated Experience Approach to Learning* (Minneapolis, Minn.: Burgess Publishing Co., 1964).

20. Benjamin S. Bloom, *Human Characteristics and School Learning* (New York: McGraw-Hill Book Co., 1976).

21. Fred S. Keller, "Goodbye, Teacher . . . ," *Journal of Applied Behavioral Analysis* 1 (1968): 79-89.

22. D. E. Hursh, "Personalized Systems of Instruction: What Do the Data Indicate?" *Journal of Personalized Instruction* 1 (1976): 91-105; Kent R. Johnson and Robert S. Ruskin, *Behavioral Instruction: An Evaluative Review* (Washington, D.C.: American Psychological Association, 1977); James A. Kulik, Chen-Lin Kulik, and Beverly B. Smith, "Research on the Personalized System of Instruction," *Programmed Learning and Educational Technology* 13 (1976): 23-30; Arthur L. Robin, "Behavioral Instruction in the College Classroom," *Review of Educational Research* 46 (1976): 313-354; B. A. Ryan, *Keller's Personalized System of Instruction: An Appraisal* (Washington, D.C.: American Psychological Association, 1974); Thomas C. Taveggia, "Personalized Instruction: A Summary of Comparative Research, 1967-1974," *American Journal of Physics* 44 (1976): 1028-1033.

23. Charles J. Morris and G. McA. Kimbrell, "Performance and Attitudinal Effects of the Keller Method in an Introductory Psychology Course," *Psychological Record* 22 (1972): 523-530.

24. Chen-Lin Kulik and James A. Kulik, "PSI and the Mastery Model," in *Personalized Instruction in Higher Education,* ed. B. A. Green, Jr. (Washington, D.C.: Center for Personalized Instruction, 1976).

25. Ernest T. Pascarella, "Aptitude-Treatment Interaction in a College Calculus Course Taught in Personalized System of Instruction and Conventional Formats," paper presented at the annual meeting of the American Educational Research Association, New York, April 1977.

26. David G. Born and Michael L. Davis, "Amount and Distribution of Study in a Personalized Instruction Course and in a Lecture Course," *Journal of Applied Behavior Analysis* 7 (1974): 365-375.

27. Kulik, Kulik, and Smith, "Research on the Personalized System of Instruction."

28. *Ibid.*

29. L. L. Haberock *et al.*, "Theory of PSI Evaluated for Engineering Education," *IEEE Transactions on Education*, E-15 (1972): 25-29.

30. Born and Davis, "Amount and Distribution of Study in a Personalized Instruction Course and in a Lecture Course."

31. Kulik, Kulik, and Smith, "Research on the Personalized System of Instruction."

32. David Dustin, "Some Effects of Exam Frequency," *Psychological Report* 21 (1971): 409-414; Mildred L. Fitch, A. J. Drucker, and J. A. Norton, Jr., "Frequent Testing as a Motivating Factor in Large Lecture Classes," *Journal of Educational Psychology* 42 (1951): 1-20; Noel Keys, "The Influence on Learning and Retention of Weekly as Opposed to Monthly Tests," *ibid.*, 25 (1934): 427-436; Sidney L. Pressey, "Development and Appraisal of Devices Providing Immediate Automatic Scoring of Objective Tests and Concomitant Self-instruction," *Journal of Psychology* 29 (1950): 417-447; Austin H. Turney, "The Effect of Frequent Short Objective Tests upon the Achievement of College Students in Educational Psychology," *School and Society* 33 (1931): 760-762.

33. James F. Calhoun, "The Combination of Elements in the Personalized System of Instruction," *Teaching of Psychology* 3 (1976): 73-76; George Semb, "Personalized Instruction: The Effects of Grading Criteria and Assignment Length on College Student Test Performance," *Journal of Applied Behavior Analysis* 7 (1974): 61-69.

34. A. A. Prohuit, M. J. Kulieke, and H. R. Manasse, "Relationship between the Number of Units and the Amount of Time to Complete the Units across Courses," paper presented at the Fourth National Conference of the Center for Personalized Instruction, San Francisco, April 1977.

35. Calhoun, "Combination of Elements in the Personalized System of Instruction."

36. Pressey, "Development and Appraisal of Devices Providing Immediate Automatic Scoring of Objective Tests and Concomitant Self-instruction."

37. Calhoun, "The Combination of Elements in the Personalized System of Instruction."

38. See, for example, John Farmer *et al.*, "The Role of Proctoring in Personalized Instruction," *Journal of Applied Behavior Analysis* 5 (1972): 401-404; Kent R. Johnson and Beth Sulzer-Azaroff, "The Effects of Different Proctoring Systems upon Student Examination Performance and Preference," in *Research and Technology in College and University Teaching*, ed. James M. Johnston and George W. O'Neill (Gainesville, Fla.: Society for Behavioral Technology and Engineering, Psychology Department, University of Florida, 1975).

39. James A. Kulik, Peter Jaksa, and Chen-Lin Kulik, "Component Features of Keller's Personalized System of Instruction," unpub. MS, Center for Research on Learning and Teaching, University of Michigan, 1977).

40. Raymond W. Kulhavy, "Feedback in Written Instruction," *Review of Educational Research* 47 (1977): 211-232.

41. Pressey, "Development and Appraisal of Devices Providing Immediate Automatic Scoring of Objective Tests and Concomitant Self-instruction."

42. Kulik, Jaksa, and Kulik, "Component Features of Keller's Personalized System of Instruction."

43. Dustin, "Some Effects of Exam Frequency."

44. Dubin and Taveggia, *The Teaching-Learning Paradox*, 35.

PART TWO
Recent Studies
in
Research on Teaching

5. Emotional Climate and Management

Robert S. Soar and *Ruth M. Soar*

For more than a decade we have been studying the effectiveness of teachers. In this chapter we have organized four studies completed during that time around a paradigm for thinking about classroom management and an environment that is related to pupil learning. Developmental changes have occurred in the instruments and the design, but parallels across the studies are considerable, which means that similarities in findings across the studies may be more meaningful than is typically true.

THE STUDIES

Study SC 3-6 involved fifty-five urban classrooms in central South Carolina, grades three through six, all white pupils spanning all socioeconomic levels but with the upper levels overrepresented.[1] Study FT 1 involved twenty first-grade classrooms in Project Follow Through, with both black and white pupils, predominantly disadvantaged.[2] Study Fla 5 involved fifty-nine fifth-grade classrooms in northern Florida, where all socioeconomic levels were represented but the lower levels were more strongly represented, and where the ratio between black and white, boys and girls, rural and urban was approximately even.[3] Study Fla 1, also done in northern Florida, was of twenty-two first-grade urban classrooms, with black and white pupils, that spanned the socioeconomic levels.[4]

In all of the studies pupil standing was measured in the fall and in the spring, and these measures were reduced to measures of mean regressed gain for each classroom. The achievement measures emphasized skills, but, in three of the four studies, both measures of lower cognitive-level attainment and noncognitive measures were included. In the last two studies, measures of socioeconomic status were collected as well.

In all the studies, classroom observation was carried out during the middle of the year. Study SC 3-6 used two observation instruments, the Flanders system[5] and a low-inference sign system that stressed nonverbal behavior and expression of affect. In the latter three studies, four observation instruments were used: one examined classroom management by the teacher, the response of pupils to it, and the expression of affect in the classroom; another identified the development of subject matter in ways that were consonant or dissonant with Dewey's experimentalism; a third looked at the cognitive level of the interaction between teachers and pupils following Bloom's taxonomy;[6] and the fourth observation instrument was a category system that was an extension of the Flanders system. In all studies, the observation items were factor analyzed to pool items into measures that reduced redundancy, and the classrooms were then factor scored on the resulting dimensions.

The central focus of the research was *observable* behavior in the classroom. As such, it has little to say about curriculum or the organization of subject matter for presentation to pupils except as those are reflected in behavior in the classroom. Similarly, it says nothing about the particular subject matter being worked on or the present level of knowledge of the pupils.

THE PARADIGM

The paradigm used to organize these results was not the starting point for the research; rather, it emerged both from the behavior measures that had been differentiated by factor analysis and also from differences in the ways in which these measures were related to pupil outcomes. It is an inductively derived system for organizing portions of the results of these studies in a way that may be more comprehensible. We hope the paradigm will serve as a set of "spectacles," by providing a set of concepts through which one can view the classroom environment, thereby giving order and coherence to this set of research findings and others. It is presented first, followed by descriptions of classrooms as a means of clarifying the terms employed and the distinctions being made. Finally, the results of the four studies are presented.

The paradigm appears in Figure 5-1. The major headings, "emotional climate" and "teacher management" (or control) are parallel to factors that emerged from earlier studies of leadership in adult work groups[7] and were found to be relatively independent.[8] However, "emotional climate" is not often separated from "management" in the thinking of educators; nor are the three areas of pupil activities distinguished from each other. But there is some evidence that such distinctions are useful when one is attempting to identify effective teaching.

Emotional climate and teacher management are combined in the traditional concept of permissiveness, which suggests that the permissive teacher is warm and supportive and shares decision making with pupils. The nonpermissive teacher is seen as negative and critical, directing the activities of the classroom with firmness. Our early work indicated, however, that classrooms with a positive emotional tone either may be tightly organized and teacher directed (as the typical contingency-management classroom is), or may have little organization or task direction. The negative classroom may be one in which the teacher uses negative affect and criticism of pupils to "run a taut ship," or it may be the occasional classroom where the teacher spends the day screaming at pupils but never establishes enough order to teach. Thus, it seems important to distinguish emotional climate from management and control.

Teacher management consists of three areas of classroom activity. "Pupil behavior" refers to such things as the amount of physical movement, frequency of pupil socializing, and fluidity of groupings—the nontask, behavioral aspects of the classroom. "Management of learning tasks" refers to the way learning tasks are selected and carried out in the classroom—the degree of control exercised by the teacher. "Thinking processes" refers to the manner in which thought

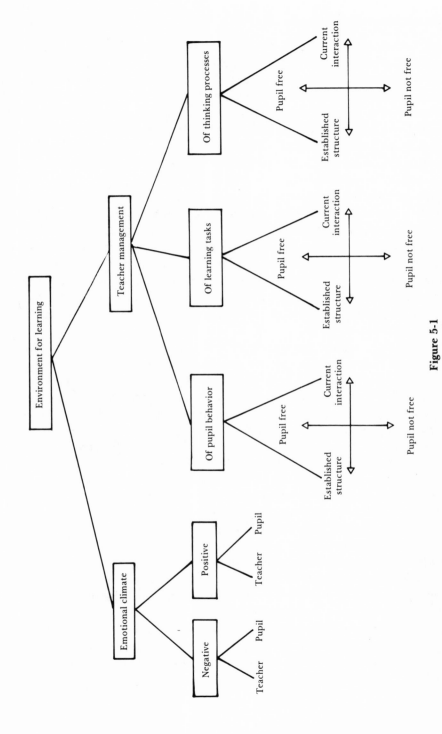

Figure 5-1

Paradigm of the environment for learning

is developed in the classroom—the freedom (or lack of freedom) the pupil has to explore related ideas, or even divergent ones, and the cognitive level of the thinking processes permitted or encouraged by the teacher. These three areas of teacher management are not often separated. As extreme examples, contingency management class-rooms (which use conditioning principles and programmed learning) typically control all three areas closely. Open classrooms, on the other hand, attempt to free thinking processes and learning tasks, but, in doing so, usually free behavior as well—sometimes to the point of chaos.

Under each of the management subheads, there is a continuum, the ends of which are identified as "established structure" and "current interaction," representing a dimension along which the classroom may be placed. Established structure represents internalization by pupils of limits to behavior, patterns of behavior that are carried out, and sequences of activities that have been established in the past. Examples would be a pupil putting materials away without being instructed, building with blocks on the rug but not on the floor, or leaving for the bathroom without asking permission but writing his or her name on a sign-out sheet. In contrast, "current interaction," verbal or nonverbal, is a here-and-now attempt by the teacher to support or modify pupil behavior. Established structure represents activities or limits that are not the result of teacher inter-vention at a particular moment; they are the consequences of earlier interaction between the teacher and pupil that make further inter-action unnecessary. In effect, structure is interaction written in the past.

The vertical continuum from "pupil free" to "pupil not free" represents the varying amount of freedom pupils have, which has been established by some balance between established structure and interaction with the teacher. We assume that a given amount of freedom can be established by different combinations of structure and interaction.

Making a distinction between these two continua seems important since the interaction occurring in the classroom at any point in time has different meanings, depending on the established structure. That is, a teacher may make an occasional gentle management statement either in a classroom that is chaotic (high pupil freedom) or in one that is task-oriented and runs smoothly (less pupil freedom). The effect on pupil learning would be quite different in the two class-rooms. To observe or conceptualize only current interaction ignores the "backdrop"—the setting against which the interaction is taking place. The studies were not designed to distinguish between inter-action and established structure, but, after the fact, the observation data that were gathered do reflect the difference to varying degrees, and an attempt will be made to interpret the results in this light.

Descriptions of several classrooms may clarify the meanings of these terms and differences in dimensions. In Ms. Anderson's second-grade classroom, the day begins with a pattern followed by all the children. After the pupils have hung up their coats and perhaps spent a few seconds talking with other pupils, they go to their desks, read the assignment on the blackboard, get out paper and pencil, and start work. By the time the bell rings, most of the pupils are at their desks hard at work. Pupils spend most of the day working at their seats, and the classroom is so quiet that, even though the teacher speaks quietly, she can be heard anywhere in the classroom. There is very little physical movement, with pupils leaving their seats only to sharpen their pencils, to put paper in the wastebasket, or to get materials, and they go and come directly, without dawdling. As the day proceeds, the teacher, still speaking in a low voice, calls one group after another to work with her at one side of the room. Each lesson begins with the assumption that pupils have done what was assigned yesterday and ends with a new assignment that is to be completed before tomorrow.

This classroom description illustrates an established structure in which the freedom of behavior of pupils is sharply limited, with only rare interactions by the teacher concerning behavior. Minutes often pass without one child whispering to another. Movement is sharply limited. Social groupings rarely occur and are fleeting when they do. It is also clear that pupils have little or no freedom to choose the task that they are to do next; rather, the teacher assigns it and will know tomorrow whether it has been done satisfactorily. The emo-tional climate of the classroom is essentially neutral, with little affect being expressed, either positive or negative. On the other hand, it is clear that pupils have some freedom and support for exploring ideas in relation to their assignments. In reading lessons the teacher often asks questions like: "What else do you suppose Jimmy might have done?" "What do you suppose will happen next?" "Would it have been better if Jimmy had done something different?" In arithmetic she often asks, "There's another way to do this—how else might you get that answer?" A set of papers all describe a space voyage, but it is clear that the teacher values descriptions that are essentially poetic as much as papers which are reportorial. Thus, it seems clear that, although the behavior of pupils and their learning tasks were under the close control of the teacher, their thinking processes were relatively free.

In Ms. Baxter's kindergarten, many pupils, as they enter, come to the teacher to give and receive a hug before they move off into the classroom. After this interchange, one little girl asks, "What should I do today, Ms. Baxter?" She answers, "Well, you know what we do; we shop around and look at the materials that are laid out and see if there's something we'd like to do." The little girl straggles off and shortly is at work. Soon after, a little boy breaks into a trot crossing the room, and the teacher is with him in a moment, reminding him "We don't run in the classroom." As the day proceeds, the limits for behavior become clear. Running, talking above a quiet level, interfering with other people's activities—all are off limits. But at the same time, it is clear that the choice of the learning activity and the thinking processes are up to the pupil within the limits of the materials available.

In Ms. Cunningham's first grade, the day begins with a game in which two girls are identified by the teacher as princesses for today, and the other pupils are to identify two aspects of the girls' dress that are common to them but to no one else. After this, the teacher and the aide each spend a considerable part of the day working with one small group after another, and the remainder of the pupils work on assigned tasks individually at their seats or in small groups, but with freedom to do the tasks in any order. When pupils are interacting with the teacher, they receive frequent smiles, compliments, and praise. When we left at lunchtime, we waved good-bye to the teacher who was working with a small group. She got up and came to the door to say good-bye. The pupils whom she left and the other pupils in small groups looked at the clock, got up, put away their materials and went to their desks. When the teacher turned around, all the pupils were in their seats, smiling, chatting quietly, waiting for her to give the signal to line up for lunch. Clearly, the pupils have internalized the routine, the established structure, but the structure is one in which pupils have more freedom than they had in Ms. Anderson's second-grade classroom. This is a classroom in which the expectations for behavior are clear, and pupils assume considerable responsibility for meeting them. Learning tasks are assigned daily, can be done in any order and at any time, but must be done before the next day. Responses at a high cognitive level are encouraged. Thus, this is a classroom where the limits for behavior are clearly defined and reflect established structure; learning tasks are assigned, but with some freedom, and there is support for activities at a higher cognitive level.

In Ms. Wilson's first-grade classroom, pupils enter noisily, some running, and with considerable horseplay. There are no assigned tasks. Some pupils choose materials to work with; others play. The teacher moves among individual pupils and small groups, pausing to ask questions. To a girl stringing beads, she asks, "What would you do next to repeat the pattern?" Direction of behavior by the teacher is infrequent but strong, dealing only with the most deviant behavior. Small groups are occasionally called together for an activity set by the teacher, but the activities are brief. This is a classroom in which the established structure permits a great deal of freedom for pupil behavior, for learning tasks, and for thinking processes.

In contrast to these classrooms in which there was some support for activity at a higher cognitive level, an incident in a contingency-management classroom following one of the popular sets of programmed materials illustrates the "not free" end of the continuum. The concept "container" is being taught, with the teacher pointing to pictures of different objects on a flipchart and asking whether they are containers or not. After the group has agreed that a glass is a container, and that a jar is a container, a little girl comments "The jar is glass," to which the teacher responds, "That's right, but that's not what we're concerned with now." Presumably, it would not take many responses of this sort before pupils would cease attempting to relate ideas. The established structure for thinking processes would be reflected in activity at a lower cognitive level.

RESULTS AND DISCUSSION

All of the studies from which results will be reported were correlational in nature, so that causal conclusions cannot be drawn.

For ease of communication, interpretations of results may seem to imply cause, but this is not intended. Table 5-1 lists the factors from each study, classified according to the paradigm, along with the direction of the relationship with pupil gain.

Emotional Climate

Probably no aspect of the classroom has been more central to the concept of "good" teaching than a warm emotional climate. Although these studies offer support for the undesirability of negative affect, they offer none for the importance of positive affect. In study SC 3-6, a measure of teacher criticism was negatively related to two measures of gain in arithmetic, and a measure of pupils' negative affect was negatively related to gain on the same arithmetic measures, and also to gain on vocabulary and creativity. In study Fla 1, a factor that included negative affect by both teacher and pupils was negatively related to gain in two measures of readiness. But in none of the four studies was there a significant relation between positive affect and gain.

In addition to these correlations, study Fla 5 found an interaction between negative affect and pupil socioeconomic status that indicated a slight trend for pupils of high socioeconomic status to learn more with negative affect, but a stronger trend for pupils of low socioeconomic status to learn less. It does not seem surprising that a detrimental effect should be found for pupils who may already be alienated from learning and who often expect failure. There is also support for this interaction from the work of Brophy and Evertson.[9] This finding suggests a problem for education. If, as seems reasonable, pupils of low socioeconomic status come to school with patterns of behavior that the teacher dislikes and responds to with negative affect, a vicious circle is created that makes it difficult for such pupils to learn.

The results of our studies provide no support for the widely held belief that it is necessary for a classroom to provide a warm emotional climate for learning. The results do suggest that an affectively neutral classroom can be functional. What is apparently crucial, however, is that the climate not be negative.

Table 5-1

Relations of behavior measures to pupil gain

Behavior measure	Study	Factor	Pupil gain	
			Positive	Negative
Emotional climate				
	SC 3-6	Teacher criticism	—	L[a]
	SC 3-6	Pupil hostility versus pupil interest-attention	—	L
	Fla 1	Teacher-pupil negative affect (versus positive climate)	—	L
Teacher management—			Established structure	Current interaction
Of behavior				
	SC3-6	Pupil physical freedom	L	—
	FT 1	Pupil talk (versus teacher talk)	—	L
	Fla 5	Pupil disorder[b]	L	—
	Fla 5	Pupil freedom[b]	L	—
	FT 1	Teacher neutral control (versus teacher support in task settings)	—	L
Of learning tasks				
	Fla 5	Seatwork without the teacher	H	—
	Fla 5	Order, and pupil interest-attention[b]	H	—
	SC 3-6	Discussion (versus rapid interaction)	—	H
	FT 1	Pupil interruption (versus teacher direction)	—	H
	Fla 5	Recitation	—	H
	Fla 1	Order and teacher indirect (versus criticism)	—	H
	FT 1	Drill (versus pupil initiation)	—	H
	FT 1	Teacher-directed (versus pupil-selected) activity	M	M
	Fla 5	Recitation	—	M

Of thinking				
	SC 3-6	Indirect (versus silence and confusion)	—	H
	SC 3-6	High cognitive level, positive affect, and pupil central	—	H
	FT 1	Highly focused learning task	—	H
	FT 1	Broad (versus narrow) answer	—	L
	FT 1	Moderately focused learning tasks	—	H
	FT 1	Information giving and receiving	—	H
	Fla 1	Teacher asks hard question, pupils mull	—	L
	Fla 1	Teacher-pupil translation	—	H
	SC 3-6	Indirect (versus silence and confusion)	—	M
	Fla 1	Teacher-pupil translation	—	M

[a] L indicates low values of the behavior measure were associated with greatest gain; H high amounts; M, moderate amounts (a non-linear relationship).

[b] Subfactors, derived rationally, confirmed empirically.

Management of Behavior

A current belief in education is that, unless pupils have considerable freedom to move about, to work with one another, to talk to each other, and to work in subgroups, pupils' growth in complex learning objectives, such as problem solving, abstracting, generalizing, and especially creativity, will be minimized. The results of our studies consistently indicate that greater amounts of freedom of behavior are associated with a decrease in the amount of learning.

We believe that varying degrees of freedom of behavior for pupils may be created either by established structure or by current interaction. In study SC 3-6, a behavior measure that reflected freedom of physical movement of pupils and included no indication of teacher involvement was considered to fall at the established structure end of the continuum. It was negatively related to growth in creativity. A factor identified as current interaction from study FT 1, which represented a balance between pupil talk and teacher talk with no reference to task, was also negatively related to a complex achievement measure. The greater the amount of pupil talk permitted by the teacher, the less the gain made by pupils.

In study Fla 5 an attempt was made to clarify the meaning of two complex factors by scoring separately subsets of items that logically were internally consistent in meaning. One of these measures represented a disorderly kind of pupil freedom, including pupil behavior that was out of bounds by the teacher's definition, frequent socialization, and aimless wandering. That measure, which appeared to reflect established structure, was negatively related to growth in reading and spelling. The second measure appeared to be considerably more constructive. It involved free movement by the teacher among pupils while attending pupils briefly, pupils seeking reassurance or support, reporting a rule or giving a reason to another, and aimless wandering (the only item common to the two measures). This measure also appeared to reflect primarily established structure. Even though this second measure was constructive in appearance, it had just as strong a negative relation to growth in reading and spelling as the measure of pupil disorder. The comparison of results from these two measures raises the question of whether the use pupils make of freedom is relevant or whether the simple existence of greater amounts of freedom of behavior may be the major component negatively associated with pupil outcomes.

In study FT 1, a factor that represented an attempt by the teacher to stop all physical movement or to direct activities of pupils one step at a time was negatively related to a factorially derived measure of complex achievement. The factor appeared to be a clear measure of current interaction. This negative relation between teacher control and gain appears to be contradictory. These extreme control behaviors, which occurred in just a minority of classrooms, occurred infrequently. It is surprising that the classrooms where they did occur were primarily open ones. In retrospect, the setting was one in which the level of pupil noise and activity grew over a period of time, unsupervised by the teacher. Eventually, the teacher stepped in firmly, brought the activities to a stop, and stepped out of control again. After a while, the noise and activity began to build again, and the cycle was repeated. Probably this negative relation between teacher control and pupil gain was a reflection of settings in which pupil behavior was usually free, and the control that occurred was infrequent and inconsistent. Further, the occurrence of this pattern in open classrooms suggested that some minimum structuring was necessary and that, in its absence, the teacher replaced it with current interaction which, although infrequent, was strong in nature. The contrast between this cyclical pattern of behavior and Ms. Cunningham's first grade described earlier, in which pupils carried on activities largely undirected, is a compelling one; it illustrates the distinction between established structure and current interaction in the paradigm. Apparently, freedom of behavior is negatively related to learning. Whether this freedom is determined by established structure or current interaction seems, however, to be of secondary importance.

These results raise serious question about the soundness of the popular belief that considerable freedom of activity is important for pupil growth in complex outcomes. Perhaps that belief is ill founded. Most adults, when faced with a hard mental task, seek a setting in which distractions are minimized. It seems strange, then, that anyone should expect pupils to work effectively where the level of distraction is high.

Our results suggest that the typical teacher does not distinguish the management of behavior from the management of learning tasks or the management of thinking. In a study that was not one of the four reviewed here, one behavior factor seemed to reflect management of behavior and another a mixture of the management of learning tasks and thinking from a Deweyan viewpoint. The correlation between these two measures was .87, which is probably as high as the reliability of either measure. This correlation indicates that the teachers in that study who controlled behavior closely also controlled the learning tasks closely. That is, the teacher defined the tasks narrowly and limited pupils' freedom to explore ideas. Conversely, the teacher who gave pupils freedom to explore ideas and a degree of choice in the task typically also gave them considerable freedom of behavior. Probably the failure to make this distinction is the reason educators expect pupils to do hard mental work in a distracting environment.

The several measures of freedom of behavior that have been reported were negatively related with gain in achievement and creativity, but, to anticipate results, some degree of freedom in the task setting is likely to relate positively. This may be an important distinction teachers do not make and that is not usually made in educational thought.

Management of Learning Tasks

The factors that describe management of learning tasks and management of thinking seem to be less clearly differentiated in general than was true of the measures of emotional climate and management of behavior. As a consequence, the classification of some of the measures may be arbitrary and the distinctions between them less important.

Two measures from study Fla 5 seemed to reflect established structure. One involved the pupil doing seatwork without the teacher, but with evidence that the pupil was free to choose another activity when finished, and with freedom for groups to emerge spontaneously. It related positively to gain in vocabulary and reading. The second measure of established structure reflected pupils' task involvement, self-control, following of classroom routine, and working without supervision; it related to gain in spelling. Both measures reflect pupils' involvement in tasks without immediate supervision by the teacher and some, although limited, freedom.

For current interaction, one factor from study SC 3-6 was related to gain in achievement. One pole of the factor was made up of interaction in which teacher and pupils alternated talking for fifteen or twenty seconds, while the other pole represented rapid interaction such as occurs in drill. This kind of leisurely interaction, rather than drill, was positively related to gain in vocabulary, reading, and arithmetic concepts. A measure from study FT 1 represented the pupil interrupting while the teacher was communicating information or ideas. It was positively related to the factorially derived measure of complex achievement. In study Fla 5, recitation appeared to be more narrowly focused than the two previous measures of leisurely interaction and pupil interruption. It may be meaningful that the only measure of achievement to which it was related was spelling, with a positive relation. A measure from study Fla 1 involved orderliness and teachers' indirect interaction with pupils, which afforded pupils some degree of freedom. It was positively related to gain in readiness.

One implication of the results for management of learning tasks discussed so far is that on-task behavior by the pupil is important to learning. It is important to point out that three of the studies involved regular classrooms rather than special programs, with the data being collected between 1962 and 1971. The classrooms were little affected by the movement toward either open classrooms or contingency management teaching, so they did not represent the extremes of classroom procedures. It is reasonable to expect that results from classrooms that included the extremes would be likely to show even stronger relationships. At the same time, it is important to recognize that, with the exception of recitation, from study Fla 5, the measures generally reflected at least some pupil freedom, but not large amounts, whether under established structure or current interaction. As illustrations, "seatwork without the teacher" involved task behavior, but with pupil freedom to subgroup and to choose a new task; "pupil interruption" of the teacher clearly reflected some freedom, but in the context of a substantive interaction. The clear exception was "recitation," which reflected little pupil freedom. In addition to its positive relation with spelling, which is a low cognitive-level outcome, it showed nonlinear relations with vocabulary, reading, and spelling. These relationships, indicated by an "M" in the table, showed that a moderate or intermediate amount of recitation was associated with greatest learning, with greater or lesser amounts associated with decreased learning. These and other nonlinear relations will be discussed later.

The set of relations for management of learning tasks, taken as a whole, suggests that task focus is important, but that an intermediate position on the dimension representing pupil freedom is associated with greatest gain, whether determined by structure or interaction. The set of relations does not suggest that teacher monitoring and close control are functional; nor do the relations indicate that high degrees of pupil choice and self-direction are useful.

Management of Thinking

The uncertainty of the classification of some of the measures of management of thinking should be noted here. This uncertainty raises the question of whether the distinction between learning task and thinking is useful, or even defensible. The basic difficulty seems to be that thinking is embedded in the learning task and that the teacher often shifts from one to the other, or that the same inter-action has consequences for both. A drill session, for example, sets the learning task and monitors pupil involvement so as to leave little freedom of task and simultaneously leaves little freedom for explora-tion of ideas. Indirect interaction may tend to free both, yet main-tains teacher participation so as to limit pupil freedom to a degree. The measures of cognitive level of interaction, however, are specific to the thinking process, and the measures of order and task involve-ment seem more clearly to reflect task management so that there does seem to be some basis for the distinction.

All of the measures here fall under current interaction. We are not suggesting that an established structure, or set, does not exist with respect to thinking processes, but only that our measures did not record it. The example of the pupil's idea ("The jar is glass.") and the teacher's rejection of it probably would establish a structure in which pupils no longer explore ideas. As another example, the work by Rowe suggests that the teacher can increase materially the amount and quality of pupil exploration of ideas by waiting at least three seconds after asking a question, or after a pupil response, before intervening again.[10] That is, the teacher can create an environment in which there is freedom for pupils to explore ideas. At the end of a year, the established structure for thinking in this classroom would be quite different from the one in which the pupil's idea was rejected.

In first- through twelfth-grade classrooms, Wood found that pupils' higher cognitive-level interaction tended to occur when two other kinds of interaction were present: the teacher asked higher-level questions, and other pupils accepted and built on each other's ideas.[11] This pattern of interaction also suggests an established structure for thinking.

In study SC 3-6, a measure of indirect teacher behavior was positively related to gain in creativity. This same measure of gain in creativity from the same pupils was found to be negatively related to freedom of pupils' behavior. Thus, for this measure of creativity, for these pupils, freedom in thinking was positively related with gain, but freedom of behavior was negatively related. This contrast underscores the usefulness of distinguishing control of behavior from control of learning tasks and thinking. Another measure from study SC 3-6 involved teachers' asking high cognitive-level questions, pupils' positive affect, and the centrality of the pupil in classroom activity and was positively related to growth in arithmetic concepts.

Several measures from study FT 1 that were based on the cognitive level of teacher-pupil interaction were related to achievement. A measure that represented a close focus on skills-related activities was positively related with gain in a factorially derived measure of simple achievement. Three other measures from the same study produced internally consistent relations with the measure of complex achievement: information giving, a low cognitive-level activity, was positively related, and another measure representing an intermediate cognitive level was also positively related. But a measure of the frequency of broad questions (high cognitive level) was negatively related. These data suggest that lower and middle cognitive-level activities were positively related to complex gain, but higher cognitive-level activities were negatively related.

In study Fla 1, a measure of the teacher's asking of questions that expected pupils to go beyond what was given, and to "sit, think, and mull," was negatively related to gain in a readiness measure, and it also interacted with socioeconomic status in a way that indicated that the decrease in learning was greater for pupils from low socioeconomic backgrounds. Also from study Fla 1, a measure of teacher-pupil interaction at the second lowest cognitive level ("teacher-pupil translation") was positively related with gain in the same measure of readiness.

The results from study SC 3-6 seem to contrast with the others. They indicated that indirect teaching (which tends to support

exploration of ideas) and the measure of high cognitive-level interaction with a positive climate are both positively related to gain.
Studies FT 1 and Fla 1, however, showed negative relationships
between higher cognitive-level interaction and gain, and positive
relationships between lower cognitive-level activity and gain. The
explanation for this difference may lie in the nature of the pupil
groups. The pupils in study SC 3-6 were in grades three through six,
disproportionately upper socioeconomic status, and their average
achievement was advanced a grade level. Pupils in the other two
studies, however, were in first grade, predominantly disadvantaged in
study FT 1, and mixed in study Fla 1. In study Fla 5, pupils were in
fifth grade, but a grade level behind expectation, and the measures
of cognitive level of interaction were unrelated to gain. Thus, study
SC 3-6 involved upper-elementary, able pupils, and high cognitive-
level interaction was positively related; study Fla 5 involved upper
elementary, less able pupils, for whom there was no relationship; and
studies FT 1 and Fla 1 involved young children, some less able, and
the relationships were negative. The pattern of relationships suggests
that greater amounts of high cognitive-level interaction are dysfunctional for young pupils, especially those of lower ability, but
may become functional for older elementary pupils, especially those
of higher ability.

The negative relationships for first-grade pupils sometimes pro-
voke the response that everyone knows that young children cannot
carry out higher-level thinking. But it seems clear that the child who
evolves the concept of conservation or abstracts the meanings of
words such as "over," "under," or "beside" has engaged in higher
cognitive-level activities. The results may mean that these teachers
used too much higher cognitive-level interaction for these young
children or that they were not sensitive to the many pupils who were
not keeping up with the class and went ahead with the small number
of children who were. What is clear is that the "universal prescrip-
tion" implied in some educational writing, that all teachers should
ask all children more higher-order questions, is an oversimplification.

A final comment has to do with the adequacy of the paradigm to
deal with management of thinking. The dimension of freedom has
been used to represent both freedom of thinking and cognitive level,
but the two may in time need to be distinguished. It is usually
assumed that higher cognitive activity will occur in an environment

of freedom, but this assumption may not be true. In Ms. Baxter's kindergarten, in which pupils chose their activities, the materials available had been selected to support high-level activity, but pupils were free to use them at a low level, and some did. On the other hand, in study Fla 1 there was an example of high cognitive level and low freedom ("teacher asks hard question, pupils mull"). We have not included an additional dimension to distinguish freedom and cognitive level since it has seemed preferable to accept a degree of "fuzziness" of the paradigm at this point rather than to complicate it further.

Nonlinear Relations

In most research on classroom behavior to date, the analysis has used product-moment (linear) correlations, which assume that, if some of a behavior is good, more is better. Since it does not seem reasonable that the "more is better" assumption should fit all classroom behavior, nonlinear relations were also calculated for some measures in all our studies. In general, the nonlinear relations seem to amplify the conclusions that were reached from the linear relations. In the area of teacher management of learning tasks, from study FT 1, the relation between a measure of "drill (versus pupil initiation)" and gain in achievement was represented by a curve in the form of an inverted "U." Beginning with the least amount of drill, gain tended to increase as drill increased. But at a point approximately midway through the range of teacher behavior, increases in gain leveled off, and, as drill increased even more, the curve fell more and more sharply. Most gain was associated with a moderate amount of drill, as shown by an "M" in the table, rather than with higher or lower amounts. A measure of "teacher-directed (versus pupil-selected) activity" from the same study was related to gain in the same way, indicating that most gain occurred with a balance between direction by teachers and freedom of pupils. The similar nonlinear relation between recitation and three measures of achievement from study Fla 5 has already been cited, and the similarity between the activities of drill and recitation should be noted. Moderate amounts of either were associated with greatest pupil gain.

In the area of teacher management of thinking, from study SC 3-6, the same measure of indirect teacher interaction that was related in linear fashion to gain in creativity was also related in nonlinear form to both vocabulary and reading. In study Fla 1, the measure of "teacher-pupil translation," the second lowest cognitive level, was related similarly to two readiness measures. These non-linear relationships for measures that were classified under both management of learning tasks and thinking support the conclusion reached earlier for learning tasks—an intermediate amount of teacher control and pupil freedom was associated with greatest learning.

In addition to these findings of nonlinearity, there were indications that the curves were different for different outcome measures. The differences were consistent with the interpretation that greater amounts of pupil freedom were functional for complex, high cognitive-level learning objectives, but lesser amounts of pupil freedom were functional for simpler, low cognitive-level outcomes. The results suggest that when the teacher is concerned with pupils' memory for facts, such as the multiplication table, spelling or dates in history— certainly necessary goals—a highly focused drill session that gives pupils little freedom in learning task or thinking will result in most learning. But when the teacher is concerned with more complex objectives, such as understanding arithmetic operations, solving complex problems, organizing ideas in writing, or generalizing historical relationships to the future, then more freedom for pupils in exploring ideas and carrying out the task is functional. But even here a certain amount of teacher management is necessary, and the results suggest that many teachers fail to supply that amount.

But these are minor variations on the more general conclusion that teacher management of learning tasks and thinking in which the teacher selects and directs activities, yet permits a degree of freedom for pupils, is more functional for learning than either greater or lesser amounts of teacher direction and control.[12]

Implications

A paradigm has been proposed that focuses attention on separate domains in the learning environment of the classroom. The results from four studies were classified in terms of the paradigm in the attempt to clarify relations between classroom behavior and pupil gain.

The major domains identified by the paradigm are: emotional climate, separated into positive and negative affect; and teacher management (or control) of three areas of pupil activity. Pupil behavior includes such activities as amount of physical movement, fluidity of groupings, and socialization; learning tasks refer to the degree of control exercised by the teacher over the choice and conduct of learning tasks; and thinking processes include pupil freedom to explore ideas and the cognitive level of interaction. Each of these areas of teacher management is further separated into the dimensions of the relative freedom that pupils have, and the extent to which that freedom is brought about by established structure, an internalization of rules and procedures by pupils, or by current interaction with the teacher.

When the results of the four studies were summarized and organized in this way, the results seemed consistent and coherent, and the distinctions made by the domains seemed to provide a useful way of thinking about classrooms. There is evidence, however, that some teachers do not make these distinctions; nor do some currently popular innovative programs.

For emotional climate, the conception of good teaching that emerges from this synthesis of results is that the avoidance of negative affect is important to pupil gain, but the expression of positive affect is not related. With respect to teacher management, rather than advocating freedom in all areas, as some educational theories seem to do, the results suggest that each area should be considered separately. For the management of pupil behavior, the synthesis suggests that a teacher should limit pupil freedom to move about, to form subgroups, and to socialize, and that, unless a teacher has established a minimum of structure, relatively strong interactions that are not functional for pupil learning are likely to occur. For learning tasks, the synthesis suggests that teacher selection and direction, but with some degree of pupil freedom, is related to pupil gain, whether brought about by established structure or current interaction. The fact that some teachers created effective learning settings in which pupils were orderly and task involved without the presence of the teacher was evidence that close teacher monitoring of pupils' learning activity is not necessary. For management of thinking, as for learning tasks, the synthesis suggests that some degree of pupil freedom, within a context of teacher involvement that maintains focus, was related to gain. There also are indications that, for lower-grade pupils, greater amounts of high cognitive-level interaction are not functional. Although it has been less clearly established, all four studies suggest that the amount of pupil freedom that is most functional for both learning tasks and thinking depends on the complexity of the learning task—for more complex tasks, a somewhat greater degree of freedom is functional, but even then it may be too great.

These results, viewed in terms of the paradigm, raise a question about the usefulness of typical educational recommendations. Terms like "pupil centered," "democratic," or "permissive" as descriptors of classroom behavior are too global and nonspecific to be useful. It seems possible that innovative programs may also fail to make the distinctions among domains that are important. Both progressive education and at least some open classrooms, in the attempt to free pupil thought and inquiry, have probably also freed behavior in ways that are destructive of pupil learning. It seems clear that the teacher who has pupils working quietly in their seats, or who holds a drill session on memory for facts, should not be looked down on as old fashioned or unprofessional. On the other hand, some findings suggest that learning activities and thinking processes can be too closely controlled for greatest pupil gain in the more complex outcomes.

These results raise questions about the usefulness of the "universal prescriptions" common in educational advocacy in which teachers are encouraged: to give pupils more freedom, without specifying to what degree, or in what respect, or toward what objective; to provide a warm, supportive emotional climate; to ask more higher-order questions without specifying the pupil group, the frequency of the behavior, or the relevant outcome.

Finally, the results should not be viewed as providing prescriptions for precise amounts of the several teacher behaviors that have been discussed. Rather, we hope the paradigm and the results of the studies organized around it will provide a framework for thinking about teaching. Within this framework, the sensitivity of the teacher to the response of the pupil remains an essential ingredient.

NOTES

1. Robert S. Soar, *An Integrative Approach to Classroom Learning,* NIMH Project Nos. 5-R11 MH 01096 and 7-R11 MH 02045 (Philadelphia: Temple

University, 1966). ERIC No. ED 033 749; *id.*, "Optimum Teacher-Pupil Interaction for Pupil Growth," *Educational Leadership Research Supplement* 1 (1968): 275-280.

2. Robert S. Soar and Ruth M. Soar, "An Empirical Analysis of Selected Follow-Through Programs: An Example of a Process Approach to Evaluation," in *Early Childhood Education*, Seventy-first Yearbook of the National Society for the Study of Education, Part II, ed. Ira J. Gordon (Chicago: University of Chicago Press, 1972), 229-259.

3. Robert S. Soar and Ruth M. Soar, "Classroom Behavior, Pupil Characteristics, and Pupil Growth for the School Year and for the Summer," *JSAS Catalog of Selected Documents in Psychology* 5 (1975): 200 (Ms. No. 873).

4. *Ibid.*

5. Ned A. Flanders, *Analyzing Teaching Behavior* (Reading, Mass.: Addison-Wesley, 1970).

6. Benjamin S. Bloom, *Taxonomy of Educational Objectives: The Classification of Educational Goals, Handbook 1: Cognitive Domain* (New York: David McKay Co., 1956).

7. Edwin A. Fleishman, "The Description of Supervisory Behavior," *Journal of Applied Psychology* 37 (1953): 1-6.

8. Soar, *Integrative Approach to Classroom Learning.*

9. Jere E. Brophy and Carolyn M. Evertson, *The Texas Teacher Effectiveness Project: Presentation of Nonlinear Relationships and Summary Discussion*, Report No. 74-6 (Austin: Research and Development Center, University of Texas, 1974).

10. Mary B. Rowe, "Reflections on Wait-time: Some Methodological Questions," *Journal of Research in Science Teaching* 11 (1974): 263-279.

11. Samuel E. Wood, "An Analysis of Three Systems for Observing Classroom Behavior," unpub. diss., University of Florida, Gainesville, 1969.

12. A more detailed discussion is available in Robert S. Soar and Ruth M. Soar, "An Attempt to Identify Measures of Teacher Effectiveness from Four Studies," *Journal of Teacher Education* 27 (1976): 261-267.

6. *Tempus Educare*

David C. Berliner

Since the early 1970s, the Beginning Teacher Evaluation Study (BTES) has promoted inquiry into teaching and learning in the elementary school. The design of the study was influenced by the research literature and those methodological paradigms for research that were available in the middle of the 1970s, and it was these factors that led to an investigation of various aspects of instructional time. Three measures of time—allocated time (the time a teacher provides for instruction in a particular content area), engaged time (the time a student is attending to instruction in a particular content area), and academic learning time (the time a student is engaged with instructional materials or activities that are at an easy level of difficulty for that student)—were considered to be important variables

The ideas and data presented in this chapter emerged from work performed while conducting the Beginning Teacher Evaluation Study. That study was funded by the National Institute of Education and administered by the California Commission for Teacher Preparation and Licensing. The research was conducted by the Far West Laboratory for Educational Research and Development. The study represents a joint effort on the part of David C. Berliner, Leonard S. Cahen, Nikola N. Filby, Charles W. Fisher, Richard N. Marliave, Marilyn Dishaw, and Jeffry E. Moore.

through which teacher behavior and classroom characteristics influence student achievement. This chapter opens with an explanation of how the inquiry into use of instructional time began. It goes on to investigate the three measures of time considered important in the educational process and concludes with a summary of why the three time variables deserve the attention of those who study classroom teaching and learning.

THE BTES DESIGN

Many flaws in design and logic are apparent in the literature on teaching and learning in the elementary schools. Nevertheless, a cluster of variables that related consistently to achievement did emerge.[1] They are called direct instructional variables.

—One variable was the goal-setting or structuring behavior provided by the teacher. Teachers identified as being effective in eliciting achievement from their students made more verbal statements directing students to the tasks in which they should be engaged.[2] They clearly informed students what they should be doing, where to do it, and for how long, which ensured that students did not lose time because they were confused or because they were waiting for decisions to be made.

—Another variable was absence from school. Absence of either teacher or student was usually negatively related to student achievement, indicating that the time spent in school contributes to achievement. Additional data support the belief that instructional time is an important predictor of student achievement in academic areas.[3]

—The focus of the time spent in the classroom also emerged as an important variable. An academic focus was found to result in consistently higher achievement. When, on the other hand, large amounts of time were spent in telling stories or in art, music, or play activities, as opposed to reading and mathematics activities, correlations with achievement were found to be negative.

—As for coverage of content, this was also considered to be a positive predictor of achievement. Particularly in mathematics, the more content that was covered, the greater the achievement.

—The importance of monitoring by the teacher was another variable that emerged as significant. When monitoring was carefully done, the teacher was able to keep children engaged in their assigned tasks and correlation with achievement was positive.

—Yet another variable that demonstrated a positive relation with achievement outcomes was the type of question asked by teachers. Factual, concrete questions were associated with higher achievement in the elementary grades than evaluative, abstract ones.

—The type of feedback that teachers provide to students also seemed to be important. Feedback that was academic in nature correlated positively with achievement.

—And, finally, the classroom environment was found to be important. A classroom environment characterized as warm, democratic, and convivial showed up as a positive predictor of achievement.

The conclusion reached after reviewing the literature was a simple one: Elementary school teachers who find ways to put students into contact with the academic curriculum and to keep them in contact with that curriculum while maintaining a convivial classroom atmosphere are successful in promoting achievement in reading and mathematics. It was this simple summary statement that led us to design the BTES study so that the student and curricular materials were focal points in collecting and analyzing data.

MODIFYING THE PARADIGMS

Research on teaching had not received much attention before 1960. By 1975, however, a number of team and individual research efforts had been completed or were under way, almost all of which were cast in the form of process-product analyses. This means that teacher behavior and classroom characteristics were observed and subsequently related to measures of student achievement and attitude. Correlation was the most frequently used statistic in such studies. It was expected that the BTES would reflect this traditional approach. As the study progressed and the research literature was examined, however, the investigators became increasingly dissatisfied with the process-product approach since it appeared that certain illogical elements were inherent in the design of a process-product study of classroom teaching. For example, how could the number or percentage of teacher verbal communications coded as praise statements in November influence results on achievement test items given in May? Without imposing strict experimental controls, how can one evaluate the effects of teachers' questioning behavior in a particular subject area when one teacher devotes five hours a week to that area and another teacher devotes one and one-half hours per week to the same area? How could anyone expect to discover a relationship between a variable such as time spent lecturing on ecology and achievement test items that measure dictionary usage? The latter occurs when investigators use instruments that code teacher behavior of various sorts and correlate that behavior with broad-spectrum tests of reading achievement.

At first it appeared that correlational approaches using the process-product research paradigm were inherently deficient. Some of our colleagues argued that only by recourse to true experiments could the situation be remedied. But true experimental designs used in the investigation of teaching and learning in classrooms also have certain flaws. The most serious of these are that such designs do not reflect the complexities of the classroom, with its myriad inter-actions; they do not reflect the dynamic quality of the classroom, with its ever-changing events; nor can they, typically, develop an appropriate time perspective since the acquisition of knowledge in the classroom is best conceived of as a multiyear process.[4] Thus, experimental designs that reflect the process-product framework often suffer from problems of ecological validity.[5]

If correlational studies were to be conducted in natural classroom environments, which would appear to give them more potential external validity, then the logical and hypothetical causal flow of events in the process-product model needed to be modified. Re-searchers on the Beginning Teacher Evaluation Study proposed a simple modification of the process-product approach to the study of classroom learning. This modification is based on the belief that what a teacher does at any one moment while working in a cir-cumscribed content area affects a student primarily at only that particular moment and in that particular content area. The link between teacher behavior and student achievement is, therefore, the ongoing student behavior in the classroom learning situation. The logic continues in this way. What a teacher does to foster learning in a particular content area becomes important only if a student is engaged with *appropriate* curriculum content. Appropriate curric-ulum content is defined as curriculum that is logically related to the criterion and is at an easy level of difficulty for a particular student.

Thus, a second-grade student engaged in the task of decoding blends in reading, either by means of a workbook or by watching the teacher at the chalkboard, is engaging in processes that can lead to proficiency in decoding blends if the task requires a low rate of error on the part of the student. The variable used in BTES research is the accrued engaged time in a particular content area using materials that are not difficult for the student. This complex variable is called Academic Learning Time (ALT). Although the relationship is probably not linear, the accrual of ALT is expected to be a strong positive correlate of achievement.

It was originally believed that engagement with curriculum materials of an intermediate level of difficulty would lead to greater achievement. The data, however, show that young children trying to learn in traditional classroom settings need to work on academic tasks that give rise to low error rates. A low error rate occurs when about 20 percent or fewer errors are noted for a student engaged with workbook pages, tests, or classroom exercises. When a student's responses are not overt, an observer must estimate the level of difficulty of the activities in which the student is engaged.

Certainly trying to keep students engaged for too long with too many easy tasks will not improve academic performance. Engagement is likely to drop off, and content coverage will be reduced. Knowing when to move a student to new materials and activities is a complex diagnostic decision that teachers must make. That must always be kept in mind. Still, for the conception of classroom learning proposed here, it is when teachers put students into contact with academic materials and activities that are relatively easy that learning is hypothesized to take place.

This variable of ALT, which is measured in real time, has some roots in the works of Carroll, of Bloom, of Harnischfeger and Wiley, and of others.[6] The effort to develop a variable focusing on students' use of time and the curriculum, simultaneously, comes from the earlier literature, as has already been discussed. The concern for the easy level of difficulty, where low error rates are noted or inferred, has some roots in the literature of instructional design, particularly that concerned with programmed instruction. Investigating the relations of ALT to teacher behavior and to student achievement requires, as was noted, that a change be made in the process-product research paradigm. This modification is shown in Figure 6-1.

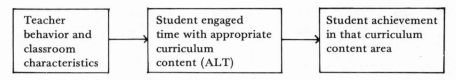

Figure 6-1

Simple flow of events that influence achievement
in a particular curriculum content area

In this conception of research on teaching, the content area the student is working on must be specified precisely, the task engagement of the student must be judged, the level of difficulty of the task must be rated, and time must be measured. The constructed variable of ALT, then, stands between measures of teaching and measures of student achievement. A design for research using this approach requires the construction of two correlational matrices. The first is used to study how teacher behavior and classroom characteristics affect ALT. The second is used to study how ALT and achievement are related.

Essential to this conception of how teachers influence student achievement is the variable of engaged time. The upper limit on measures of engaged time in classrooms, for a particular content area, is the time the teacher has allocated for instruction in that area. The remainder of this chapter is concerned with allocated time, engaged time, and ALT in different content areas. The thesis is that the marked variability in allocated time, engaged time, and ALT, between and within classes, is the most potent explanatory variable to account for variability in student achievement—after intial aptitude has been removed as a predictor variable. A corollary of this thesis is that interactive teaching behavior (praise, questioning, use of organizers, feedback, and so forth) can only be understood through its effect on ALT. In this conception of classroom learning, interactive teaching behavior or teaching skills are not thought to be directly linked to achievement.

A STUDY OF INSTRUCTIONAL TIME

Allocated time, engaged time, and ALT were studied during a recent school year in twenty-five second-grade and twenty-five fifth-grade classes in California. Teachers were trained in log-keeping procedures so that the daily time allocations for selected students could be recorded within particular content areas of reading and mathematics. In addition, a trained observer was present approximately one day a week for over twenty weeks of the school year. The observer recorded engaged time and provided data to compute estimates of ALT, as well as providing data about a number of other facets of classroom life.[7] Selections from this larger data set are used to illustrate some of the within- and between-class variability in allocated time, engaged time, and ALT.[8]

Allocated Time

Table 6-1 presents allocated time in content areas of second-grade mathematics and Table 6-2 presents allocated time for content areas of fifth-grade reading. These data were obtained from teachers' logs over an average of ninety days of instruction from October to May of the school year. The logs were filled out daily for six students in each of the classrooms. Within each grade level the students were of comparable ability levels in reading and mathematics, both within and across classes.[9] The data from the six students who were studied intensively in each class will be used to generalize about the whole class.

With the data from both second-grade mathematics and fifth-grade reading, one can notice widespread variation in how teachers spend their time. Different philosophies of education yield different beliefs about what is important for students to learn. These beliefs, along with the teacher's likes and dislikes for teaching certain areas, result in some interesting differences in the *functional* curriculum of a class. For example, from Table 6-1 it can be seen that students in class 13 had an average of 400 minutes each to learn the concepts and operations involved in linear measurement, while students in class 5 had an average of 29 minutes each to learn those operations and concepts. Class 21 received very little time in the content area of fractions and in the content area of money, while class 13 received markedly more time in these areas. From Table 6-2 it can be seen that class 11 spent dramatically more time on comprehension in reading than any of the other three fifth-grade classes. In class 25 silent reading and spelling were emphasized, to judge from the

Table 6-1

Time (in minutes) spent in content area of mathematics and related variables
for students in four second-grade classes

	Time (in minutes)			
Content areas and related variables	Class 5	Class 21	Class 8	Class 13
Content areas of the curriculum				
Computation				
Addition and subtraction, no regrouping, short form	835	420	1,839	540
Addition and subtraction, no regrouping, instructional algorithm	172	177	131	596
Addition and subtraction, with regrouping, short form	0	357	246	736
Addition and subtraction, with regrouping, instructional algorithm	43	464	138	723
Speed tests	232	31	71	100
Other computation	0	3	68	15
Concepts-applications				
Computational transfer	453	185	580	130
Place value and numerals	416	352	684	692
Word problems	109	226	416	132
Money	98	9	228	315
Linear measurement	29	130	107	400
Fractions	0	21	63	399
Developmental activities	0	76	111	40
Other concepts or applications	145	237	54	309
Related variables				
Total time in minutes	2,530	2,687	4,736	5,127
Number of days data collected	93	83	94	96
Average time per day in minutes	27	32	50	53
Percent of time students engaged	71	62	61	78
Engaged minutes per day	19	20	31	41
Percent of time students are in material of easy difficulty level	67	59	65	55
Academic learning time per day in minutes	13	12	20	23
Engaged hours per 150 days in school year	48	50	78	103
Academic learning time in hours per 150-day school year	33	30	50	58

Source: Marilyn Dishaw, *Descriptions of Allocated Time to Content Areas for the A-B Period,* Technical Note IV-11a; *id., Descriptions of Allocated Time to Content Areas for the B-C Period,* Technical Note IV-11b; and Nikola N. Filby and Richard N. Marliave, *Descriptions of Distributions of ALT within and across Classes during the A-B Period,* Technical Note IV-1a—all publications of the Beginning Teacher Evaluation Study (San Francisco: Far West Laboratory for Educational Research and Development, 1977).

Table 6-2

Time (in minutes) spent in content area of reading and related variables
for students in four fifth-grade classes

Content areas and related variables	Time (in minutes)			
	Class 1	Class 3	Class 11	Class 25
Content areas of the curriculum				
Word structure				
Root words and affixes	250	112	126	103
Syllables	67	60	102	212
Word meaning				
Synonyms	95	152	10	119
Pronoun reference	0	0	9	56
Other word meaning	558	949	1,042	615
Comprehension				
Verbatim (no rephrasing)	206	329	188	325
Translation (paraphrase)	122	151	1,649	383
Inference-synthesis	235	252	1,432	306
Identifying main items	153	243	943	326
Evaluation of fact and opinion	5	0	66	56
Other comprehension	196	325	1,368	239
Reading practice				
Oral reading	604	63	885	305
Silent reading	1,083	724	956	3,640
Reading in content areas	505	256	400	284
Related reading				
Spelling	694	847	664	1,415
Grammar	242	183	859	413
Creative writing	56	343	98	573
Study skills	472	669	270	171
Other	207	687	1,317	426
Related variables				
Total time in minutes	5,749	6,344	12,383	9,965
Number of days data collected	97	96	87	74
Average time per day in minutes	59	66	142	135
Percent of time students engaged	82	77	84	75
Engaged minutes per day	48	51	119	101
Percent of time students are in material of easy difficulty level	51	61	47	58
Academic learning time per day in minutes	24	31	56	59
Engaged hours per 150 days in school year	120	128	298	283
Academic learning time in hours per 150-day school year	60	78	140	148

Source: Dishaw, *Descriptions of Allocated Time to Content Areas for the A-B Period; id., Descriptions of Allocated Time to Content Areas for the B-C Period;* and Filby and Marliave, *Descriptions of Distributions of ALT within and across Classes during the A-B period.*

dramatically greater allocation of time to those content areas, in contrast to the average amount of time each student of classes 1, 3, and 11 received. And oral reading hardly seemed to be of interest to the teacher of class 3; at least that could be inferred if the data from class 3 were compared with the data from the other fifth-grade classes.

These rather significant differences in the functional classroom curriculum should, from all we know about learning, result in considerable differences in achievement. If students in these second-grade classrooms were tested at the end of the year on linear measurement, one might wager that students in class 13 would demonstrate better performance than students in class 5. If the fifth-grade classes were part of some end-of-year statewide testing program where drawing inferences from paragraphs of prose was tested, as it often is, one might well expect that students in class 11 would show superior performance when contrasted with similar students in the other fifth-grade classes.

The broad-spectrum standardized achievement test may be a social indicator from which state or national policy can be illuminated. But as long as teachers have the freedom to choose what areas they will emphasize in their classrooms, these tests can never be used as fair measures of a teacher's effectiveness. It simply is not fair to teachers to evaluate their students in areas that the teacher did not cover or emphasize. On the other hand, it may not be fair to students and their parents to let teachers arbitrarily choose what is to be taught. Tighter control of the functional curriculum of the classroom may be desirable. This problem is recognized by many, and has led some curriculum developers to insist upon stringent control of teacher behavior in order to implement the program that they would promote.[10]

Another interesting aspect of allocated time is the average daily time devoted to mathematics and reading. States and school districts usually insist upon a certain minimum number of minutes per day or hours per week for certain subject matters. Let us suppose, by law, that forty minutes a day is the minimum amount of time to be devoted to mathematics in the second grade within a particular school district. Let us also suppose that this mathematics time begins at 11:15, after a recess, and that the time period devoted to mathematics ends at noon. The teacher, principal, and superintendent may well feel that the state minimum requirements are being met and exceeded. But careful observation will reveal otherwise. A ten-minute delay in the start of work, called transition time in the Beginning Teacher Evaluation Study, may occur before the mathematics curriculum is really in effect. Toward the end of the allocated time students are putting workbooks, contracts, and Cuisenaire rods away, getting lunches out, and lining up for dismissal at noontime. Another ten minutes may be lost. Functional time for mathematics is now twenty-five minutes, which is 60 percent under the legal requirements.

The data presented in Table 6-1 reflect the difficulty of managing time in the classroom. Classes 5 and 21 have, on the average, a daily allocation totaling about thirty minutes per day for mathematics, while classes 8 and 13 show, on the average, an allocation of over fifty minutes per day for mathematics. From other data collected as part of this study, we estimated that the students in class 5 and class 21 spend an average of 42.5 minutes per day in transitions from activity to activity, while students in classes 8 and 13 spend about half that time, approximately 22 minutes per day, in transitions. The average number of minutes per day devoted to fifth-grade reading, as presented in Table 6-2, shows similar variability. Teachers in classes 11 and 25 allocated over 100 percent more total time to reading than teachers in classes 1 and 3. Other data from our full fifth-grade sample reveal that the teachers with the lower rate of allocated time had a higher than average amount of class time spent in transitions and the management of behavioral problems. What this indicates is that the time allocated for academic instruction in a school day can easily slip away when a teacher cannot keep transitional time and behavioral problems to a minimum. Any sensible manager knows that. Somehow, in some classes, there is a casualness about classroom management that results in considerable inefficiency.

This brief examination of selected data presenting estimates of time allocated in the classroom shows clearly that some teachers spend considerably more time instructing in particular content areas than other teachers, and some teachers allocate considerably more total time for instruction than other teachers. These differences, put into experimental terminology, represent clear differences in the type and in the duration of treatment. One can expect, therefore, considerable variability on the outcome measures used to assess these vastly different treatments.

Engaged Time

Tables 6-1 and 6-2 also present data on the average percentage of time students are engaged in reading or mathematics instruction. These data are from observer records, and not from teacher logs. Previous work revealed that teachers can keep accurate records of allocated time, but that classroom observers were necessary to obtain accurate records of engaged time.[11] In examining these data it appears that the percentage of time students are engaged is relatively high. This is an artifact of the observational system that was in use. The system required that transition time and other classroom phenomena be coded as separate events. Thus, the data on engagement rates are for the time spent in mathematics and reading, after a class has settled down and before the class starts to put away their work. If engagement were coded for the entire time block denoted by teachers as mathematics or reading time, the engaged time rates would be considerably lower because most of the class is not engaged during transitions. Still, variation among classes is noted for an important variable. The engagement rates in the four second-grade classes vary from 61 percent to 78 percent during mathematics instruction. In the four fifth-grade classes engagement rates vary from 75 percent to 84 percent during reading instruction. These ranges were much larger in the total sample of classes studied.

The average number of minutes per day allocated for instruction, multiplied by the engagement rate, provides liberal estimates of the number of engaged minutes per day for each student. These data are found in Tables 6-1 and 6-2. In the second-grade data for mathematics, at the lower end of the range, 20 minutes of engaged time per day is noted. At the higher end of the range, 40 minutes per day is noted. For fifth-grade reading, the range in the four classes is between 48 and 119 minutes of engaged time per day. These are dramatic differences of 100 percent or more in the amount of engaged time students allot to learn mathematics and reading. For reasons that we do not yet fully understand, some combination of teacher behavior and students' socialization to school interacts to produce classes where most of the children are attending to their work most of the time. And these same factors sometimes result in classes where less than half of the children are attending to their work during the time allocated for instruction.

In most districts we may assume that a school year is about 180 days. This figure must be reduced by absences of teachers and students, strikes, busing difficulties, the difficulties of instructing before Christmas and Easter breaks, testing at the beginning and end of the school year, and other factors. A reasonable estimate of the "functional" school year may be about 150 days. Accumulating the engaged minutes per day over these 150 days gives an estimate of the engaged instructional time allotted by students to the academic curriculum during the entire school year. Tables 6-1 and 6-2 present these data for the four classes in each grade level. Between 50 and 100 hours per year of active student involvement in classroom instruction in mathematics is noted in the four second-grade classes. In the four fifth-grade classes, with more mature and more independent learners, between 120 and 298 cumulative hours per school year are noted for all areas of reading. When these and other data collected as part of the study are examined, it is evident that many second-grade classes have cumulative engaged time, in *both* reading and mathematics, of under 100 hours for the entire school year. In the fifth grade, these data provide considerably higher estimates of engaged time for the school year.

As these data come to light, some important questions must be asked. For example, what should be expected in the way of engaged time for thirty students and one teacher, working together throughout the school year? What are the expectations for instructional time held by parents and school board members as they make policy to educate the young of a community? Because these new estimates of classroom allocated and engaged time do not conform to the prevailing beliefs that exist among the people who manage and support education, either those beliefs must be changed, or instructional practices must be altered.

Academic Learning Time

As noted above, academic learning time is the research variable of most interest in the Beginning Teacher Evaluation Study. One component of ALT is the level of difficulty of the material that is attended to by a student. It is the belief of the investigators that learning occurs primarily with materials that are at an easy level of difficulty. Materials that are too hard for a student do not add much to his acquisition of the concepts, skills, and operations that are required at a particular grade level. Nor do they allow for practice, repetition, and overlearning. These are important concerns if retention is to be maximized. Tables 6-1 and 6-2 present information on the percentage of time that students are working with relatively easy material. These data are ratings made by observers in classrooms. As shown in Table 6-1, for second-grade mathematics the range is between 55 percent and 67 percent. In fifth-grade reading the range is between 47 percent and 61 percent. Multiplying the engaged minutes per day by the percentage of time students are assigned work that yields low error rates provides an estimate of ALT per day. These data are also provided in the tables.

As noted above, the typical academic school year of 180 days may be considered to be a functional school year of 150 days. The last line in Tables 6-1 and 6-2 presents academic learning time, in hours, for a school year of 150 days. In these four classes, at each grade level, differences of many hundreds of percent in accumulated ALT are noted. In second-grade mathematics, the range is from 30 hours per school year to 58 hours per school year. In fifth-grade reading, the range is from 60 hours per school year to 148 hours per school year. In the total sample studied the range of ALT is considerably larger. It should also be noted that all of the elementary school teachers in this sample were volunteers. These data, if they could be obtained from a nonvolunteer sample, would most likely show even more between-class variability.

If academic learning time is the key to acquiring the knowledge and skill required to master the curriculum of a particular grade level, for a particular content area, one can see that the school year does not contain as much ALT as might be desired. If our concerns about instruction are correct, there are many classes where there is not sufficient time for students to master the curriculum that has been chosen for them.

IN SUMMARY

Descriptive data on allocated time, engaged time, and academic learning time have been presented. Data from four second-grade and four fifth-grade classes were chosen to reflect differences in the variables of interest. If the type of treatment and the duration of treatment are crucial variables in the determination of what is learned and how much is learned, then between-class differences in allocated time in content areas, and in total allocated time per day or per school year, become important operationally defined behavioral indicators of the instructional treatment. If learning is likely to occur only when students attend to the instruction offered them, then between-class differences in engaged time become an important operationally defined behavioral indicator of the effective stimulus situation, as opposed to the nominal stimulus situation. And, finally, if learning primarily takes place when students are engaged with materials and activities that are of an easy level of difficulty for that particular student, then ALT becomes an important operationally defined behavioral indicator of student learning. The construct of ALT has an intriguing virtue. One does not need to wait until the end of the school year to decide if learning has taken place. One can study learning *as it happens* if the construct of ALT is accepted as it has been defined. In the conception of instruction that has guided the research that has been conducted and on which this chapter is based, ALT and learning are synonymous.

The commonsense logic of the above statements is appealing. Even without data relating allocated time, engaged time, and ALT to achievement, these descriptive data have a certain obvious validity, and they can, moreover, lead teachers and supervisors of teachers to examine classroom processes in ways that logically relate to student achievement. Without turning classes into authoritarian factories of learning, many teachers can improve their effectiveness by attending to these variables and reorganizing classroom practices to maximize teaching time and learning time—resources over which they have considerable personal control.

NOTES

1. David C. Berliner and Barak V. Rosenshine, "The Acquisition of Knowledge in the Classroom," in *Schooling and the Acquisition of Knowledge,* ed. Richard C. Anderson, Rand J. Spiro, and William E. Montague (Hillsdale, N.J.: Erlbaum, 1977), 375-396; Barak V. Rosenshine and David C. Berliner, "Academic Engaged Time," *British Journal of Teacher Education* 4 (1978): 3-16.

2. W. J. Tikunoff, David C. Berliner, and R. C. Rist, *An Ethnographic Study of the Forty Classrooms of the Beginning Teacher Evaluation Study Known Sample,* Technical Report No. 75-10-5 (San Francisco: Far West Laboratory for Educational Research and Development, 1975).

3. David E. Wiley and Annegret Harnischfeger, "Explosion of a Myth:

Quantity of Schooling and Exposure to Instruction, Major Educational Vehicles," *Educational Researcher* 3 (1974): 7-12; Jane A. Stallings and David H. Kaskowitz, *Follow Through Classroom Observation Evaluation, 1972-73* (Menlo Park, Calif.: Stanford Research Institute, 1974).

4. Charles W. Fisher and David C. Berliner, *Quasi-clinical Inquiry in Research on Classroom Teaching and Learning*, Technical Report VI-2, Beginning Teacher Evaluation Study (San Francisco: Far West Laboratory for Educational Research and Development, 1977).

5. Glenn H. Bracht and Gene V Glass, "The External Validity of Experiments," *American Educational Research Journal* 5 (1968): 437-479.

6. John B. Carroll, "A Model of School Learning," *Teachers College Record* 64 (1963): 723-733; Benjamin S. Bloom, *Human Characteristics and School Learning* (New York: McGraw-Hill, 1976); Annegret Harnischfeger and David E. Wiley, "Teaching-Learning Processes in Elementary School: A Synoptic View," *Curriculum Inquiry* 6 (1976): 5-43.

7. Beginning Teacher Evaluation Study, *Proposal for Phase III-B of the Beginning Teacher Evaluation Study, July 1, 1976-June 30, 1977* (San Francisco: Far West Laboratory for Educational Research and Development, 1976).

8. Marilyn Dishaw, *Descriptions of Allocated Time to Content Areas for the A-B Period*, Technical Note IV-11a, Beginning Teacher Evaluation Study (San Francisco: Far West Laboratory for Educational Research and Development, 1977); id., *Descriptions of Allocated Time to Content Areas for the B-C Period*, Technical Note IV-11b, Beginning Teacher Evaluation Study (San Francisco: Far West Laboratory for Educational Research and Development, 1977); Nikola N. Filby and Richard N. Marliave, *Descriptions of Distributions of ALT within and across Classes during the A-B Period*, Technical Note IV-1a, Beginning Teacher Evaluation Study (San Francisco: Far West Laboratory for Educational Research and Development, 1977).

9. Leonard S. Cahen, *Selection of Second- and Fifth-grade Target Students for Phase III-B*, Technical Note III-1, Part 2, Beginning Teacher Evaluation Study (San Francisco: Far West Laboratory for Educational Research and Development, 1977).

10. Wesley C. Becker and Siegfried Engelmann, "The Direct Instruction Model," in *Encouraging Change in America's Schools: A Decade of Experimentation*, ed. Ray Rhine (New York: Academic Press, 1978).

11. Richard N. Marliave, Charles W. Fisher, and Nikola N. Filby, "Alternative Procedures for Collecting Instructional Time Data: When Can You Ask the Teacher and When Must You Observe for Yourself?" paper presented at the annual meeting of the American Educational Research Association, New York, 1977.

7. Teachers' Decision Making

Hilda Borko, Richard Cone, Nancy Atwood Russo,
and *Richard J. Shavelson*

THE CLASSROOM SCENE

(A second-grade teacher is seated at a round table with five students. She shows them a flash card with a subtraction problem: 14 − 5 = _____.)

Teacher: Who can tell me the answer to this problem?

Cliff: Zero. Four and one makes five. Five take away five is zero.

Teacher: No. Remember that the one in the tens column is equal to one bundle of ten sticks.

Kathy: I can't do it. I don't know how to take five from four.

Teacher: Use your bundles of sticks and the individual sticks if you need to.

Martha: Yo no comprendo.

(Teacher turns to help Martha by showing her how to use the sticks to solve the problem.)

Phillip: The answer is nine.

Teacher: That's right, Phillip. Show us how you figured it out.

Phillip: I needed one more one so I took one stick from the bundle of ten sticks and that left nine.

Teacher: Very good. Now let's try thirteen minus seven.

Cliff: I still don't get it.

(The teacher walks around to help Cliff. Martha gets up and goes to the drinking fountain without permission.)

Kathy: The answer is sixty.

Teacher: How did you get sixty?

Kathy: I took three away from this three and that left zero. Then I took four away from the ten and that left six.
(The teacher walks over to help Kathy.)
Michael: Cliff has one of my sticks.
Teacher: Cliff, did you take one of Michael's sticks?
Cliff: Well, he was teasing me.
Teacher: Please give it back and keep your hands off other people's property.
(The teacher continues to help Kathy. Suddenly students throughout the room begin to laugh. The teacher looks over to Phillip who has used two of the sticks to make fangs and is pretending to be a monster.)
Teacher: Phillip! O.K., everyone, get back to work. Michael, did you get the answer?
Michael: I don't know how to do it.

Students are losing interest in the lesson. What should the teacher do to capture their interest again? Let's take a look at two teachers to see what each might do.

Teacher (Ms. Hilbern): O.K., everyone, put your sticks in the box. Then take one of these worksheets.
(Ms. Hilbern passes out a worksheet which reviews single-digit subtraction.)
Teacher: I want you to work alone on these problems. If you have any trouble, raise your hand, and I'll come around and help you. When you finish, raise your hand, and I'll correct your work.

The second teacher might deal with the situation as follows:

Teacher (Ms. Gilborg): Let's put away our sticks and papers and play a little game.
(Ms. Gilborg goes to the closet and takes out a box of play money.)
Teacher: Let's pretend that this is a grocery store and I am the clerk. Everybody gets fifteen dollars to start with. *(She gives each child except Phillip a ten and five ones. She gives Phillip a large stack of ones.)* Now, Phillip is a banker. When you buy something, I will only take the correct amount; I don't keep change because I am afraid of burglars. When you pay me, I drop the money into this closed safe. If you don't have the right amount of change, you'll have to get change from Phillip. Whenever you buy something, write down how much money you are starting with, how much your bill is, and how much you have left over when you have paid your bill.
(The teacher allows each child three turns to buy something and pay the bill. Only Martha has difficulty with the problems.)
Teacher: Now, let's see if you can work these problems in your head.
(The teacher gives hypothetical transactions to the students, beginning with single-digit subtraction and proceeding to subtraction requiring regrouping.)

Why did these two teachers' strategies differ so in dealing with the same classroom situation? We think that differences in teachers' strategies result from differences in their *decisions*. Teaching, then, can be characterized as a process of decision making; sometimes teachers are aware of their decisions, and sometimes they make them automatically. From this perspective, each teacher has a repertoire of teaching strategies and materials that are potentially useful in a particular teaching situation. The choice of a particular strategy depends on the teacher's goals for the lesson, beliefs about teaching, and information about the students.

In the classroom situation just described, both teachers decided to have the children put the sticks away and begin a new activity. The activities that they selected were, however, very different. These differences may have arisen from differences in what the teachers knew about the students' abilities and interests, differences in their beliefs about teaching, or differences in their goals for the lessons. The following sections of this chapter will present several specific explanations for the different choices and will present research bearing on these explanations.

A MODEL FOR TEACHERS' DECISIONS

When teaching is viewed as a decision-making process, the teacher is seen as an active agent who selects a teaching skill or strategy in order to help students reach some goal. This choice may be based on one or more factors. If all of the types of information mentioned above were used, teachers would need to integrate the large amount of information about students available from a variety of sources and somehow combine this information with their own beliefs and purposes, the nature of the instructional task, the constraints of the situation, and so on, in order to select an appropriate instructional strategy.

We are proposing a model for decision making that identifies some important types of information that might influence teachers' instructional decisions (see Figure 7-1). This model is simply a heuristic device that provides one way of thinking about teaching from a decision-making perspective. It has, in addition, proved helpful in explaining and integrating previous research findings and in planning our own research. As such, the model is really a set of

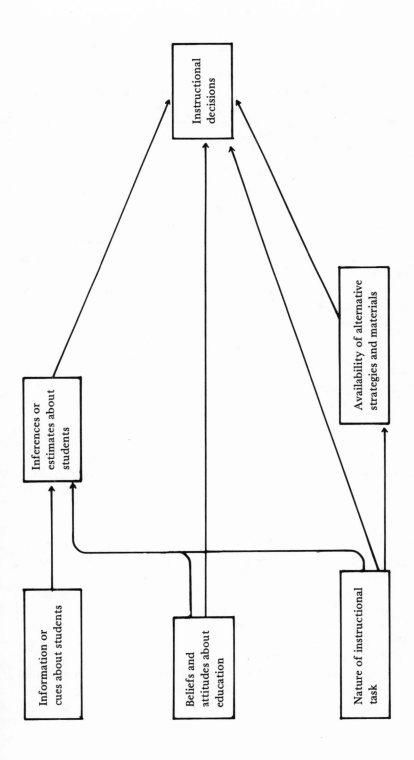

Figure 7-1

Some factors contributing to teachers' preinstructional decisions

hunches or hypotheses about important factors in teachers' decisions. We expect that the model will be revised as more is learned about this process.

The decision model identifies several important factors that are expected to affect teachers' decisions about instruction. Teachers deal with a large amount of information about their students from many sources (for example, their own informal observations, anecdotal reports of other teachers, standardized test scores, school records). The model suggests that, in order to handle the "information overload," teachers integrate this information into a few "best guesses" (estimates) about the student's learning, feelings, and behavior. These estimates may influence teachers' plans for instruction and the decisions they make, consciously or unconsciously, during instruction. As the model indicates, plans and decisions may also be influenced by the teachers' educational beliefs and the nature of the instructional tasks. The instructional task may also indirectly affect instructional decisions by limiting the alternative strategies that the teacher considers. Finally, the availability of strategies and materials may influence decisions by limiting or expanding the number of alternatives from which the teacher can choose.

Information and Inferences about Students

One type of information that teachers consider when making instructional decisions relates to the characteristics of their students. Teachers know a lot about the students—more than they can possibly use in making a decision. We know, however, that people often handle an "information overload" by paying attention to only a small portion of the information available to them.[1]

One method that people use to simplify information is to classify or categorize people, events, or objects in some way.[2] Teachers probably combine available information into a few inferences or estimates about students and use these estimates to guide instructional decisions. Several studies support this view and indicate the types of information teachers use. In some of these studies, teachers identified the characteristics of students that they considered most important[3] or most desirable.[4] In other studies, teachers indicated the types of information they sought when making instructional decisions such as planning a reading program,[5] forming reading groups,[6] planning a social studies lesson,[7] or recommending students for different tracks in junior high school English.[8] Other studies have focused on student characteristics that teachers notice while teaching a lesson.[9] In most of these studies teachers sought the following types of information about students: general ability or achievement, class participation, self-image, social competence, classroom behavior, and work habits.

Several other studies suggest ways in which teachers may categorize students. For example, elementary teachers have used the following dimensions to categorize students: ability, motivation, classroom behavior, social competence, and personality problems.[10]

If teachers differ in the information or cues about students to which they attend, their inferences about students will be based on different pieces of information. The salience of a particular dimension would depend on what information the teacher considered, and differences in inferences about students may lead to differences in the choice of teaching strategy. For example, Ms. Hilbern may have recalled that Michael and Martha are quiet, withdrawn children who seem to lack self-confidence and become easily frustrated when lessons are difficult. She may have remembered also that Kathy often has difficulty with mathematics. From this information and the students' behavior during the lesson, Ms. Hilbern may have inferred that the activity was too difficult. This is the inference that may have led to her decision to have the students complete worksheets reviewing material that had been learned previously.

Ms. Gilborg, on the other hand, may have noticed that Phillip and Cliff had often been instigators of disruptive behavior. She may have recalled as well that Cliff, although he is a capable student, becomes bored easily and, when bored, often attempts to distract other students. Phillip, on the other hand, is the class clown. In his attempts to be the center of attention, he does many of the same things that Cliff does when he is bored. Ms. Gilborg may have inferred that Cliff and Phillip were disruptive because the lesson did not sustain their interest. She may have selected the grocery store game because it required more active involvement on the students' part. She may have asked Phillip to be the banker, so that his desire to be the center of attention could be put to constructive use.

Educational Beliefs

Several studies conducted over the past twelve years suggest that teachers' beliefs affect their instructional decisions. Sontag found that teachers' beliefs fall into one of three groups: traditional, progressive, and mixed (teachers who hold both traditional and progressive beliefs).[11] Other studies have reported that teachers' educational beliefs are related to their views about desirable teacher behavior[12] and teacher personality traits.[13] Still other studies have found that teachers' beliefs about important educational goals are related to their reports of their own teaching styles.[14]

Differences in Ms. Hilbern's and Ms. Gilborg's beliefs about education may also have led to differences in their instructional decisions. Ms. Hilbern may believe that academic learning is the most important goal of education; she may also stress the importance of discipline and control in the classroom. The decision to assign worksheets to the children may have reflected these concerns.

Ms. Gilborg, on the other hand, may see social and emotional growth, in addition to academic learning, as important educational goals. Her major concern may be getting students interested in learning, and she may be less concerned than Ms. Hilbern about classroom control and her role as the central figure in class activities. Selection of the grocery store activity may reflect these views about education.

Nature of the Instructional Task

Instructional decisions may also be influenced by the nature of the instructional task. Two important aspects of the instructional task that affect teachers' decisions are the nature of the subject matter and the goals of instruction. For example, a lesson on addition imposes different limitations on a teacher than a lesson in art. Similarly, a lesson for which the major objective is cognitive imposes different limitations than a lesson for which the major objective is affective.

Unfortunately, research has not been done on how the nature of the instructional task affects teachers' decisions. Research on judgment and problem solving suggests, however, that the characteristics of the task may influence the set of alternatives that a person considers. Newell and Simon argue that, because people can use only a limited amount of information at one time, they construct a "problem space" to simplify the process of selecting a strategy for completing a task.[15] This problem space consists of a set of potential solutions from which the person will choose when faced with that particular task.

One study of teaching style showed that the types of classroom management strategies used by teachers are greatly influenced by the type of instructional activity.[16] For example, teachers attempted to control students' behavior more during recitation lessons than during multitask activities involving small groups and independent projects. Teachers also tended to handle misbehavior on a more individualized basis during multitask activities than during recitation activities.

The nature of the instructional task may also indirectly affect teachers' decisions by influencing the cues to which the teachers attend and their estimates about students. Since different student abilities may be required for success at different instructional tasks, teachers may consider different cues and make different estimates about students when planning different instructional tasks. For example, teachers' estimates about their students' ability in mathematics may play an important role in determining the strategy used to teach a lesson on fractions, but have little to do with decisions about how to teach a lesson on creative writing.

Differences in Ms. Hilbern's and Ms. Gilborg's primary objectives for the mathematics lesson may have led to differences in their instructional decisions. For example, Ms. Hilbern's major objective may have been a cognitive one—that the students correctly solve the subtraction problems without using their wooden sticks. When she realized that the task was too difficult, she may have selected another, easier cognitive objective—that students correctly solve problems involving single-digit subtraction. Use of the review worksheets may have been intended to achieve this revised objective. In contrast, Ms. Gilborg's major objective may have been an affective one —interest in mathematics through active participation in the lesson. When the children began to lose interest in the activity, she may have decided to use the grocery store game as an alternative strategy for attaining the same objective.

Ms. Hilbern's and Ms. Gilborg's decisions may have been affected as well by the problem spaces they constructed. For example, Ms. Hilbern may have in her repertoire of teaching strategies a set of possible techniques for teaching subtraction with regrouping. If activities such as the grocery store game were not included in this set of potential solutions, she would not have been able to consider this activity when selecting an alternative instructional strategy.

Other Possible Explanations

Teachers' instructional decisions may be influenced by a number of other factors. Such things as educational facilities, material resources, school politics, pressure from the community or administration, and teacher training undoubtedly affect instructional decisions, but such factors, which may limit or extend the alternative strategies from which teachers may choose, will not be further considered in this chapter.

HOW TEACHERS MAKE DECISIONS

Our approach to studying decision making by teachers has been experimental. The experiments investigate relationships hypothesized in the model in Figure 7-1. In order to study the model, we systematically varied different parts of it by simulating actual classrooms in the laboratory. This was done by providing descriptions of fictitious students and their classroom conduct to teachers with different educational beliefs. These teachers were then asked to make several different types of instructional decisions for a variety of instructional tasks.

There are two major advantages to this experimental, laboratory-based approach. First, it allows us to isolate the effects of important factors on teacher decision making in a simple, straightforward way. The complexities and interrelationships between factors found in the real world can be disentangled in the laboratory. Second, this method provides a relatively inexpensive way to test some basic hypotheses about teachers' decision making before more expensive experiments in actual classrooms are conducted.

The major limitations of this approach relate to the extent to which our findings in the laboratory generalize to the actual classroom. Since there are great differences between actual classrooms and our simulations, it is not clear that the results apply to real teaching situations. For example, it may be that the types of information about students used by teachers in our studies are different from the types of information that teachers actually use in their own classrooms.

Four studies described below investigate the effects of some of the factors identified in Figure 7-1 on different types of instructional decisions in different contexts. Study I examines the accuracy of teachers' estimates about students and the effects of these estimates on instructional decisions. Study II investigates the importance of several of the factors specified in the figure on decisions about planning instruction in reading and mathematics. Study III focuses on the effects of these factors in determining decisions about planning classroom organization and management. Finally, Study IV explores interactive decisions (decisions made in the course of interaction with students) about classroom management in the context of a reading lesson.

Our plans for future research are directed at the concerns about generalizability. Once we have completed a series of laboratory studies to isolate critical factors in the decision-making process, we plan to do research in the classroom. In this way we can verify our laboratory findings in the field. In addition, we will be able to investigate the impact of instructional strategies selected by teachers on students' achievement and their feelings about school.

Study I: Accuracy of Teachers' Estimates and Their Effects on Decisions

Study I focused on the accuracy of teachers' estimates of student aptitudes and the influence of these estimates on teachers' instructional decisions.[17] One purpose of the study was to examine whether teachers make optimal use of information when estimating student aptitudes. In particular, how accurately do teachers estimate a student's ability when given some initial cues about the student? Further, when teachers receive additional information about the student's performance, how accurately do they revise their initial estimate of the student's aptitude? A second purpose of the study was to examine the influence of teachers' estimates of student aptitudes on their decisions. In particular, do teachers take into account their initial estimate of the student's ability when making instructional decisions? Further, do teachers revise their initial decisions when provided additional information about student performance? A third purpose was to determine the influence of reliable and unreliable and positive and negative information on teachers' estimates and decisions.

Teachers were given a story about a hypothetical student named Michael. Sixteen different stories were constructed. Each teacher, however, read only one of the sixteen versions. These stories contained initial information about Michael that varied in terms of reliability (reliable or unreliable information) and valence (high or low in ability and effort). The base story for the initial information was:

Michael is ten years old and beginning the fifth grade. He lives with his parents, an older brother, and two younger sisters.

Reliability and valence of initial information were varied along three dimensions: father's occupation, Michael's use of time, and Michael's intelligence. For example, the reliable and positive insert was:

. . . In an interview with his parents, his father gave his occupation as an engineer in an aerodynamics firm. In the interview his parents also noted that Michael spent about two hours each evening on his homework and reading books. On an individual test, Michael scored quite high.

The unreliable and negative insert was:

. . . In an interview, a classmate stated that, while he did not know Michael well, he thought Michael's father worked on airplanes. He also thought Michael never did any homework, spent a lot of time watching television, and was not very smart.

Subjects read a version of this initial story and were asked to estimate the probability that Michael would earn grades of B or better in the fifth grade and to make one preinstructional and two interactive decisions. (We refer to these judgments as decisions at "time one.")

Teachers were then given additional information about Michael. This additional information also varied on three dimensions: academic ability, curiosity, and attitude toward school. For example, the unreliable and positive insert was:

. . . When interviewed, some of Michael's classmates said that they liked him and that they thought he was a good student. Cathy Robbins, an education student at a nearby college, had been hired as a substitute aide at Michael's school. She had assisted in Michael's class for a few days and had decided to administer an inkblot test to the class. She interpreted the results to mean that Michael was curious and enthusiastic about academic activities and that he had a positive attitude toward school.

Subjects read the additional information and were asked to make the probability estimate and instructional decisions a second time. (We refer to these judgments as decisions at "time two.")

The results suggested that, in making estimates about student ability, teachers were sensitive to the reliability and valence of the information they received. For example, when information was positive and reliable, teachers indicated that the probability was high that Michael would earn grades of B or better at the end of the fifth grade. Similarly, when information was negative and reliable, teachers indicated that the probability was low. However, when information was unreliable, teachers tended to ignore this information and provided more moderate estimates. Moreover, teachers revised their initial estimates in the appropriate direction when given additional information.

The preinstructional decision required teachers to select the appropriate level of instructional materials for Michael. Results indicated that, at time one, teachers' estimates of Michael's ability were the important factors in making this decision. At time two, additional information had a strong influence on revisions of this decision made by the teacher. Again, the additional information indirectly influenced the teachers' decisions via their estimates of Michael's ability. This finding indicates that the teachers formed composite estimates of Michael rather than using each piece of information, and they were quite willing to revise their initial decision based on new information.

A different pattern of results was found for the two interactive instructional decisions. When teachers were asked what they would do if Michael failed to answer a question during a mathematics lesson, they tended to ignore the information about Michael and their estimates of his ability in making this decision. Further, when given additional information about the student, teachers tended to ignore it and base their revised decision on their initial one. This makes sense since information about general ability had little relevance to the particular situation. It appears that the teachers' responses to the decision depended on factors not measured in the experiment, such as their personal preference for teaching method or philosophy of teaching.

A similar picture was found for the second interactive decision, which concerned the importance of reinforcement for Michael. Ability, as well as the other information contained in the story, played a minor role in the decision. Again, the prior decision was the most influential factor in the revised decision.

In summary, this study suggests that teachers may use different kinds of information to make different kinds of decisions. For the initial, preinstructional decision—choosing material at the appropriate grade level—teachers based their decisions primarily on their estimate of Michael's ability and much less on other specific information contained in the story. They revised their initial decisions when new information became available. In contrast, for the two interactive decisions—questioning and reinforcement strategies—teachers tended to give little or no weight to the information available in their estimates and in the stories. Rather, their decisions at time one and time two were influenced by factors not measured in the study. One possible explanation for this finding involved the relevance of the information to the instructional decision.

Study II: Preinstructional Decisions in Reading and Mathematics

Study II examined the effects of student cues, teacher beliefs, and types of lessons (see Figure 7-1) on preinstructional decisions in reading and mathematics. In particular, the following questions were investigated: What informational cues do teachers take into account when making estimates about students? How do these estimates affect teachers' preinstructional decisions? How do their beliefs affect preinstructional decisions? How do beliefs about education influence the cues and estimates about students to which teachers attend in making these decisions? How does the nature of the instructional task influence the cues and estimates about students to which teachers attend in making these preinstructional decisions?

Teachers with experience at the primary level (grades one to three) first completed a questionnaire concerning their beliefs about education. They were then given descriptions of hypothetical second-grade students who systematically varied on the following dimensions (cues): sex, reading achievement, mathematics achievement, class participation, and appropriateness of classroom behavior. After reading each description, teachers made three estimates about each student concerning:

1. the likelihood that the student would master most of the concepts and skills typically included in the second-grade reading curriculum by the end of the school year;
2. the likelihood that the student would master most of the concepts and skills typically included in the second-grade mathematics curriculum by the end of the year; and

3. the likelihood that the student would be a behavior problem
in the classroom.

Next, they placed students into reading groups and then into mathematics groups. Finally, subjects were given descriptions of three reading and three mathematics lessons (instructional tasks) that are commonly taught in the second grade. Two of the reading lessons dealt with cognitive objectives: a decoding lesson on phonics skills and a comprehension lesson on sequencing of events. The third lesson was aimed at an affective objective: encouraging students to read for fun. Two of the mathematics lessons also involved cognitive objectives: a lesson on place value of two-digit numbers and a lesson introducing two-digit addition with carrying. The third mathematics lesson was directed toward an affective objective: encouraging students to play mathematics games and puzzles in their free time.

Teachers were asked to make a series of preinstructional decisions about appropriate strategies for teaching each of these lessons to each group. These decisions involved planning an instructional strategy for teaching the objective, selecting materials for the lesson, selecting follow-up activities to provide practice for students, allowing time in the lesson for motivation, and assessing the importance of mastery of the objective for the group.

We found that teachers based their estimates primarily on the one cue most relevant to the estimate. For example, teachers' estimates of the likelihood that a student would master the skills and concepts included in the second-grade reading curriculum were based on the student's prior achievement in reading. Similarly, estimates of the likelihood of mastering mathematics skills and concepts were based primarily on the student's achievement in mathematics. In addition, estimates of the likelihood that a student would be a behavior problem in the classroom were based primarily on accounts of the student's prior behavior in the classroom.

Teachers' grouping strategies were based primarily on students' achievement. Furthermore, teachers differed in their grouping strategies. Some teachers, for example, used only information about reading achievement in forming reading groups. Other teachers took into account both achievement in mathematics and achievement in reading.

Finally, teachers' decisions about appropriate strategies for teaching reading and mathematics were based on several factors: educational beliefs, the nature of the group being taught, and the type of instructional objective. For example, in deciding on a strategy for teaching each lesson, progressive teachers tended to select alternatives involving an inquiry approach while more traditional teachers tended to favor lecture or recitation approaches. In making decisions about instructional materials, teachers tended to select manipulative materials for mathematics lessons and more abstract materials (for example, pictures or verbal representations) for reading lessons. In addition, teachers tended to allot more time to motivational activities for groups of low-achieving students than for high-achieving ones.

Study III: Preinstructional Classroom Organization and Management Decisions

Study III focused on the influence of three critical factors in the decision model on preinstructional decisions about classroom organization and management strategies. In particular, the study explored the effects of educational beliefs and cues and estimates about students on these decisions at the fifth-grade level.

Teachers with experience at the upper-elementary level (grades four to six) first completed a questionnaire about their educational beliefs. They then read descriptions of hypothetical, fifth-grade students who systematically varied on six dimensions: sex, achievement, social competence, self-confidence, rule-following behavior, and ability to work independently. After reading each description, teachers made three estimates about the student concerning:

1. the likelihood that the student would master most of the skills and concepts typically included in a fifth-grade curriculum by the end of the school year,
2. the likelihood that the student would be highly motivated during most class activities, and
3. the likelihood that the student would be a behavior problem in the classroom.

Teachers were then asked to make a series of decisions about appropriate classroom organization and management strategies and long-term educational goals for the student. These decisions involved recommendations about referral for special testing or consideration for placement in a special program, participation in a peer-tutoring program as a tutor or a tutee, appropriate degree of involvement of students in planning their own instructional activities, and the importance of long-term objectives for the student in the following areas: basic academic skills, social competence, and emotional growth.

The results from this study are currently being analyzed and, at present, only tentative, preliminary findings can be presented. As in Study II, teachers based their estimates primarily on the single student cue most relevant to the estimate. For example, teachers' estimates of the likelihood that a student would master the skills and concepts included in a fifth-grade curriculum were determined primarily by the student's prior academic achievement. Other, less important cues were the student's classroom behavior and the ability to work independently. Similarly, estimates of the likelihood that a student would be a behavior problem were based primarily on the student's prior behavior in the classroom. Estimates of the likelihood that a student would be highly motivated were determined by a combination of several characteristics—achievement, behavior in the classroom, and ability to work independently.

Analyses of the teachers' decisions about classroom organization and management strategies are not yet completed. Preliminary analyses indicate that these decisions are based primarily on estimates about the students. In addition, student characteristics that do not play an important role in determining the estimates appear to influence directly those decisions for which they are most relevant. For example, teachers' decisions about the importance of long-term objectives in basic academic skills appear to be based primarily on their estimates of the likelihood that a student will master most of the skills and concepts included in a fifth-grade curriculum by the end of the school year. Decisions about the importance of long-term objectives in the area of social competence seem to be determined primarily by a student's ability to get along with peers, and decisions about the importance of long-term objectives in the area of emotional growth seem to be based primarily on a student's self-image.

Study IV: Interactive Decisions About Classroom Management

Study IV focused on interactive decisions about classroom management in the context of a reading lesson at the fifth-grade level. One purpose of this study was to examine teachers' use of information about students in deciding how to respond to deviant behavior. A second purpose was to examine how beliefs about education affect these decisions. Teachers with experience at the upper-elementary level first completed questionnaires concerning their beliefs about education. Scenarios that described an incident as it allegedly occurred within a particular classroom setting systematically varied information about the organizational structure of a fifth-grade reading lesson (large-group recitation or independent small-group activities), the sex of the deviant child (as designated by a relatively common, Anglo name), background information about the deviant student (a history of deviancy or no such history), and a description of the deviant act (out of seat, noise, vocalizations, physical aggression). After reading each description, teachers estimated the probability that the deviant behavior would disrupt classroom instruction. They were then asked to indicate the type of management technique they felt would be most effective in dealing with the student's deviant behavior. These techniques included the following strategies: ignoring the deviant behavior; using a nonverbal technique, such as establishing eye contact; requesting politely that the deviant behavior cease; using reprimands, rebukes, demands, or other strong verbal approaches; punishing by taking away privileges or giving extra work; isolating the child; referring the child to a counselor or the principal; recommending suspension or transfer to another teacher or school; and using corporal punishment.

Data from Study IV are currently being analyzed. Preliminary analyses indicate that the factor primarily responsible for teachers' estimates of the probability of disruption is the previous history of the deviant child. For example, an abrasive and hard-to-manage student was considered more likely to disrupt the class with a given deviant act than a quiet and considerate student. The type of deviant act, while not having much effect on the estimates of the probability of disruption, appears to affect the decisions, with acts of violence consistently being met with more severe managerial techniques. Management decisions also seem to be affected by the estimates of the probability of disruption. As the probability of disruption increases, managerial techniques become increasingly severe. Finally, teacher beliefs, the organizational structure of the classroom, and the sex of the deviant child do not appear to be significant factors.

What the Studies Suggest

Together, these four studies suggest that teachers making decisions in laboratory settings base their decisions on the most relevant information at hand. They look at reading scores to make estimates of the likelihood of mastering certain reading objectives and, in turn, look at these estimates to make decisions about forming reading groups. They look at previous behavior to form estimates of disruptiveness and use these estimates to make management decisions. These findings provide preliminary support for the usefulness of the model proposed in this chapter as a way of helping us to understand the teaching-learning process.

IMPLICATIONS OF THE MODEL

All too frequently educational researchers are faced with the fact that their "latest discovery" is common knowledge to the classroom teacher. Such may be the case with the decision-making approach presented here, in which teaching is viewed as a complex and demanding task requiring almost constant decision making. Teachers are aware of the complexities of using the "right material" with the "right student" at the "right time." They know the difficulty of deciding which program is most likely to be effective for a particular student. They are aware that all techniques do not work with all students. Why, then, spend time investigating a model of teaching about which teachers already seem knowledgeable? We have examined the decision model because:

1. It is a model that offers a broader perspective of the teaching-learning process than traditional approaches and leads to a reconceptualization of other research and an integration of apparently contradictory findings.
2. It is a model that looks at the rationality of the teaching process rather than prescribing a single "best" way of teaching.
3. It is a humanistic model that depicts teachers as professional decision makers who are competent in their field, rather than as black boxes to be programmed with teaching skills.
4. It is an instructional model that, we hope, will give teachers more specific information about how and why they make certain decisions.
5. It is a model with direct implications for both preservice and in-service training.

Much research in education has focused on a particular, narrowly defined aspect of teaching or learning. The research is certainly valuable in contributing to an understanding of specific components of the teaching-learning process. Results from individual studies are often contradictory, however, and the studies themselves offer no way of resolving these contradictions.[18] The model of teaching and the research studies reported here view teaching not merely as a process of asking higher-order questions, using a discovery mode, or enhancing motivation, but as a process of integrating all of our knowledge and skills into a decision that best suits the situation at any given moment. Thus, the model offers a broader perspective of the teaching-learning process than traditional approaches and provides a framework for understanding and integrating previous research findings.

In the past, many educators have tended to view teaching methods, materials, and programs as "effective" or "ineffective" based on their own conceptions of what constitutes good teaching. Only recently has there been a move away from this unidimensional view that there is one best way to teach (and to learn).[19] But, for the most part, educators tend to believe that different teaching techniques should only be used in response to individual differences in students. The model proposed in this chapter suggests that certain methods, materials, and programs might be better for one teacher than another, even given the same set of students. The model also implies that there are optimal ways for teachers to make instructional and managerial decisions, but these methods might vary from teacher to teacher. Thus, the model emphasizes the importance of considering individual differences in teachers as well as individual differences in students when making educational decisions. The research reported in this chapter examined one such individual difference—teachers' beliefs about education. Our preliminary analyses indicated that the measure of educational beliefs we used did not predict teachers' decisions, perhaps because this measure was not sensitive enough to the differences in beliefs of the teachers participating in the studies. We still believe that individual differences in teachers do affect their decisions, and we plan to continue to explore the role of individual differences in our future research.

Unfortunately, many models of teaching lead to the belief that teachers can and should be programmed so they can effectively use "desirable" methods, materials, and programs. Efforts to train teachers stemming from these models are often met by failure, particularly when teachers attempt to integrate the individual skills they have been taught. These failures are sometimes blamed on resistance or ignorance on the part of the teacher. As a result, some curriculum developers have gone so far as to suggest that teachers should be given "teacher-proof" materials and programs so that they can teach effectively. The decision-making model suggests that these failures may not be because of the teachers at all. Rather, they may result from the erroneous assumption underlying training efforts that a particular program will work in any given classroom, under any circumstances. More specifically, the decision-making model suggests that, for particular strategies to be successful, teachers should be involved in deciding if and when the strategies are appropriate for them and their students.

But the model should not be judged solely on how well it helps researchers reconceptualize research or how effective it is in altering our conceptualization of teaching and teachers. Like all models of teaching, this approach must address the question: How can it help teachers in the classroom?

It is our belief that simply making teachers more aware of their own decision-making strategies may enhance their ability to make professional decisions. There are several reasons why this may be true. Perhaps most important is realizing that teachers, like everyone else, are limited in the amount of information they can handle at any one time. Because of this limitation, simplifying strategies are not only used, but are probably essential. This leads to an examination of personal strategies for dealing with large amounts of information. Under what conditions do individual teachers simplify information? How is it simplified? How effectively is it simplified? Who, if anyone, is helped or hurt by these strategies? Such an examination has the same effect as an examination of personal prejudices. The prejudice may remain, but it is never quite the same once examined.

Much of the literature about the effects of teacher expectancies on students is highly moralistic in tone; teacher expectations for students are seen as potentially harmful and damaging to students.[20] From the decision perspective, however, expectations are essential in handling the information overload. Furthermore, teachers' expectations are often accurate.[21] If students get into trouble every time they leave their seats, should not the teacher expect those same students to get into trouble the next time? This is not to condone all expectations held by teachers. Many teachers, perhaps all teachers, have some expectations for students that are erroneous, that is, they are founded on insufficient or inaccurate information. These less-than-optimal simplifying strategies can be more realistically examined once we understand that simplifying strategies are a common response to "information overload" and that it is not simplifying strategies per se, but particular ineffective strategies, that should be eliminated or revised.

Familiarity with this conceptualization of teaching may also help teachers to understand better the interplay between student behavior, task, demands, and instructional decisions. For example, one watch-word among experienced teachers is to "be consistent." Frequently this is interpreted by new teachers to mean "treat students the same under all conditions." Teachers either attempt to be consistent in this way and are frustrated in their efforts, or they vary their behavior according to the situation and suffer moments of guilt for their lack of consistency. The decision-making model of teaching suggests an alternative view of consistency, one which takes into account the elements entering into a teacher's decisions (for example, student behaviors, task demands) as well as the decisions themselves. According to this model, teachers act consistently when they utilize the same strategy to reach a series of instructional decisions. For example, a teacher may be acting consistently in allowing a great deal of discussion among students who are taking turns solving mathematic problems at the chalkboard, but expecting students to remain seated and quiet when the correct solution is demonstrated on the board. It may be that the objective of allowing student discussion is to reduce tension and create an atmosphere in which students do not fear trying. In contrast, the objective of the more structured follow-up may be to allow everyone an opportunity to see the correct way to solve the problem. These differing task demands call for quite different decisions about the appropriate way for the students and teacher to relate to each other. A single decision strategy that takes into account both task demands and student behavior can lead to two quite different instructional practices.

One additional way of using the decision model would be to train teachers in the use of decision-making strategies in preservice and in-service training programs. Currently the primary training in decision making that teachers receive occurs when they are actually in their own classrooms. Teacher-training programs provide a lot of information about the subject matter, curriculum, and principles of learning and development. They also frequently provide opportunities to try out specific skills under simulated conditions. Until teachers are actually face to face with students in a classroom (usually their first student-teaching experience), however, they seldom get an opportunity to try to integrate their knowledge and skills into a lesson taught to a large number of students in an actual classroom situation. Frequently this lack of actual experience in the classroom means that student teachers venture into the classroom with a simplistic view of teaching and with a sorely inadequate basis for using the knowledge they possess.

One way of providing teachers and prospective teachers with less painful and perhaps more beneficial practice in making instructional decisions has been suggested by Shavelson.[22] Teachers could be asked to state how they make decisions about grouping, assigning lessons, selecting programs, managing students, and so on. These stated policies could be compared to responses to written descriptions of teaching situations similar to those used in the studies described above. Discrepancies between actual policies and stated policies could be reported back to the teachers. Given this information, teachers could either revise their decisions to match their stated policies or review and alter their policies.

One drawback of this procedure is that the determination of actual decision policies currently requires considerable time. It has been suggested that simulations that make use of interactive computers could provide immediate information on the decision strategies used by teachers.[23] In addition to providing immediate feedback on the discrepancies between stated and actual policies, computers could be programmed to demonstrate discrepancies between the teacher's strategies and other strategies proposed as effective or optimal. In this way, teachers could continue working with simulations until satisfied that their actual decision policy would be personally most effective.

The model of teaching as decision making that we have proposed is, at the present, in its formative stages. Results of our initial studies, described in this chapter, suggest that teaching can, in fact, be conceptualized as a decision-making process. Specifically, our findings indicate that teachers actually do make complex decisions, carefully weighing information in light of their own beliefs about teaching and the task demands. In addition teachers, in some cases, seem to simplify the complexity of the decision-making task by forming estimates of students that, in turn, influence their decisions. Finally, results from these studies suggest that teachers may be reasonably good decision makers when making instructional decisions since they base their decisions primarily on reliable and relevant information.

A word of caution is essential at this point. To date, all of our studies have been conducted in controlled laboratory situations. Thus, the generalizability of our results to the actual classroom situation remains to be demonstrated. Teachers who have participated in these experiments have, however, said that the experiments do begin to simulate the process they go through countless times a day when making planning decisions, on-the-spot instructional decisions, and behavior-management decisions. Thus, we are optimistic that research with this model in actual classroom situations will provide an important framework for understanding and improving the teaching-learning process.

NOTES

1. Paul Slovic, "From Shakespeare to Simon: Speculations—and Some Evidence—about Man's Ability to Process Information," *Oregon Research Institute Monograph* 12 (1972): 1-29; Paul Slovic, Baruch Fischhoff, and Sarah C. Lichtenstein, "Cognitive Processes and Societal Risk Taking," in *Cognition and Social Behavior*, ed. John S. Carroll and John W. Payne (New York: Halsted Press, 1976), 165-184.

2. Jerome Bruner, Jacqueline Goodnow, and George Austin, *A Study of Thinking* (New York: John Wiley and Sons, 1956).

3. Barbara Long and Edmund Henderson, "The Effects of Pupils' Race, Class, Test Scores, and Classroom Behavior on the Academic Expectancies of Southern and Non-Southern White Teachers," paper presented at the annual meeting of the American Educational Research Association, Chicago, 1972; Arnold Morrison and Donald McIntyre, *Teachers and Teaching* (Baltimore, Md.: Penguin Books, 1969).

4. Kaoru Yamamoto, "Images of the Ideal Pupil Held by Teachers in Preparation," *California Journal of Educational Research* 20 (1969): 221-232; Charles Schaefer, "An Exploratory Study of Teachers' Descriptions of the 'Ideal' Pupil," *Psychology in the Schools* 10 (1973): 444-447.

5. Greta Morine, *A Study of Teacher Planning*, Technical Report, Beginning

Teacher Evaluation Study (San Francisco: Far West Regional Laboratory for Educational Research and Development, 1976).

6. Rebecca C. Barr, "How Children Are Taught to Read: Grouping and Pacing," *School Review* 83 (1975): 478-498.

7. Penelope L. Peterson, Ronald W. Marx, and Christopher M. Clark, *Teacher Planning, Teacher Behavior, and Student Achievements*, (Madison, Wis.: School of Education, University of Wisconsin, 1977), mimeo.

8. Harley M. Albro and Emil J. Haller, "Teachers' Perceptions and Their Tracking Decisions," *Administrator's Notebook* 20 (1972): 1-4.

9. Christopher Clark and Penelope Peterson, "Teacher Stimulated Recall of Interactive Decisions," paper presented at the annual meeting of the American Educational Research Association, San Francisco, 1976; Greta Morine and Elizabeth Vallance, *A Study of Teacher and Pupil Perceptions of Classroom Interation*, Technical Report, Beginning Teacher Evaluation Study (San Francisco: Far West Laboratory for Educational Research and Development, 1976).

10. Gerald Rubenstein and Lawrence Fisher, "A Measure of Teachers' Observations of Student Behavior," *Journal of Consulting and Clinical Psychology* 42 (1974): 310; G. W. Herbert, "Teachers' Ratings of Classroom Behavior: Factorial Structure," *British Journal of Educational Psychology* 44 (1974): 233-240.

11. Marvin Sontag, "Attitudes toward Education and Perception of Teacher Behaviors," *American Educational Research Journal* 5 (1968): 385-402.

12. *Ibid.*

13. Fred N. Kerlinger and Elazar J. Pedhazur, "Educational Attitudes and Perceptions of Desirable Traits of Teachers," *American Educational Research Journal* 5 (1968): 543-559.

14. P. Ashton *et al.*, *The Aims of Primary Education: A Study of Teachers' Opinions* (London: Macmillan and Co., 1975); Neville Bennett, *Teaching Styles and Pupil Progress* (London: Open Books, 1976).

15. Arthur Newell and Herbert A. Simon, *Human Problem Solving* (Englewood Cliffs, N.J.: Prentice-Hall, 1972).

16. Steven T. Bossert, "Tasks, Group Management, and Teacher-Control Behavior: A Study of Classroom Organization and Teacher Style," *School Review* 85 (1977): 552-565.

17. Richard J. Shavelson, Joel Cadwell, and Tonia Izu, "Teachers' Sensitivity to the Reliability of Information in Making Pedagogical Decisions," *American Educational Research Journal* 14 (1977): 83-97.

18. Oded Erlich and Richard J. Shavelson, "The Search for Correlations between Measures of Teacher Behavior and Student Achievement: Measurement Problem, Conceptualization Problem, or Both?" *Journal of Educational Measurement* 15 (1978): 77-89.

19. Lee J. Cronbach and Richard E. Snow, *Aptitude and Instructional Methods* (New York: Irving Publishers, 1977).

20. Robert Rosenthal and Lenore Jacobson, *Pygmalion in the Classroom* (New York: Holt, Rinehart and Winston, 1968).

21. Shavelson, Cadwell, and Izu, "Teachers' Sensitivity to the Reliability of Information in Making Pedagogical Decisions."

22. Richard J. Shavelson, "Teachers' Decision Making," in *The Psychology of Teaching Methods,* Seventy-fifth Yearbook of the National Society for the Study of Education, Part I, ed. N. L. Gage (Chicago: University of Chicago Press, 1976), 372-414.

23. *Ibid.*

8. Curriculum, Instruction, and Materials

Harriet Talmage and *Maurice J. Eash*

Many variables interact in complex ways to give each educational setting distinctive characteristics.[1] Studies of some of the variables are reported elsewhere in this and the companion volume (*Educational Environments and Effects: Evaluation, Policy, and Productivity*, edited by Herbert J. Walberg). In this chapter we narrow the examination to three determinants of classroom learning environments: curriculum, instruction, and instructional materials. Learners' perceptions of their classes, as measured by scales found in two inventories, the *Learning Environment Inventory* (LEI) and the *My Class Inventory*, are used as indicators of learning environments in classrooms.[2]

Ideally, curriculum, instruction, and instructional materials make different but essential contributions to an educational program. Curriculum identifies what is taught; instruction encompasses planning and implementing the teaching-learning transactions; and instructional materials provide the physical media through which the intents of the curriculum, mediated instructionally, are experienced. It would be convenient if their separate impact on the learning environment were measurable, as well as their relationships to specific environmental characteristics. A clear-cut distinction among the three components of an educational program, however, is not readily apparent in practice. We propose a paradigm for sorting out the components to facilitate the study of their impact on learning environments in schools and classrooms.

We first explore each of the three determinants independent of the learning setting and of each other. A discussion of the interactions among the three that interfere with parceling out their separate effects follows, with a paradigm for studying the relationships and interactions. Finally, we describe four evaluation research studies to illustrate ways of studying the separate and interactive effects of curriculum, instruction, and instructional materials in naturalistic settings within the framework of the paradigm.

THE THREE DETERMINANTS VIEWED INDEPENDENTLY

Curriculum

The emergence of curriculum as an area of study under the more encompassing heading of education is generally attributed to Bobbitt.[3] His work technically marks curriculum as a field of study embedded in practice, as distinct from the work of philosophers of education or political policy makers. The latter are concerned with the purpose and goals of education rather than with selecting and organizing a body of knowledge, skills, and understandings, and attendant activities for ensuring experiences that fulfill these purposes and goals. While Bobbitt opened an area of study over a half century ago, curriculum specialists are still unable to agree on what constitutes curriculum as a field of study.[4]

Despite the inability of curriculum workers to arrive at an agreed-upon definition of curriculum, we propose a generic definition to provide a conceptual focus for our discussion. *Curriculum results from a preconceived idea or value position about the purpose of education and constitutes an educational program for fulfilling that purpose.* This definition of curriculum allows for all possible value positions, which in turn will determine what content is selected and how that content is intentionally organized through learning activities as an educational program to fulfill the articulated purposes. The values identified, the content selected and organized, the learning activities, and the procedures for evaluating the effectiveness of the curriculum in fulfilling the purposes of education—all contribute to a milieu for learning, as well as imposing in some measure constraints on the learning environment.

The point is illustrated by two examples: one a curriculum laid out by Stratemeyer and her colleagues[5] based on the notion that the purpose of education is to assist students in their efforts to resolve "persistent life situations," and a physics curriculum developed under the leadership of Zacharias.[6]

Efforts to resolve persistent life situations required a curriculum that emphasized the learner and his need to acquire skills needed to cope in society, including topics and subjects thought to be of most benefit to students in the course of living their normal lives. Given this curricular purpose, areas for study were grouped under three major headings: situations calling for growth in individual capacity; situations calling for growth in social participation; and situations calling for growth in ability to deal with environmental factors or forces. The typical subject-centered curriculum gives way to a curricular organization designed around the three-area framework. Under such a design, students are encouraged to explore, question, and select among alternatives. Students engaged in supporting learning activities possibly view their learning environment as cohesive, goal directed, and cooperative.

The Physical Science Study Committee (PSSC) curriculum was developed by Zacharias and other scientists in an effort to encourage political policy makers to update the teaching of physics, thereby preventing the United States from lagging behind Soviet Russia in the exploration of space during the 1950s. They saw a need to channel the brightest students into science and engineering in order to provide the United States with high-powered scientists and technicians. The purpose of education, thus, was to strengthen the United States in its role as the foremost world power. The physics curriculum was designed "to provide a sound foundation in high school for those students who plan to study science or engineering in college."[7] A curriculum designed to serve this purpose would tend to encourage students to excel as individuals, to master challenging and difficult scientific problems, and to build strong quantitative skills. A type of learning environment different from that based on persistent life situations is likely to result.

As seen from these two examples, a curriculum developed with a given educational purpose in mind can encourage a particular learning environment.

Instruction

Ideally, curriculum design dictates instruction. In the case of a biology curriculum in which the organizing focus or rationale builds upon an exploratory approach, we would expect the learning environment to be perceived differently by students than one in which the approach to science is based on acquiring an organized body of information. In the first case, the students are involved principally in open-ended activities; in the second case, the body of knowledge is usually acquired through attending lectures, reading, viewing audio-visual presentations, and recitation.

Instruction is further mediated by the goals of each curriculum regarding the social aspects of learning. If a goal of the exploratory curriculum were acquired through cooperative inquiry, we would expect the students' perceptions of their learning environment to differ from those of students engaged in an exploratory curriculum utilizing individualized, self-paced, and self-instructional exercises.

Instructional decisions that affect the learning environment arise from factors other than curricular considerations. Other possible influences include: school and classroom organization, scheduling, teacher variables, pupil variables, administrative support and constraints, and the general physical plant. For instance, the custodial staff has been known to dictate the physical arrangement of the classrooms in ways that alter how the teacher groups students for various learning activities. Such interference can shift the instructional emphasis from "hands-on" activities, with students working together in small groups, to less active forms of involvement in learning. This in turn would create a different learning environment.

Instructional Materials

Over the past hundred years, textbooks have played a singular role in education. To this day they *are* the curriculum in many classrooms. As such, the philosophy of education, the curriculum, and the instructional practices in a school district emanate from them.[8] As teachers and administrators delegate this decision-making authority to instructional materials, textbooks and other supporting instructional materials tend to determine the learning environment. A recent national survey conducted by the National Survey and Assessment of Instructional Materials found that more than 90 percent of the time that students are engaged in learning activities in the classroom is spent with instructional materials.[9]

Contrasting learning environments can be expected if teachers follow textbooks as they are designed. Comparison of two reading classes using two different reading series suggests two different types of learning environments. *McGuffey's Eclectic Primer* served for many generations as the reading curriculum of school districts across the United States.[10] It was more than a reading curriculum, or even a language arts curriculum. It laid out the lessons, the instructional sequence, the activities and response modes, teaching approaches, and the evaluation of student progress. In addition, it set a moral tone for expected social behavior. Visions of the learning environment in a class using the McGuffey reader suggest lack of disorganization but also lack of diversity and democracy, and a high degree of formality, goal directedness, and competitiveness.

A present-day class using the Scott, Foresman Systems becomes an entirely different learning environment. Materials are directed toward a number of different levels. The teacher moves from direct instruction to facilitation as the need arises, students are grouped and regrouped according to specific activities, and the pace of learning varies according to the individual needs of the students. The media employed also vary to accommodate learning styles. If these materials are used in the classroom as they were designed to be used, the learning environment might be characterized as cohesive, diverse, and democratic, but could possibly be perceived as difficult and disorganized by some students.

Curriculum, instruction, and instructional materials can and do exert separate influences on the learning environment.

RELATIONSHIP AND INTERACTION AMONG THE DETERMINANTS

Hypothetically the effects of each of the three determinants being discussed in terms of the classroom learning environment can be examined independently of the others by holding constant the other two determinants. This is shown as the open area labeled Level 1 in

Figure 8-1. At that level, curriculum, instruction, and instructional materials have an independent existence apart from each other and from the classroom. The dotted portions of the diagram, Level 2, represent the relationship between any two determinants apart from classroom practice. The horizontally striped lines, Level 3, represent each determinant as it interacts with the classroom independently of the other two (for example, curriculum and the class; instruction and the class; instructional materials and the class). Level 4, shown as vertically striped zones, indicates the interaction of two of the determinants within the classroom setting (for example, curriculum-instruction and the classroom; curriculum-instructional materials and the classroom; instruction-instructional materials and the classroom). Level 5, the solid portion of the diagram, is set within the classroom and is intersected by all three determinants.

To study systematically the effects of curriculum, instruction, and instructional materials on the classroom learning environment, the researcher needs not only to identify the level but also to designate the dependent and independent variables and the direction of the

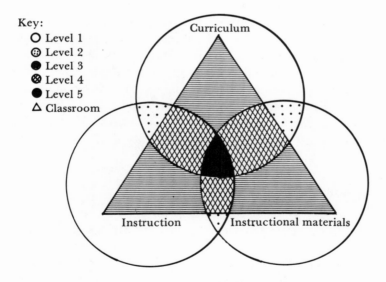

Figure 8-1

Three determinants of the classroom learning environment

relationship. As an example, does the study involve a single determinant in a single direction, that is, the effects of curriculum on the classroom, with changes in learning environment as by-products? Using a single determinant involving two-way directionality (effects of curriculum on the class and class on curriculum) increases the complexity of a study, but moves toward a more realistic representation of studying the learning environment in a naturalistic setting. As another level is added to a study with multidirectionality, studies of the learning environment in the classroom setting show additional complexity.

Figure 8-1 suggests a paradigm for generating designs for studies of learning environments. Studies at Level 1 in the figure are self-analytical inasmuch as none of the determinants is studied in a classroom context. Such studies could be used to predict possible effects on the learning environment, but a body of empirical data needs to be accumulated before predictive statements gain plausibility. Examples discussed in the first part of the chapter are of this nature. The same is true of studies at Level 2, which are still outside the naturalistic setting. These studies may be one-way or two-way directional studies. In one-way studies, a determinant is the dependent variable and another determinant is the independent variable. Or, the determinants could be interactive, as in two-way studies. Level 3 places the studies in the naturalistic setting—the classroom. Level 4 studies involve two of the three determinants in the naturalistic setting. Level 5 brings all three determinants together in the classroom context, with all possible interactions.

LEARNING ENVIRONMENT STUDIES IN THE NATURALISTIC SETTING

Using the paradigm for designing studies of learning environments, we turn now to a discussion of four studies carried out in naturalistic settings. The first study examined the impact of an instructional approach in the learning environment—a Level 3 design. The second study focused on the impact on the learning environment of instructional materials in reading classes—also a Level 3 design. The third study involved a total school district undergoing desegregation. The interactive effects of the two determinants on the classroom learning environment became the educational program as the school district responded to internally mandated desegregation—a Level 4 design.

The last study examined the impact of curriculum, instruction, and instructional materials, developed and implemented as an alternative educational program, on the learning environment—a Level 5 design.

Investigative Teaching: A Level 3 Study[11]

Under a grant from the National Science Foundation, teachers in a large metropolitan area were engaged for a year in the study of an investigative approach to teaching mathematics from kindergarten through the eighth grade. Investigative teaching was defined operationally as an instructional approach involving the students in learning activities that pose problems for which the potential solutions require exploration in a laboratory setting. The teacher's role included posing problems, asking probing questions, and fostering a learning environment in the mathematics class that encouraged sharing of ideas without fear of failure or ridicule.

It was hypothesized that a conscious awareness of the characteristics of investigative teaching would transfer to the participants' own classroom teaching as measured by changes in the learning environment. The subjects were students in forty-six public and parochial classes in metropolitan Chicago; the unit of study was the class. The schools in which the classes were located varied widely in terms of physical plant, availability of instructional materials, and support provided to the teachers. The teachers participating in the study taught twenty-three of the classes; teachers who were not participating in the study taught twenty-three other classes and served as the control group. Each Saturday morning throughout the academic year, the participating teachers spent two hours actively involved in building their understanding of basic mathematical concepts through investigative instructional encounters. Another two hours were devoted to analyzing the teaching and learning approaches that characterize investigative teaching in mathematics.

The design of this study conforms to a Level 3-type design, with the focus on instruction as the determinant of the learning environment and the classroom as the setting for learning. Directionality was two-way, with instruction holding potential for modifying the learning environment and the initial classroom learning environment interacting with instruction. Five learning environment scales from the *My Class Inventory* defined the environmental press: cohesiveness, competitiveness, difficulty, friction, and satisfaction.

The findings from a stepwise multiple regression analysis indicated that the variable, "group," contributed significantly to the cohesiveness of the learning environment. After the effects of the pretest scores of the classes on their perception of cohesiveness were removed from the regression equation, the variable "group" accounted for a significant amount of the variance. The experimental classes perceived greater cohesiveness in their mathematics learning environment than the control classes did at the end of the year.[12] Experimental gains in cohesiveness, however, were somewhat modified by grade level. The primary classes exposed to investigative learning situations showed dramatic increase in cohesiveness, while both intermediate groups and the control primary group showed decreases in the classes' perception of cohesiveness from pretest to posttest. Regardless of the school system (public or parochial), the experimental group showed gains in cohesiveness, while the control group in both public and parochial systems decreased in cohesiveness from pretest to posttest. Other significant changes in the learning environment were observed, but these changes were due to factors other than investigative teaching.

The outcome of this study suggests that a Level 3 design for studying the impact of instruction on the learning environment can assist in separating out the effects of instruction from curriculum and instructional materials.

A District Reading Series: A Level 3 Study [13]

Instructional materials in the form of basal reading series for grades one through six was the subject of this study. The investigators were charged with the task of designing and implementing an evaluation research study to assist personnel of the district in making a decision on the adoption of a textbook. In addition to considering the effects of five reading series on achievement, the study examined grade level, teacher characteristics, instructional characteristics, and the learning environment press.

Learning environment was examined from two perspectives: the students' perceptions of their reading class as measured by five *My Class Inventory* scales and observational data on instructional characteristics as these related to reading classes using the five reading series. Specifically, the questions asked were: What effects does a given reading series have on students' perceptions of the environment in which they learn to read? What are the effects on formal and informal classroom procedures?

If reading series do differ from one another, then differences among series should be observable in the behavior of teachers and students. Differences in the students' perceptions of their learning environment, in turn, should obtain from series to series. The portion of the study being reported can be categorized as a Level 3 design for evaluation research, with instructional materials as the determinant of the classroom environmental press. Data on what modifications in the materials or methodology teachers needed to consider in order to implement the series make this a two-way directional study.

Prior to initiating the study, the staff of the district narrowed selection to four series put out by Ginn; Holt, Rinehart and Winston; J. B. Lippincott; and Scott, Foresman. Pilot tests were conducted on the four series in twelve schools, grades one, two, three, and six. A fifth series put out by Scott, Foresman (Basic) was the one being used at the time, and it was the source of baseline data. A total of sixty classes participated in the study. Teachers received in-service training from the respective publishers and the reading staff of the school district during the summer; further in-service assistance was provided during the school year. During the winter, participating teachers responded to a questionnaire; many of the responses formed items on an observation schedule and an interview instrument. In early spring all sixty classes were observed, and teachers and administrators were interviewed. Pretests and posttests of achievement in reading were administered to the students in the fall and spring, respectively. The *SRA Reading Tests,* the instruments used in the district to measure achievement in reading, were administered as pretests and posttests in grades two, three, and six. For grade one, the *Metropolitan Reading Readiness Test* was used as the pretest measure and the *SRA Reading Tests* as the posttest. Data on students' perceptions of the environment of their reading classes were obtained in May.

Observable Behavior within the Learning Context. An observation instrument used to collect data on the reading classes focused on three aspects of instruction: locus of instructional decisions, variety and utilization of instructional materials, and students' learning behavior. If a series were implemented as designed, the methodological approach to teaching reading should have been reflected in the teaching-learning process and be observable in the classes.

The methodological approaches built into the design of the materials assigned varying roles to the teachers and to the students, and called for different classroom procedures in implementing the lessons. Reading classes by series could be considered on a continuum that ranged from formal to informal. For locus of instructional decisions, the continuum ranged from "material-teacher" as the primary source of instructional decisions to "students." For variety and utilization of instructional materials, the continuum ranged from "limited" to "extensive." For students' learning behavior, the continuum ranged from "passive-dependent" to "active-independent."

A pattern of instructional behavior was observed that differed somewhat among the reading series. Although these differences were not statistically significant among the series, either on a majority of items in the observation instrument or on the cluster of items subsumed under the three aspects of methodology, the observed differences did tend to reflect the designs of the respective reading series. The Scott, Foresman Systems had the highest observation mean rating, while the Lippincott series had the lowest mean rating. Generally, classes using the Scott, Foresman Systems were more informal than the other classes; students in these classes had more choice as to their partners in learning activities; students' work on display showed more originality; activities reflected multiple modalities; and inquiry (as contrasted with a single, right response) was encouraged.

Students' Perceptions of the Environment. The five *My Class Inventory* scales used to measure students' perceptions of their reading environment constituted one set of a number of independent variables entered into a guided, setwise, stepwise regression analysis. The other variables included reading series, teacher characteristics, grade level, and pretest reading scores; posttest reading achievement was the dependent variable. Each set of independent variables was studied in turn as a dependent variable, and the five learning environment scales were examined as dependent variables, with reading series entered into the regression equation as independent variables.

In the first set of regression analyses, after the effects of pretest reading achievement were removed, only one variable emerged as a significant predictor of posttest reading achievement, and that was competitiveness. Low competitiveness scores were associated with higher reading achievement. The implications of this finding for reading instruction are beyond the scope of this chapter.[14] No significant findings were observed when reading series, as the independent variables, were entered into regression equations, with each learning environment scale serving in turn as a dependent variable. Reading series did not significantly affect the learning environment.

While differences in degree of formal and informal procedures were observed, these differences were compressed within a narrow band on the continuum. We can assume from this that formal-informal differences among the series are not sufficient to influence significantly the environment in which students learn to read. Furthermore, we can conclude that the reading series alone does not significantly change students' perceptions of their learning environment.

A Level 3, two-way directional design for studying the impact of instructional materials on the learning environment helps parcel out the effects of curriculum and instruction in analyzing effects of instructional materials on how students perceive their learning environment.

District-Wide Desegregation: A Level 4 Study [15]

Desegregation of a school system and the subsequent busing of students often heightens tensions among faculty, parents, and children. Often the focus for alleviating these tensions is seen to reside in some sort of training in human relations that is directed toward calming the individual's emotional stress through increased knowledge of self and more accurate perceptions of others. While this seems eminently reasonable, the result, as tallied by objective measures, has not been reassuring. For the most part, results from such approaches have not affected student achievement, which means that one of the major objectives in plans for desegregation is not realized. We believe that a directed plan that focuses on curriculum and instruction should be a basic element in the learning environment in a desegregated setting so that students can improve their academic achievement. The consequences of such a strategy spill over to aid in achieving other social and personal goals sought in a more democratic society that allow each person to achieve his growth potential.

Forrestville was a suburb that experienced rapid growth as a bedroom community after World War II. As a community, it had long served young couples who needed inexpensive housing to raise families. Within this community, a segregated area grew until one of the eight schools of Forrestville contained a black population that constituted 25 percent of the total district population. Under the watchful eye of the state, and with some encouragement, a desegregation plan adopted in 1971 reorganized schools into K-3, 4-6, and 7-8 groupings of the grades and placed the ratio of black students in each school at approximately the ratio of the racial populations in the district. This setup generated considerable tension in the district, and white flight became a distinct possibility. There was need for policy at the school board level to ensure that desegregation would bring about integration. Professional educators at a nearby university was asked to set up an evaluation research design to provide information that could be used by the school board to formulate policy and by the administrative staff to help in developing the curriculum and instruction program.

In the evaluation research design, carried out over a five-year period, a number of measures were used, including the LEI. The data were interpreted by the university and reported back to the administration and the school board. It soon became apparent that curriculum and instruction required considerable attention if the achievement of all races were to improve. Having a data base on learning environments and achievement soon established that rumors of school differences circulated to the school board were baseless and inaccurate; that in some schools black children achieved more than their counterparts in other schools; that discipline problems in the middle schools were not racial in origin; that there were not widespread discipline problems among students, but that a few students were causing most of the major problems; that in-service work in specific subjects for teachers did not result in sustained achievement, if measured across years; and that there was a need to draw principals into developing a system for instructional improvement that would give consistent attention to the interaction of instruction and curriculum.

Achievement over the first three years was limited. In the third year, an intensive study of all fourth grades that included classroom observation and interviews with a sample of students and all fourth-grade teachers was carried out, and the results showed that there were grave deficiencies in the instructional practices and that the curriculum was limited in terms of subject matter. As a consequence of this study, an in-service program on the monitoring of classroom instruction was introduced for principals in an effort to secure a data base to improve teacher and student performance.

Sharp gains in achievement resulted. As the principals became aware of curricular deficiencies and of the great differences in teacher performance, specific focuses for viewing teacher performance were identified, objectives were set, and the results were evaluated. Several of the lowest-performing teachers resigned under the new system of instructional monitoring rather than accept the commitment to meet specific objectives in instruction and curriculum. Substantial achievement gains have since been made at each grade level for both races. These gains date from direct attention to curricular and instructional concerns and their interaction. A school is a learning system where the interaction of curriculum and instruction contributes in large measure to the classroom experience. In this case, action on these determinants led to a stabilized school district where parents are now expressing greater satisfaction with the school, and the community has not experienced white flight as a result of desegregation. Because of the improved achievement of all students and the attendant pupil-parent satisfaction, the community is experiencing an increasing number of inquiries from parents who are seeking a high-achieving, integrated setting for their children.

We have concluded from our five-year study that attention to the variables of curriculum and instruction within a specified improvement effort pays greater dividends than working on the more nebulous interpersonal variables that are the focus of many organizational development projects. Improved learning environments do bring increased personal satisfaction to students and contribute to the primary mission of the school, that is, academic achievement. Parents seek both of these for their children and fear desegregation because they believe, and rightly so in many cases, that it poses a threat. We believe, based on our experience and research in Forrestville, that attention to curriculum and instruction and interaction in classrooms is a necessary first step to successful desegregation where it is the problem of classroom performance that becomes salient when social change is structurally superimposed on a school system.

A Model School Experiment: A Level 5 Study [16]

Clockville, a school district serving a number of disparate, heterogeneous communities, received a federal grant, under Title I of the Elementary and Secondary Education Act, to develop an alternative middle school. This middle school was designed to develop curriculum, instruction, and instructional materials for students who were not benefiting from, or were experiencing difficulty with, the traditional curriculum in the schools. In a planning group that included community representatives, school staff members, and university consultants, objectives were identified. These objectives, which were to serve as a guide to the school (hereafter referred to as Model School) in developing innovations in curriculum, instruction, and instructional materials with groups of students, included:

1. The Model School program, during the course of a regular nine-month school year, will demonstrate community involvement (both the Model School with the community and the community with the Model School) to a greater degree than that shown in our present school structure.
2. The learning environment of the Model School program will provide a humanized setting for students. This will be accomplished with the help of staff, rules and procedures, and attention to minority-group concerns, as well as the physical school environment.
3. Over the course of the program year, Model School students will show at least as much growth in the cognitive domain as similar students in the traditional school.
4. Over the course of a program year, Model School students will show greater growth in the affective domain than students in traditional schools.
5. Model School Pupil Personnel Service (PPS) efforts will be completely integrated with all other efforts of the total Model School team to approach a student's total educational environment as a whole in order to provide a more consistent approach toward increasing the effectiveness of the Model School's PPS effort.
6. The Model School will demonstrate by testing results that its program can raise the overall quality of education without an increase in cost per student.

From the eight junior high schools within the district, six hundred students were recruited or volunteered to attend the Model School. Due to the funding, only three hundred sixth, seventh, and eighth graders could be accepted, and these were randomly selected by the university evaluators. An evaluation research design was drawn up to gather data on each objective and to provide results for feedback to the Advisory Committee of parents and the administrators.

The primary data sources were standardized achievement tests, a classroom learning scale,[17] a self-concept measure,[18] classroom observations,[19] and interviews with teachers, students, and parents. In order to give the project guidance, results were reported twice a year to the administration, teachers, and the Advisory Committee. In addition to fulfilling state requirements on the grant, a summative evaluation of the project at the end of two years of operation was prepared. To determine whether the curriculum, instruction, and materials interactions had any carry-over, a two-year follow-up study was conducted with a randomly selected sample of students. Sixty students were interviewed (thirty experimental, thirty control), grade point averages were checked for all the sample who remained in the Clockville high schools, dropout rates for both groups were computed, descriptive questionnaire data on student activities were compiled, and learning environment and self-concept measures were administered.

The evaluation design had an unusual advantage over most research in naturalistic settings inasmuch as it had randomly assigned the subjects to the experimental and control groups and established a solid base for controlling error and attributing results to treatment. Three questions were addressed:

1. Does reorganization of curriculum for greater student choice and determination of content make a difference in student achievement and psychological outlook (short term and long term)?
2. Does change in instructional design to grant students a larger role in participation (from teachercentric to pupilcentric) make a difference in student achievement and psychological outlook (short term and long term)?
3. Do different instructional materials, chiefly more experience-centered than publisher-centered, make a difference in student achievement and psychological outlook (short term and long term)?

As the diagram in Level 5 indicated, these relationships are interactive and nonlinear, and the interaction constitutes an independent variable that influences the dependent variable of student achievement and attitudes. The data on achievement and attitudes (the latter measured by a self-concept test, learning environment scales, and interviews) were subjected to statistical analysis that compared the experimental and control groups for the two years of the Model School's existence and at the end of two years in high school.

The weight of the evidence from the study supports the conclusion that purposeful attention to design changes in curriculum, instruction, and instructional materials did have immediate and long-range consequences for the experimental students. Paper-and-pencil measures are crude tools, especially when psychological nuances that are important in human interaction are sought. Nevertheless, the multiple measures made over time found the experimental students to be responding to the interaction of a changed educational treatment on curriculum, instruction, and instructional materials. In brief, the experimental students were doing better academically, they had short-term improvements in self-concepts, and they were more effectively coping with the learning environment of the high school two years later.[20]

Several other significant findings emerged from the study. What is of particular interest methodologically is that the learning environment scales reflected subtle differences in the two groups sooner than the achievement tests and self-concept measure. The self-concept scale picked up differences in the two groups at the end of the school year, and the achievement differences emerged at the end of the two-year follow-up. The strength of randomization for control of error was apparent in the dropout rates of the two groups, in each of which there were fourteen dropouts (eight girls and six boys in one group, eight boys and six girls in the other). In interview situations, students in the experimental group were more assured and confident, seemed to be using the resources of the high school more effectively in their education, were more specifically goal oriented, and seemed to reflect less angst as they spoke of their future vocational orientation.

While the literature on the variables of curriculum, instruction, and instructional materials leans to the descriptive and is extremely limited on causal studies, these data do testify to the fact that intervention on these three variables has measurable consequences.

Moreover, the benefits conferred on this study of random assignment give us confidence in attributing these effects to the educational treatment employed and not to chance.

The role and function of curriculum, instruction, and instructional materials in an educational program have been the subject of discussion among curriculum specialists for over fifty years. While the argument continues as to whether these can be regarded as separate entities, decisions are being made outside the naturalistic setting about each determinant that affect the others as they are implemented in classrooms. Each determinant can, however, have an effect on the learning environment since they interact once they are put into practice. The paradigm presented in this chapter may help in designing studies of the effects of curriculum, instruction, and instructional materials on learning environments and in sorting out the varying relationships and interactive effects.

NOTES

1. Maurice J. Eash and Harriet Talmage, *Evaluation of Learning Environments*, TM Report No. 43 (Princeton, N.J.: ETS Tests, Measurements, and Evaluation Clearinghouse, 1975).

2. Gary J. Anderson, *The Assessment of Learning Environments: A Manual for the* Learning Environment Inventory *and the* My Class Inventory, 2d ed. (Halifax, Nova Scotia: Atlantic Institute of Education, 1973).

3. Franklin Bobbitt, *The Curriculum* (Boston: Houghton Mifflin Co., 1918); see also Hollis L. Caswell, "Emergence of the Curriculum as a Field of Professional Work and Study," in *Precedents and Promise in the Curriculum Field*, ed. H. F. Robinson (New York: Teachers College, Columbia University Press, 1966), 1-12.

4. *Curriculum-Making: Past and Present*, Twenty-sixth Yearbook of the National Society for the Study of Education, Part I, ed. Guy Montrose Whipple (Bloomington, Ill.: Public School Publishing Co., 1926); Robert S. Zais, *Curriculum Principles and Foundations* (New York: Thomas Y. Crowell Co., 1976).

5. Florence Stratemeyer *et al.*, *Developing a Curriculum for Modern Living* (New York: Bureau of Publications, Teachers College, Columbia University, 1947).

6. Jerold R. Zacharias, "Physical Science Study: Into the Laboratory," *Science Teacher* 24 (1957): 324-326.

7. Paul D. Hurd, *New Directions in Teaching Secondary School Science* (Chicago: Rand McNally and Co., 1970), 188.

8. Harriet Talmage, "The Textbook as Arbiter of Curriculum and Instruction," *Elementary School Journal* 73 (1975): 20-25.

9. *EPIEgram* 5 (1976): 1.

10. *McGuffey's Eclectic Primer*, rev. ed. (New York: American Book Co., 1886; reissued by Van Nostrand Reinhold; originally published in 1879).

11. Alice Hart and Harriet Talmage, *Instructional Improvement and Implementation Project: Final Report*, Grant No. GW-8535 (Washington, D.C.: National Science Foundation, 1976).

12. Harriet Talmage and Alice Hart, "A Study of Investigative Teaching of Mathematics and Effects on the Classroom Learning Environment," *Journal of Research in Mathematics Education* 8 (1977): 345-358.

13. Harriet Talmage and Herbert Walberg, *Pilot Reading Series Evaluation Study: Final Report* (Chicago: Office of Evaluation Research, University of Illinois at Chicago Circle, 1977).

14. Harriet Talmage and Herbert Walberg, "Naturalistic, Decision-oriented Evaluation of a District Reading Program," *Journal of Reading Behavior* (in press); Herbert Walberg and Harriet Talmage, *District-wide Research on Reading Achievement* (Chicago: Office of Evaluation Research, University of Illinois at Chicago Circle, 1977).

15. Maurice J. Eash and Sue P. Rasher, "Evaluation in Mandated Integration: Decision Making and Program Planning," paper presented at the annual meeting of the American Educational Research Association, San Francisco, April 1976.

16. Maurice J. Eash, Sue P. Rasher, and Herbert J. Walberg, "A Follow-up Study of a True Experiment: Curriculum Evaluation of a School District's Educational Alternative," paper presented at the annual meeting of the American Educational Research Association, New York, April 1977.

17. Anderson, *Assessment of Learning Environments.*

18. Ira J. Gordon, *A Test Manual for the How I See Myself Scale* (Gainesville, Fla.: Florida Educational Research and Development Council, 1968).

19. Richard Kunkel and James McElhinney, *In-Classroom Observation Form: Curriculum Evaluation* (Muncie, Ind.: Ball State University, 1970).

20. Eash, Rasher, and Walberg, "Follow-up Study of a True Experiment."

PART THREE
Directions
in
Research on Teaching

9. Classroom Tasks and Students' Abilities

Walter Doyle

Research on teaching appears to be at the threshold of fundamental conceptual reorganization. Although the outcome is difficult to predict, two developments promise to play an important role. First, there has been intensified interest in student variables among investigators in the traditional areas of teaching and curriculum research.[1] Walker, in a recent review of curriculum studies, ventures the question: "Dare we hope that the next decade will see as much attention paid to what students do in classrooms as has been paid in the past decade to what teachers do?"[2] Second, there has been vigorous study of cognition and individual differences within an information-processing framework,[3] and this approach provides a powerful analytic tool for investigating the student response variables that mediate instructional effects.

The research on which this chapter is based was supported by grants from the North Texas State University Organized Research Funds and the National Institute of Education, Department of Health, Education, and Welfare (Grant No. NIE-G-0099). The opinions expressed do not necessarily reflect the position or policy of NTSU or NIE, and no official endorsement by either institution should be inferred.

Recent work on cognition is being brought to bear on issues in the field of instructional design,[4] but more work needs to be done on the question of how student responses mediate effects in *classroom* settings. Before this question can be addressed adequately, a much richer understanding of classroom environments would seem to be necessary, and it is toward this end that the present chapter outlines some features of an ecological approach to research on teaching, with special emphasis on how student processes operate in classrooms. The work reported here is based on three years of naturalistic observations in classroom settings and on analytic reviews of research on teaching effectiveness and student mediating responses.[5] Although promising results are beginning to emerge from these efforts to analyze classroom phenomena, many of the present formulations are necessarily tentative and incomplete.

INTERPRETIVE MODELS

Any attempt to interpret evidence on relationships between instructional conditions and learning outcomes requires some assumptions about the processes that mediate these two clusters of variables. Assumptions about mediating processes, in turn, require a causal model of teaching effects, that is, a set of propositions about why instructional variables are related to achievement. In research on teaching, the causal models that guide inquiry and interpretation are most often implicit and, as a result, too readily ignored. A brief examination of the implicit models will accentuate the conceptual changes occurring in the field and clarify how an ecological perspective can contribute to an understanding of classrooms.

In traditional process-product research, that is, studies of relationships between teachers' behaviors and students' learning outcomes,[6] the implicit model that underlies interpretation has at least two features. The first is that the direction of causality is typically from the teacher to the student, despite periodic admonitions about this practice. A correlation between teacher enthusiasm and student achievement, for example, is usually interpreted as evidence that enthusiasm causes learning, presumably because this teacher characteristic is somehow contagious. In view of the correlational nature of the studies, however, it is equally legitimate to argue that teachers tend to be more enthusiastic when working with groups of high-achieving students. Given the relatively weak strength of the correlations—.40 to .60 in most studies[7]—there are likely to be instances in which enthusiasm is unrelated or even negatively related to student achievement. A more fruitful basis for ascertaining how teacher variables are associated with outcomes in classrooms, then, would result from comparative analysis of positive and negative instances of the relationship between enthusiasm and learning. This example, which can be easily multiplied, underscores the need for more attention to alternative causal models for interpreting process-product findings.

A second feature of the implicit model is that it traditionally reflects a reinforcement view of teaching effects. Considerable emphasis, for example, has been placed on the affective consequences of teacher "rewards," such as warmth, praise, and encouragement. The weight of evidence suggests, however, that "task" variables related to the way teachers structure and present lessons have a more powerful effect on academic achievement than "affective" dimensions.[8] Indeed, pupil awareness appears to be oriented more toward task features than affective aspects of teaching processes.[9] This is not to say that affective consequences do not influence behavior in classrooms, but it would appear that the reinforcement model does not provide a sufficiently rich conceptual framework to account for all classroom effects.

The recent emphasis on student variables has been accompanied by some restructuring of the underlying assumptions in research on teaching. In particular, the emphasis on reinforcement in traditional process-product research has been augmented by an interest in *practice* variables such as attention, content covered, time spent on-task, engagement, and opportunity to learn.[10] The current focus, in other words, is not simply on the supportive atmosphere of the classroom; it is also on the activities that occupy students' time during instruction. Unfortunately, the model of causality itself remains unidirectional: teaching variables are assumed to cause students' behavior. This view of how practice effects occur can, however, lead to potentially spurious interpretations, especially in correlational studies.

Although it seems self-evident that the amount of practice is related to mastery, it is important to understand how this relationship operates in classrooms. Recent studies of individual differences suggest, for one thing, that successful learners process information more efficiently, that is, they take less time to accomplish a given cognitive task.[11] Results from Shimron's classroom study confirm this finding: although high achievers spent more time on-task, they actually spent less time per learning unit.[12] In this case, the relationship between time and achievement was negative. Such evidence indicates that simply increasing time on-task under conventional classroom conditions would have an effect on the achievement mean of the class but that the effect would result primarily from an increase in the amount accomplished by the more efficient learners. At the same time, the amount of variance within the class would be expected to increase. This result would not necessarily be consistent with the goal of improving instructional effectiveness.

The question of why the amount of practice is related to learning outcomes can be analyzed from at least two perspectives that depart from the causal model underlying contemporary research. From one perspective, it is possible that high-achieving students exhibit more engaged time because they are more inclined to conform to a teacher's rules for classroom conduct and not simply because they need the time to learn. Potter found, for example, that girls initiated contacts with the teacher during seatwork assignments (and thus appeared more task oriented) because they felt that the teacher "liked that sort of thing."[13] A similar desire to please the teacher could occur in other areas of classroom behavior. Under such circumstances it is conceivable that the amount of engaged time has little relationship to learning and that students are actually spending more time learning than is necessary. Along these lines, a fourth-grade student of above-average ability reported to me that he did not like to finish mathematics assignments early because he then had to help other students in the class. In this case, avoiding what was considered to be an odious chore would certainly seem to play an important part in determining the amount of observable time engaged in learning.

From a second viewpoint, there may appear to be a relationship between time and learning in correlational studies because of teacher adaptation to the work habits of students. Harnischfeger and her colleagues reported that teachers allocated more time to reading instruction in classrooms populated with higher-achieving students.[14] This apparently contradictory practice would seem to indicate how

the reactions of students and the constraints of the classroom influence teachers' decision making.[15] Given the task of managing classroom groups over long periods of time, it is reasonable that teachers
provide more academic learning time for students inclined to engage
in academic tasks.

The point here is not whether time relates in some causal manner
to learning; it is, rather, that the relationship is considerably more
complex than most discussions suggest. Moreover, the amount of
classroom time students spend learning is not necessarily a direct
result of a teacher's procedures.

The preceding analysis of interpretive models in research on teaching illustrates the need for a broader understanding of classrooms to
serve as a guide for formulating studies and interpreting results. I
argue that a framework for understanding classrooms needs to include
at least the following four features:

1. *A concept of reciprocal causality in classroom relationships.*
There is a growing body of evidence that students have a significant
impact on determining the response opportunities they receive, the
roles they will assume in the classroom group, and the way teachers
behave.[16] Such findings need to become an integral part of interpretive work in research on teaching and more attention should be
given to determining how reciprocity moderates classroom effects.

2. *An information-processing view of the mediational strategies
students use to navigate classroom environments.* Records of overt
behavior in classrooms are simply not sufficient for explaining,
except at a very gross level, how teaching effects occur. Research on
teaching needs to draw closer to the recent work on cognitive operations that influence achievement.[17]

3. *A differential perspective for the analysis of effects in classrooms.* The common practice of determining teaching effects solely
on the basis of analyses of mean scores for a class fails to account
for the fact that teachers often direct instruction to individual
students and for the possibility of interactions between instructional
conditions and student characteristics.[18] Although mean scores are
perhaps useful for purposes of general policy, they mask much
information that would seem to be especially useful for understanding classrooms. Conceptual tools need to be devised, therefore, to
deal with a broader range of differences in both types of students and
types of classrooms.

4. *A systemic view of the natural classroom environment.* Classrooms are complex environments that exist for relatively long periods of time. As a result interrelatedness exists among classroom components to the degree that changes at one level have consequences for other components of the system. Short-term experiments or brief observations of arbitrarily selected dimensions of classroom processes are not sufficient to capture the richness of classroom events. Interpretations and recommendations based on such analyses are precarious at best.

Research on teaching needs a more comprehensive model of how classrooms work in order to integrate findings about aspects of teaching and learning. The purpose of such a model is not to dispute or disparage the results of previous studies on reinforcement and practice variables in teaching but, rather, to provide a basis for understanding the results. The ecological approach to classroom functioning outlined in this chapter, although certainly provisional, represents a step toward a more refined model to guide inquiry and interpretation in the field.

ECOLOGICAL ANALYSIS

It is useful, before turning to the details of classroom analysis, to define briefly the distinctive features of an ecological approach to research on teaching.[19] The ecological framework contains three basic dimensions. First, the perspective is vigorously *naturalistic.* As defined in the present essay, naturalistic research places primary emphasis on richly detailed, finely grained descriptions formulated on the basis of extensive unstructured experience in classrooms. To paraphrase Stenhouse, the goal is to allow the reality of the classroom to impinge upon the investigator's subjectivity until the categories for description are determined by the phenomena of the classroom itself.[20] During this process of formulating descriptions, an attempt is made to account for the meaning of events and actions from the perspective of the participants in the situation being described. This approach to description differs markedly from the common practice in research on teaching where preselected categories that have meaning primarily in an investigator's "theory" of classroom processes are used.

Naturalistic description has the advantage of capturing variables that simply do not occur in laboratory settings or are overlooked in standard category systems for observation. Naturalistic studies are often characterized, therefore, by unexpected phenomena and by terminology that is fashioned to reflect the special features of the setting being studied, for example, Kounin's term "withitness."[21] An unstructured view of classrooms would seem, however, to be an especially difficult attitude to achieve. Becker cautions that, when observing classrooms, "it takes a tremendous effort of will and imagination to stop seeing only the things that are conventionally 'there' to be seen" in order to "see or write anything beyond what 'everyone' knows."[22]

A second feature of an ecological viewpoint is, appropriately, that there is a direct focus on *environment-behavior relationships.* The model postulates that environments establish limits on the range of behavioral options and that observed behavior is in large measure a response to the demand characteristics of a given setting. In an ecological analysis of teaching, therefore, an attempt is made to account for the actions of teachers and students in terms of the demands of classroom environments. Such an analysis consists of a two-stage process of defining the dimensions of the classroom environment and identifying those strategies of teachers and students that account for success or failure in that environment. There are, of course, other "causes" of behavior related to the capabilities and interests of participants, and there are a variety of functionally equivalent ways of meeting environmental demands. Nevertheless, the texture of the setting is a powerful influence on the behavior of teachers and students.[23]

Finally, the organizing question in ecological inquiry is fundamentally diagnostic: "Why do teachers and students behave as they do in classrooms?" The focus, in other words, is on the *functional value or adaptive significance of behaviors in an environment.* This investigative thrust contrasts with the more conventional orientation in teaching research, where the question is: "How can teachers be changed to be more effective?" The answer to the more conventional question often reflects an investigator's preconceived notions of an effective classroom style, notions typically derived from studies conducted in settings other than classrooms. The diagnostic question—the "why" of behavior—is more suited to building an understanding of the constraints of a setting and focuses attention on the broader human consequences of changing physical or behavioral dimensions.

Some of the character of an ecological approach to research on teaching can be illustrated by an episode observed in a junior high school social studies classroom. For the last ten minutes of the period, the teacher assigned students to work on their homework. At this point, the following exchange occurred:

S: When is the homework due?

T: All homework is due on Tuesdays. [*This class was meeting on a Thursday.*] Are you already finished?

S: Yes.

T: Did you answer all the questions?

S: Yes.

T: Are all the lines straight?

S: (*pause*)   I guess I'd better check.

T (*to class*):   Don't be in such a hurry to finish that you aren't careful.

The last three comments require some elaboration. The observer's initial reaction to the teacher's comment "Are all the lines straight?" was one of surprise. What did this have to do with social studies? The student's reaction, however, appeared not to be one of surprise, but, rather, one of recognition, that is, the realization that some requirement had been overlooked. Moreover, the teacher's question did not seem to require further explanation for the participants in this setting. The teacher's final comment to the class ("Don't be in such a hurry . . . . ") suggests that the teacher, a fifteen-year veteran, had established contingencies that served to slow down students who began to get too far ahead on assignments.

From an ecological perspective, the teacher's behavior would seem to represent an adaptation to the demands of the classroom environment. Different work rates beyond a certain range would clearly increase the complexity of keeping records and scheduling activities for 150 students. It is not unreasonable that teachers would develop procedures for keeping students together on assignments and activities. Students, in turn, would presumably learn to adjust their work output to match teachers' preferences. Such a perspective would seem to be essential for interpreting observational data concerning pacing and time utilization in classrooms.

In summary, the ecological framework is particularly useful for illuminating the intrinsic properties of the classroom system. This emphasis counterbalances a common practice in research on teaching of extracting units of behavior from the classroom context and then imposing interpretation based on process-product assumptions or on formulations at the level of individual psychology (for example, anxiety, level of aspiration, reinforcement) to explain classroom effects. The focus on intrinsic properties of classrooms can also contribute a needed conceptual base for research on teaching and teacher education.

THE STRUCTURE OF CLASSROOM TASKS

Some interpretive propositions can result from an ecological analysis of classroom processes. Here the focus is primarily on academic achievement as one outcome of classrooms, and the result is a fairly general treatment of the formal structure of classroom environments. Attention is given first to the inherent features of classrooms as settings populated by a large number of people, designed for multiple purposes, and convened for a long period of time. An attempt is then made to conceptualize the strategies that enable students to navigate this setting. Finally, the analysis is directed to the ways in which the structure of academic tasks interacts with the strategies of students to influence achievement.

The classroom as an information system exhibits three general characteristics.[24] First, there appears to be an abundance of information resources. That is, classrooms contain a complex array of interacting objects and media, including textbooks, workbook exercises, bulletin board displays, films, and tests, besides the range of verbal and nonverbal behaviors on the part of both teachers and students. Any one of these resources may assume instructional significance, depending upon particular sets of circumstances. Second, not all elements of the classroom are equally reliable as instructional cues. Teacher instructions, for example, are sometimes ambiguous and incomplete, and teacher feedback is not always consistent or accurate.[25] There is also evidence that instructional materials used in classrooms, even in the early grades, place extraordinarily complex logical demands on students.[26] Thus, in spite of the number of sources, the information available for a particular instructional task may be inadequate. Finally, since the classroom is a mass-processing system, the degree to which the level of information and flow of activities necessarily match the individual student's interests or abilities is limited.[27] What this shows is that the classroom environment itself is problematic.

The problems of learning from classrooms would seem nearly insurmountable if one were to assume that the environment is composed of discrete entities. There would seem, however, to be a system of overlapping task structures that integrates elements of the classroom. Each of these task structures consists of a goal and a set of operations to achieve that goal, and, from the perspective of the present analysis, each task structure defines a behavior ecology. Although these task structures do not disentangle completely the problematic nature of the environment, they supply an organizing reference for interpreting events and actions in classrooms. The following paragraphs outline some general features of classroom task structures.

With special reference to academic outcomes, the formal structure of classroom tasks can be defined as *an exchange of performance for grades*.[28] This exchange seems to operate at two levels. At the first level students are required to answer questions, participate in discussions, and complete assignments, and evaluative feedback is provided on a fairly continuous basis while performing these tasks. Exchanges during class sessions are typically characterized by a degree of informality, and every student is not usually required to contribute to each exchange. At the second level worksheets are distributed, and examinations are administered periodically, to provide a more formal basis for the performance-grade exchange. Exchanges on tests differ in several respects from those conducted during class sessions: conditions are more standardized, the results are more likely to be recorded and used as formal evidence to classify a student, and students can seldom avoid participation. The distinction between these two levels of exchange is important because it is possible that differences in performance expectations can exist. A teacher might, for example, conduct "inquiry" exercises in the classroom that require students to generate answers by generalizing across a series of examples. The same teacher might also test for verbatim recall of answers that were previously generated in class. The point—to be developed in more detail shortly—is that a failure to recognize this distinction has consequences for information-processing strategies and, hence, for a student's chances of achieving a successful performance-grade exchange.

The cumulative results of participation in the performance-grade exchange can affect the way a student is classified within the school. To the extent that school records are used as screening devices by employers and college registrars, the performance-grade exchange has long-term consequences for a student's access to educational and occupational opportunity. In a more immediate sense, however, the results of the exchange would seem to be important in determining a student's role in the social system of the school. In a recent study of social organization in high schools, it was reported that "a student 'sorted' as a 'good student' is differentially allowed to negotiate both territorial rights and his adherence to the formal and informal rules of the school."[29] The existence of such immediate contingencies would seem to magnify the significance of the performance-grade exchange in a student's experience of the classroom and to connect a number of motivational factors to the exchange process.

As indicated earlier, the primary focus of the present discussion is on the structure of academic tasks. There are, of course, other task structures in classrooms that reflect both the multiple purposes of the school as an institution and the variety of individual interests and capabilities of students and teachers. As experienced teachers know, not all students choose to participate in academic tasks, and some appear to specialize in testing the formal and informal rules for conduct in the classroom. Kounin's ecology-based analysis of classroom management strategies provides important insights into this aspect of the environmental demands made on teachers.[30] A full consideration of such alternative classroom tasks is beyond the scope of the present chapter. It is important to remember, however, that classrooms are not single-purpose "learning" environments. By their very nature they afford a variety of opportunities for student engagement.

The classroom, owing to the range of purposes, number of participants, and duration of existence, is a complex environment. At the same time, the classroom is ordered by a system of overlapping task structures that reduce to some degree, but certainly do not eliminate, the problematic nature of the classroom setting. An ecological approach to research on teaching would postulate that long-term experience in a complex setting would foster strategies to deal with environmental demands. It is also reasonable to expect that these strategies would be specially adapted to the task structures that define the behavior ecologies of the classroom. To develop this point further, it is necessary to turn to the connection between the task structure of classrooms and student strategies for task accomplishment, again with special reference to academic achievement.

CLASSROOM COMPETENCIES

Given the complex nature of classroom environments, the performance-grade exchange is, from the perspective of the student, always fraught with ambiguity and risk, although the magnitude of each of these dimensions varies according to particular circumstances. Ambiguity, as used here, results primarily from gaps in information about performance expectations as to what kinds of answers will be required and which ones are considered correct. Risk, on the other hand, refers to the probability of securing a successful performance-grade exchange weighed against the consequences of failure to meet performance requirements on a particular occasion. Although risk and ambiguity are closely associated features of classroom life, they can vary independently. Classroom task structures that involve memorizing a few explicitly defined items, for example, would tend to be low in terms of both ambiguity and risk. As the amount of material to be memorized increases, risk also increases even though the amount of ambiguity concerning what is to be learned remains constant. Similarly, classroom tasks that require the generation of original solutions to previously unencountered problems would tend to be high in terms of both ambiguity and risk, assuming the teacher holds the students accountable for the quality of their solutions. There are, of course, some classroom situations that are low on both dimensions, that is, no one knows what one is supposed to do, but it really does not make any difference.

Many of the student strategies that have been described in recent naturalistic studies of classrooms would seem to be directed toward reducing ambiguity and risk in the performance-grade exchange. Noble and Nolan, for example, have described ways in which students control the number and type of response opportunities they receive in class discussions.[31] Along these same lines, Brophy and Good have reviewed several studies that document strategies students use to regulate their own levels of participation in classroom recitations, and recent evidence from the Texas Junior High School Study indicates that individual students are reasonably stable across settings in maintaining patterns of participation in classroom exchanges.[32]

In an especially rich observational study of a first-grade classroom, Mehan describes student maneuvers to achieve successful classroom exchanges despite ambiguity in the teacher's definitions of performance requirements and inconsistency in reactions to student answers.[33] In a lesson on the use of such words as "over," "under," and "beside," students would, for example, attempt to elicit the teacher's approval for a provisional answer (for example, "Under the line . . . ?"). Students would also navigate the exchange by imitating responses given previously by the teacher or classmates. Finally, students were found to hesitate during responding until someone else answered for them. For example,

S_1 : The circle . . . is . . . is . . . the circle . . .
S_2 : Under the line.

Mehan called this strategy "cohort production." Behaviors such as these obviously enable students to get "credit" for an exchange without necessarily having learned the material.

In addition to strategies for managing participation during class sessions, students also appear to be able to regulate the more formal requirements of classroom task structures. In a speculative essay on college teaching, Schellenberg calls attention to the familiar ways in which students standardize and routinize classroom requirements ("How long is the term paper?") and invoke norms of fairness and democratic justice to minimize performance expectations.[34] On this latter point, Davis and McKnight have described a case in which junior high school students actively resisted an attempt to modify the mathematics curriculum to place greater emphasis on comprehension of underlying principles rather than on routine algorithmic procedures. In this instance some students argued that they had a right to be told explicitly what they were expected to do.[35] In the language of the present analysis, it seems evident that the curriculum change advocated by the instructors substantially increased the levels of ambiguity and risk for students and thus generated efforts on their part to reduce these factors.

One final aspect of ambiguity in the classrooms needs to be mentioned briefly. Given the number of class meetings each year, it is hardly possible to hold students accountable for all of the material covered in the classroom. It is not always feasible, however, for teachers to be explicit about such matters when asked by students, "Is this stuff going to be on the test?" If the teacher responds "No," then it may be difficult to keep the students' attention on the activity at hand. If, on the other hand, the teacher responds "Yes" and, in the practical world of managing classrooms, fails to include the material on the test, there could be a major confrontation on the issue of "justice." (Students seldom forget promises about what is going to be on tests.) For most experienced teachers, therefore, direct inquiries about whether a specific unit of content will appear on a test usually warrant a reasonably vague answer, such as: "It would be well if you knew it."

Although important, students' strategies for regulating participation and the general demands of classroom tasks do not eliminate ambiguity and risk; nor do they necessarily apply to testing situations in which opportunities for negotiation are more circumscribed. It would seem, therefore, that the achievement of a successful performance-grade exchange would require an additional, and perhaps more fundamental, set of students' strategies.

An analysis of this level of mediating processes focuses on the extent to which task accomplishment depends upon an ability to utilize cues afforded by the classroom environment as resources. This utilization skill rests first on a process of selective attention. The successful student must learn, in other words, to identify from the range of available sources those cues that have instructional significance in a particular setting. To identify significant instructional cues, the student must, in turn, develop an "interpretive competence" to navigate the complexities of the classroom.[36] Recent analyses by cognitive psychologists support the view that the ability to interpret discrete entities—to assign meaning to parts of a complex system—requires a general understanding of the nature of the task environment.[37] This argument suggests that, to use the classroom environment efficiently, a student must transform the complexity of the setting by constructing a cognitive system to give meaning to the individual objects and events that occur. From this perspective, academic achievement is dependent not simply on a student's ability to learn subject matter, but also on a more general understanding of how classrooms work.

TASK STRUCTURES AND MEANING IN CLASSROOMS

It is with respect to the students' interpretive skill that the concept of task structure would seem to be especially useful for understanding how students learn from classrooms. As noted earlier, the structure of classroom tasks supplies an organizing reference that integrates elements of the system. Such a structure would seem, therefore, to assign meaning to discrete objects and events based on their relationship to the performance-grade exchange. The behaviors of teachers that are reliable indicators of the nature of performance expectations or of changes in these task demands would, according to this analysis, receive primary attention from students who consistently achieve successful exchanges. Behaviors unrelated to the task structure, on the other hand, could safely be ignored. In some situations, for example, praise from a teacher has little relation to the accuracy of a student's response.[38] Under these circumstances, praise would have little significance in defining performance expectations. Corrective feedback, on the other hand, is often used with more discrimination and would thus tend to be of more use to students in identifying the demands of classroom tasks.[39]

This approach to classroom processes is especially germane to the problem of conceptualizing treatment variables in research on teaching effectiveness. In particular, the analysis underscores the role of task structures in defining the salient features of the classroom environment for an individual. The stimuli that are effective are the ones that are relevant for accomplishing classroom tasks. Variations in features of the setting that are not connected to the task structure would be expected to have only secondary and indirect influence on what is learned in the classroom. On the other hand, "changing the subject's task changes the kind of event that the subject experiences."[40] The task structure, in other words, determines which aspects of the classroom environment affect a student.

A brief comparison with the more conventional viewpoint in examining the effectiveness of teaching will clarify the contribution of this formulation. Typically "treatment" variables in research on teaching are defined in terms of such dimensions as the frequency of certain teacher behaviors or ratings of isolated teacher characteristics. It is also common to emphasize interpersonal factors to account for teaching effects. For example, Reitman, in a recent textbook for prospective teachers, asserts: "Whether teachers succeed in facilitating genuine learning in their students is . . . largely dependent upon the quality of their social interactions with their students."[41] Finally, different curricula (for example, inquiry versus exposition) or different organizational arrangements for teaching (for example, open versus conventional classrooms) are often compared to show different effects on achievement.[42] The present argument is that the significance of particular teacher variables, the effects of interpersonal relationships, or the impact of different activities is dependent upon the nature of the tasks students are attempting to accomplish. In other words, the information-processing activities of a student are not simply a function of the range of available stimuli or even of the student's personal preferences; rather, they are shaped by the structure of tasks in a given classroom.

One clear implication of the present approach to defining classroom treatments is that setting and task variables operate independently with respect to achievement. From an ecological perspective, what students learn in a classroom is a function of the operations that they perform in accomplishing tasks. But classroom tasks are enacted in settings that differ in their degree of complexity, a factor that should influence the efficiency of task accomplishment. Differences in setting under the same task structure should not be expected to affect what a student learns, although differences in the amount learned may be apparent. The task of memorizing answers to questions, for example, will produce similar results in different contexts; the density of interfering material will, however, probably influence how much students remember. On the other hand, differences in tasks, even in similar settings, should result in different types of learning outcomes.

Differences among students are, of course, important in analyzing the effects of tasks and settings. Students would certainly be expected to vary in their dependency on explicit cues, their adaptability to different settings, and their aptitude for certain tasks. Some students appear to be able to master a variety of tasks in a wide range of settings, whereas others succeed within more restricted circumstances. It is also possible that some environments, because of both setting and task variables, can be managed adequately by just a few students. More attention to individual differences as they relate to specific features of the classroom ecology would seem to be a fruitful direction for research on teaching.

CLASSROOM TASKS AND RESEARCH ON LEARNING

The preceding argument concerning the importance of task structure in determining the effect of classroom environments on learning outcomes would seem to have far-reaching implications for efforts to relate basic research on learning to the study of teaching, implications that can only be treated briefly here. Two topics have been selected for illustrative purposes: the effect of classroom task structures on students' choice of strategies for processing subject matter; and the interaction of classroom task structures and features of prose materials.

Much experimental research has concentrated in recent years on the information-processing strategies that mediate learning on the part of the student, and much of this work has focused on the effect of such strategies as elaboration, imaging, and rehearsal on students' ability to recall items embedded in relatively simple instructional displays. Rohwer, for example, has studied the effects of elaboration (forming a connection between items on noun-pair lists, for example, "The bat is in the cup.") on recall, and the differential impact of various prompt conditions on eliciting elaborative processing.[43] Research has also been directed toward the mediational properties of such "higher-order" cognitive operations as comprehension and problem-solving skills.[44]

One interesting result emerging from this work on mediation is that different ways of processing subject matter have consequences for the form of a student's response on a criterion test.[45] If task demands require that a student reproduce an exact copy of the items encountered during instruction, then a deliberate attempt to memorize the material must be employed. Under such task demands, meaningful processing of the information for comprehension will not suffice. Processing for comprehension, in which what is remembered results automatically from efforts to understand rather than from deliberate memorizing, prepares a student to reconstruct the gist or essential features of learned material. This mode of processing does not, however, enable a student to recall exactly the items presented during instruction or even to distinguish between previously encountered items and those with a similar meaning.

This feature of memory functions suggests that a student's perception of a classroom task structure will determine how the information is processed and that the information-processing strategies selected will, in turn, determine what the student is capable of doing on the teacher's tests. Comprehension may in fact be detrimental in a performance-grade exchange that requires exact reproduction of previously encountered answers. On the other hand, it is certainly possible to accomplish many classroom tasks successfully without comprehension.[46] This point reinforces the position that learning from classrooms requires more than simply the ability to process subject matter; it also requires skill in recognizing which mode of processing is appropriate to task demands.

From a slightly different perspective, a classroom task structure would also seem to function as a system of meaning that enables students to code subject matter for memory in the absence of explicit cues—a condition that appears to occur often in classrooms.[47] To the extent that the task structure in a particular classroom is understood, a student can recognize items of content that have a high probability of appearing in performance-grade exchanges and can then direct practice toward those items. Interpretive competence based on the task system operates, in this manner, to reduce ambiguity and risk inherent in the classroom environment.

One final extension of this line of reasoning would seem to be useful. In a case mentioned earlier, Davis and McKnight reported that students in a junior high school mathematics class resisted strongly an attempt to change the task demands from a routine algorithmic process to a more conceptual or heuristic mode of thinking.[48] This more conceptual mode of processing mathematical content appeared to emphasize comprehension of the general features of the material and application of this understanding to previously unencountered situations. It would seem, however, that the form of a correct response is considerably more difficult to predict in the conceptual mode, in contrast to the algorithmic mode. This unpredictability would increase ambiguity and risk and, thus, elicit attempts by the students to regulate task demands by increasing, for example, the explicitness of instructional cues. Although more descriptive research is necessary, it may well be that task structures requiring comprehension are difficult to implement because of the nature of classroom processes. Such an interpretation would account in part for the fact that recall questions tend to dominate classroom discourse.

CHARACTERISTICS OF PROSE

In addition to the study of mediating responses, experimental work in learning has also focused on the characteristics of prose passages and their impact on memory. Along these lines Meyer, for example, found that the location of an item in the content structure of a text affected recall. An idea located high in the content hierarchy was remembered better than one lower in the structure.[49] Such findings have much intuitive appeal for research on teaching, but few attempts have been made to account for classroom variables in interpreting these results. An ecological viewpoint would emphasize that text materials are always embedded within a classroom task structure. Moreover, students can be expected to have developed some understanding, accurate or not, of this task structure after the first few weeks of a school year. One would expect, therefore, that the nature of the task structure, as represented, for example, by the items on a teacher's test, would interact with the structure of the text. The degree to which the structure of text is congruent with the task demands of a particular classroom—and there is little reason to expect high congruence here—would determine the extent to which the features of text facilitate or impede achievement. There is some evidence, however, that task demands tend to override the effects of text structure,[50] a condition that would seem to neutralize the interference of any incongruity between text materials and class-room tasks.

To push the analysis one step further, one might speculate that under certain task conditions the reading level of a passage is irrelevant to the use of the text as an instructional resource. If the performance-grade exchange in a particular classroom requires that students be able to recall the names of historical events and figures mentioned in the chapter, then it is possible to achieve a successful exchange without being able to read all of the chapter with comprehension. Motivational considerations may obviously moderate this relationship since students with reading difficulties might not be inclined to participate in academic tasks.

One final point would seem to follow from this analysis of the interaction of classroom task structure and student strategies for processing subject matter. Resnick found that students worked out their own algorithms for solving arithmetic problems, even when this was not a goal of instruction. For instance, students consistently added smaller numbers to larger numbers when summing a column, even though they had never been taught this routine. Resnick suggests that students devise problem-solving routines on the basis of their direct experience with the content.[51] In ecological terms, that is, students learn the texture of subject matter tasks. This natural student process of formulating private algorithms would seem, however, to have negative as well as positive consequences. Some idiosyncratic routines, such as counting the points on numerals rather than adding them "in the head," are very inefficient and may limit the learner's ability to acquire more complex operations, in spite of the fact that the routines suffice for relatively simple computational tasks. A dramatic illustration of this point is contained in a fascinating series of interviews by Erlwanger. He discovered junior high school students who were reasonably successful at accomplishing classroom tasks but who had evolved private systems of mathematics that were fundamentally erroneous.[52] Such an analysis calls attention to the possibility that some students may achieve successful performance-grade exchanges by using strategies that effectively "short-circuit" the intended learning process. This perspective lends support to Greeno's argument for attention to cognitive objectives rather than simply behavioral objectives in the design and evaluation of instruction.[53]

IMPLICATIONS

An ecological approach to research on teaching underscores the role of classroom task structures—defined in terms of a goal and operations to achieve the goal—in determining outcomes. What students learn is, from this perspective, a function of what tasks they select and what operations are performed in accomplishing those tasks. Dimensions of the setting or the activities that occupy classroom time influence outcomes indirectly by affecting the efficiency of task accomplishment. Finally, the structure of learning tasks in the classroom provides an integrating framework for interpreting instructional cues, selecting strategies for processing subject matter, and utilizing instructional materials. The way in which a student understands this task structure would seem to have pervasive consequences for academic achievement.

Implications for research have been drawn at several points throughout the present discussion. In particular, it has been suggested that the ecological model is useful for defining treatment variables important in classroom research, for integrating research on learning with studies of classroom processes, and for interpreting results from studies of teaching. Two additional features of the ecological approach merit special attention. First, the model would seem to provide a basis for studying a classroom as a unit rather than simply in terms of discrete elements. The analysis of task structures suggests that classroom effects are multiple and operate at a molar rather than a molecular level. Teachers, from this perspective, are not simply directors of activities or contingency managers, but rather organizers of task systems. Second, the ecological framework opens up a number of lines for inquiry concerning student response variables that function to modify and transform classroom processes. Although not always overtly active in the classroom setting, students are hardly passive recipients of instructional "treatments." Research on student processes is needed to ascertain not only how students learn but also how they adapt to the demands of the classroom environment.

Implications of the ecological approach for practice are perhaps less readily apparent. There are at least two reasons for this state of affairs. First, the ecological model is itself in process of being formulated. The quantity of hard evidence necessary to draw conclusions for policy or practice simply is not available. Second, and perhaps of greater significance, the ecological model reflects a fundamentally different conceptualization of how research can assist practitioners. Traditionally, research on teaching has been viewed as a process of isolating a set of effective teaching practices to be used by individual teachers to improve student learning or by policy makers to design teacher education and teacher evaluation programs. The emphasis in this tradition has been on predicting which methods or teacher behaviors have the highest general success rate, and much of the controversy over the productivity of research on teaching has centered on the legitimacy of propositions derived from available studies.[54] At this stage, it would not seem that the ecological approach outlined in this chapter has much to offer for increasing the predictive power of general propositions about effective teaching patterns. Indeed, the approach would seem to call into question the very possibility of achieving a substantial number of highly generalizable statements about teaching effectiveness.

What, then, is the practical utility of an ecological approach to research on teaching? It would seem that the ecological model can best be viewed as an analytical framework for understanding how classrooms work. Such an understanding would appear to be especially useful to individual teachers for interpreting problems and generating solutions to meet the practical contingencies of specific classrooms. The understanding of classrooms afforded by the ecological analysis should also be of assistance to curriculum planners in designing programs that account for the demands of the classroom environments. Finally, the ecological perspective supplies a basis for identifying points for intervention into the classroom system and for anticipating the consequences of changing architecture or curriculum. To the extent that these advantages can eventually be realized, significant progress can be made toward overcoming the piecemeal and "teacher-proof" approaches that too often characterize current efforts to improve schooling.

Although it is certainly possible to improve practice with procedures that are not fully understood, an approach that stresses improvement rather than understanding has hardly achieved impressive results in teaching. Teachers do, moreover, have understandings, albeit tacit, that come from long-term experience with the demands of the classroom environment. The fact that they cannot always communicate these understandings—they are seldom asked to—does not negate their impact on classroom practice. There is even some basis to argue that "common sense" understandings of teaching and learning are as powerful as any of the explanatory models that have been constructed in the behavioral sciences.[55] It is reasonable, therefore, to give understanding due emphasis as a goal for research on teaching and as a practical tool for teachers.

NOTES

1. See, for example, David C. Berliner, "Impediments to the Study of Teacher Effectiveness," *Journal of Teacher Education* 27 (1976): 5-13; Jere E. Brophy and Carolyn M. Evertson, *Learning from Teaching: A Developmental Perspective* (Boston: Allyn and Bacon, 1976); and Annegret Harnischfeger and David E. Wiley, "The Teaching-Learning Process in Elementary Schools: A Synoptic View," *Curriculum Inquiry* 6 (1976): 5-43.

2. Decker F. Walker, "Toward Comprehension of Curricular Realities," in *Review of Research in Education*, Volume IV, ed. Lee S. Shulman (Itasca, Ill.: F. E. Peacock, 1976), 278.

3. For useful collections, see David Klahr, ed., *Cognition and Instruction* (Hillsdale, N.J.: Lawrence Erlbaum Associates, 1976); and Lauren B. Resnick, ed., *The Nature of Intelligence* (Hillsdale, N.J.: Lawrence Erlbaum Associates, 1976). A technical review is available in John W. Cotton, "Models of Learning," in *Annual Review of Psychology*, Volume XXVII, ed. Mark Rosenzweig and Lyman W. Porter (Palo Alto: Annual Reviews, Inc., 1976), 155-187. For a helpful introduction to this work, see David E. Rumelhart, *Introduction to Human Information Processing* (New York: John Wiley and Sons, 1977).

4. See, for example, Richard C. Anderson, Rand J. Spiro, and William E. Montague, eds., *Schooling and the Acquisition of Knowledge* (Hillsdale, N.J.: Lawrence Erlbaum Associates, 1977); Robert Glaser, "The Processes of Intelligence and Education," in *Nature of Intelligence*, ed. Resnick, 341-352; and M. C. Wittrock and Arthur A. Lumsdaine, "Instructional Psychology," in *Annual Review of Psychology*, Volume XXVII, ed. Rosenzweig and Porter, 417-459.

5. See Walter Doyle, "Learning the Classroom Environment: An Ecological Analysis," *Journal of Teacher Education* 28 (1977): 51-55; and *id.*, "Paradigms for Research on Teacher Effectiveness," in *Review of Research in Education*, Volume V, ed. Lee S. Shulman (Itasca, Ill.: F. E. Peacock, 1978), 163-198. The latter paper contains a more complete analysis and documentation of many of the points made in the present discussion. Portions of this chapter were presented at a colloquium at the Graduate School of Education, University of California, Santa Barbara on May 23, 1977. The author is grateful to Willis D. Copeland for arranging this session and for his helpful comments. Sandy Behrens and Charlotte Gelineau assisted in the preparation of the manuscript.

6. Barak Rosenshine, *Teaching Behaviors and Student Achievement* (Windsor, Eng.: National Foundation for Educational Research in England and Wales, 1971).

7. *Id.* and Norma Furst, "Research on Teacher Performance Criteria," in *Research in Teacher Education: A Symposium*, ed. B. Othanel Smith (Englewood Cliffs, N.J.: Prentice-Hall, 1971), 46.

8. Barak Rosenshine, "Classroom Instruction," in *The Psychology of Teaching Methods*, Seventy-fifth Yearbook of the National Society for the Study of Education, Part I, ed. N. L. Gage (Chicago: University of Chicago Press, 1976), 335-371; and Wittrock and Lumsdaine, "Instructional Psychology," esp. 442-445.

9. Greta Morine-Dershimer, "Teacher Judgments and Pupil Observations: Beauty in the Eye of the Beholder," *Journal of Classroom Interaction* 12 (1976): 31-50.

10. David C. Berliner and Barak Rosenshine, "The Acquisition of Knowledge in the Classroom," in *Schooling and the Acquisition of Knowledge*, ed. Anderson, Spiro, and Montague, 375-396.

11. John B. Carroll, "Psychometric Tests as Cognitive Tasks: A New 'Structure of Intellect,'" in *Nature of Intelligence*, ed. Resnick, 27-56.

12. Joseph Shimron, "Learning Activities in Individually Prescribed Instruction," *Instructional Science* 5 (1976): 391-401.

13. Ellen F. Potter, "The Classroom Environment and Children's Participation," *Administrator's Notebook* 24 (No. 8, 1976), n.p.

14. Annegret Harnischfeger *et al.*, "Instructional Time Allocations for Content Areas and Settings in Fifth-grade Reading," paper presented at the annual meeting of the American Educational Research Association, New York, 1977.

15. For this perspective on the task of teaching, see Dan C. Lortie, *Schoolteacher: A Sociological Study* (Chicago: University of Chicago Press, 1975); and Doyle, "Learning the Classroom Environment."

16. See Carolyn M. Evertson *et al.*, *Investigations of Stability in Junior High School Mathematics and English Classes: The Texas Junior High School Study*, Report No. 77-3 (Austin: Research and Development Center for Teacher Education, University of Texas, 1977); Carol G. Noble and John D. Nolan, "Effect of Student Verbal Behavior on Classroom Teacher Behavior," *Journal of Educational Psychology* 68 (1976): 342-346; Martha L. Fiedler, "Bidirectionality of Influence in Classroom Interaction," *Journal of Educational Psychology* 67 (1975): 735-744; and Willis D. Copeland, "The Nature of the Relationship between Cooperating Teacher Behavior and Student Teacher Classroom Performance," paper presented at the annual meeting of the American Educational Research Association, New York, 1977.

17. See Klahr, ed., *Cognition and Instruction*; and Ernst Z. Rothkopf, "Writing to Teach and Reading to Learn: A Perspective on the Psychology of Written Instruction," in *The Psychology of Teaching Methods*, ed. Gage, 91-129.

18. Jere E. Brophy, *The Student as the Unit of Analysis*, Report No. 75-12 (Austin: Research and Development Center for Teacher Education, University of Texas, 1975); Lee J. Cronbach and Richard E. Snow, *Aptitudes and Instructional Methods: A Handbook for Research on Interactions* (New York: Irvington, 1977).

19. The present approach to classroom ecology has been influenced by the formulations of Tinbergen as well as the work in ecological psychology. See N. Tinbergen, "Functional Ethology and the Human Sciences," *Proceedings of*

the *Royal Society of London, Series B,* 182 (1972): 385-410; and Edwin P. Willems, "Behavioral Ecology," in *Perspectives on Environment and Behavior: Theory, Research and Applications,* ed. Daniel Stokols (New York: Plenum, 1977), 39-68.

20. David Stenhouse, *The Evolution of Intelligence: A General Theory and Some of Its Implications* (New York: Barnes and Noble, 1974), 353.

21. Jacob S. Kounin, *Discipline and Group Management in Classrooms* (New York: Holt, Rinehart and Winston, 1970).

22. Howard S. Becker, quoted in Murray L. Wax and Rosalie H. Wax, "Great Tradition, Little Tradition, and Formal Education," in *Anthropologic Perspectives on Education,* ed. Murray L. Wax, Stanley Diamond, and Fred O. Gearing (New York: Basic Books, 1971), 10n.

23. Steven T. Bossert, "Tasks, Group Management, and Teacher Control Behavior: A Study of Classroom Organization and Teacher Style," *School Review* 85 (1977): 552-565; and Jacob S. Kounin, "Some Ecological Dimensions of School Settings," paper presented at the annual meeting of the American Educational Research Association, New York, 1977.

24. See, for example, Paul V. Gump, "Intra-setting Analysis: The Third-grade Classroom as a Special but Instructive Case," in *Naturalistic Viewpoints in Psychological Research,* ed. Edwin P. Willems and Harold L. Rausch (New York: Holt, Rinehart and Winston, 1969), 200-220; Philip W. Jackson, *Life in Classrooms* (New York: Holt, Rinehart and Winston, 1968); and Louis M. Smith and William Geoffrey, *The Complexities of an Urban Classroom* (New York: Holt, Rinehart and Winston, 1968).

25. Hugh Mehan, "Accomplishing Classroom Lessons," in *Language Use and School Performance,* ed. Aaron V. Cicourel *et al.* (New York: Academic Press, 1974), 76-129.

26. Walter H. MacGinitie, "Difficulty with Logical Operations," *The Reading Teacher* 29 (1976): 371-375.

27. Robert Glaser, "Individuals and Learning: The New Aptitudes," *Educational Researcher* 1 (1972): 5-13.

28. Howard S. Becker, Blanche Geer, and Everett Hughes, *Making the Grade* (New York: John Wiley, 1968), 79. Although perhaps less formal, this exchange process is reflected in the evaluative atmosphere of the elementary classroom. See Jackson, *Life in Classrooms,* 3-37.

29. Francis A. J. Ianni, *Social Organization of the High School Study,* Final Report, National Institute of Education Grant No. NEG-00-3-0079 (New York: Horace Mann-Lincoln Institute for School Experimentation, Teachers College, Columbia University, 1975), 114. ERIC: ED 129 711).

30. Kounin, *Discipline and Group Management in Classrooms.*

31. Noble and Nolan, "Effect of Student Verbal Behavior on Classroom Teacher Behavior."

32. Jere E. Brophy and Thomas L. Good, *Teacher-Student Relationships: Causes and Consequences* (New York: Holt, Rinehart and Winston, 1974); and Evertson *et al., Investigations of Stability in Junior High School Mathematics and English Classes,* 52-67.

33. Mehan, "Accomplishing Classroom Lessons."

34. James A. Schellenberg, "The Class-Hour Economy," *Harvard Educational Review* 35 (1965): 161-164.

35. Robert B. Davis and Curtis McKnight, "Conceptual, Heuristic, and S-Algorithmic Approaches in Mathematics Teaching," *Journal of Children's Mathematical Behavior,* Supplement No. 1 (Summer 1976): 271-286.

36. For a general discussion of this point, see Aaron V. Cicourel, "Some Basic Theoretical Issues in the Assessment of the Child's Performance in Testing and Classroom Settings," in *Language Use and School Performance,* ed. Cicourel *et al.*

37. See Klahr, ed., *Cognition and Instruction;* and Frank Smith, *Comprehension and Learning* (New York: Holt, Rinehart and Winston, 1975).

38. Arno A. Bellack *et al., The Language of the Classroom* (New York: Teachers College Press, 1966), 165-191.

39. William H. Redd, "The Effects of Adult Presence and Stated Preference on the Reinforcement Control of Children's Behavior," *Merrill-Palmer Quarterly* 22 (1976): esp. 94-95.

40. James J. Jenkins, "Remember That Old Theory of Memory? Well, Forget It!" in *Perceiving, Acting, and Knowing: Toward an Ecological Psychology,* ed. Robert Shaw and John Bransford (Hillsdale, N.J.: Lawrence Erlbaum Associates, 1977), 425. For a similar emphasis on the influence of task variables, see Rothkopf, "Writing to Teach and Reading to Learn"; and Eleanor J. Gibson and Harry Levin, *The Psychology of Reading* (Cambridge, Mass.: MIT Press, 1975).

41. Sandford W. Reitman, *Introduction to the Foundations of American Education* (Boston: Allyn and Bacon, 1977), 40.

42. Decker F. Walker and Jon Schaffarzick, "Comparing Curricula," *Review of Educational Research* 44 (1974): 83-111; and Ross Traub, Joel Weiss, and Charles Fisher, *Openness in Schools: An Evaluation Study,* Research in Education Series 5 (Toronto: Ontario Institute for Studies in Education, 1976).

43. William D. Rohwer, Jr., "Elaboration and Learning in Childhood and Adolescence," in *Advances in Child Development and Behavior,* Volume VIII, ed. Hayne W. Reese (New York: Academic Press, 1973), 1-57.

44. James G. Greeno, "Cognitive Objectives of Instruction: Theory of Knowledge for Solving Problems and Answering Questions," in *Cognition and Instruction,* ed. Klahr, 123-159; Richard E. Mayer, "Information Processing Variables in Learning to Solve Problems," *Review of Educational Research* 45 (1975): 525-541.

45. John D. Bransford *et al.,* "Toward Unexplaining Memory," in *Perceiving, Acting, and Knowing: Toward an Ecological Psychology,* ed. Shaw and Bransford, 431-466; Ann L. Brown, "The Development of Memory: Knowing, Knowing about Knowing, and Knowing How to Know," in *Advances in Child Development and Behavior,* Volume X, ed. Hayne W. Reese (New York: Academic Press, 1975), 103-152.

46. Stanley Herbert Erlwanger, "Case Studies of Children's Conceptions of Mathematics—Part I," *Journal of Children's Mathematical Behavior* 1 (1975): 157-283.

47. Mehan, "Accomplishing Classroom Lessons."

48. Davis and McKnight, "Conceptual, Heuristic, and S-Algorithmic Approaches in Mathematics Teaching."

49. Bonnie J. F. Meyer, *The Organization of Prose and Its Effects on Memory* (New York: American Elsevier Publishing, 1975).

50. James W. Pichert and Richard C. Anderson, *Taking Different Perspectives on a Story*, Technical Report No. 14 (Urbana, Ill.: Center for the Study of Reading, University of Illinois, 1976).

51. Lauren B. Resnick, "Task Analysis in Instructional Design: Some Cases from Mathematics," in *Cognition and Instruction*, ed. Klahr, 51-80.

52. Erlwanger, "Case Studies of Children's Conceptions of Mathematics—Part I."

53. Greeno, "Cognitive Objectives of Instruction."

54. N. L. Gage, *The Scientific Basis of the Art of Teaching* (New York: Teachers College Press, 1978).

55. John B. Carroll, "Promoting Language Skills: The Role of Instruction," in *Cognition and Instruction*, ed. Klahr, 3-22.

10. Perceptual Problem Solving

Philip H. Winne and *Ronald W. Marx*

Teachers strive to help students achieve a variety of goals, both personal and academic. Prominent among these many aims is that students will learn how to approach, sustain, and achieve learning outside school. Whether this objective is phrased as "learning how to learn," "achieving self-directed inquiry," or "promoting positive transfer," the emphasis given it in recent curricular and instructional reforms has been welcomed warmly.

As educational psychologists, we, too, are strongly interested in teaching and how teachers might foster such abilities in students. Although we shall speak of mental events as cognitive processes, of learning as changes in cognitive structure, and of "getting the hang of things" as acquiring perceptual schemata, our aim is the same as that of teachers: we want to be able to lay out workable plans for teaching that encourage students to learn in school and in later life.

The student is an intriguing puzzle for teachers and for us. Sometimes, when we have arranged the most stellar teaching imaginable, students do not get the point. And, fortunately, even when we feel we have botched instruction, they often learn in spite of our failure. Why? At this time, neither the teacher nor the educational psychologist can fully explain these mismatches of instructional prowess and instructional effectiveness. Perhaps one reason for this gap in the ability to explain effects of teaching stems from neglecting an essential feature of school learning, namely, how students perceive how to learn from teaching. Several questions arise: What does the student interpret as his task as he experiences teaching? How closely related are the student's interpretations and the teacher's intentions about what the student should "do" to learn? What might teachers do before and while teaching to help students more adequately perceive how to learn from teaching?

We have three goals in this chapter. First, we attempt to clarify the role of student perception of teaching, showing it to be one of the cognitive events in which students engage while learning in school. Second, we speculate about teaching events that hinder or aid the student in perceiving how to learn from the teaching that is the vehicle for whatever is to be learned. Where possible, we use empirical research to support and illustrate our claims. But, as research on teaching is still undergoing major development (some would say serious growth pains), our third goal is to comment upon the focuses for such research and the paradigm that guides it.[1]

COGNITION, PERCEPTION, AND LEARNING

Like all human beings, students in schools are constantly thinking. If we grant the assumption, however tenuous, that their thinking is focused on school learning, it seems reasonable to expect that there are probably at least three goals of their cognitive processes, whether they are consciously recognized or not. One goal is to determine what is supposed to be learned, that is, the curriculum that will be tested. A second goal is to achieve an understanding of how the teaching events that convey this curriculum point toward how learning should happen, that is, the mental processes students should use to learn the curriculum. Third, once the student has decoded teaching to make clear what is to be learned and how one might go about learning it, then thinking centers on actually applying those mental operations to the content so that actual learning takes place.

The mental paths to the first two kinds of goals are labeled "perceptual processing" by psychologists.[2] In both cases, the end product of these processes is an understanding of what stimuli in the teaching environment portend for learning. According to Gibson, the act of perceiving requires that the perceiver purposefully extract information from the environment.[3] One way that students do this is by forming "cognitive questions" about the role that stimuli in the teaching environment play in learning from teaching.[4] Answers to successively more refined questions about these roles guide the student to more useful perceptions of what to learn and how to learn it before he actually executes the learning routine itself. Thus, as Neisser puts it, "perceiving is the basic cognitive activity out of which all others must emerge . . . perception is where cognition and reality meet."[5]

This characterization of students' cognitive questions about and responses to teaching suggests that teaching should be examined for ways that it affects perception as much as, or maybe even more than, ways that it affects learning. The role of student perception, and the influence of teaching events on perceptual processing, has not received much attention in educational research in typical classroom settings. Although some exception to this generalization can be found in research on learning disabilities,[6] students' views of trait-like characteristics of their school environments,[7] and phenomenological studies of interactions between one's interpretation of "self" and situational variables,[8] we know little about perceptual phenomena and teaching.

What follows is an exploration of the role of student perceptual processing in the context of learning from teaching. An essential starting point is to describe more fully what perception is and how it functions. Our ultimate objective is to offer some defensible speculations about how students' perceptual questions about teaching might be more easily answered by the teacher.

PERCEPTION AND PERCEPTUAL LEARNING

The two basic issues facing perceptual psychologists are how humans sense information in their environment and how they attach psychological meaning to these sensations.[9] In the context of our earlier analysis of students' cognitive questions that bear on learning from teaching, little emphasis need be placed on the first issue. What is of concern regarding the second issue is whether our proposal about the existence of cognitive questions has some validity, and how it shapes a conception of teaching.

In teaching undergraduate educational psychology courses, we have noticed an interesting phenomenon when students take notes. Specifically, whenever something is written on the overhead projector, nearly all the students scamper to get that material, whatever it is, into their notebooks.[10] The correlation between what appears on the overhead projector and students' learning of those concepts, however, is less than might be hoped for. Clearly, students "perceive" the importance of material appearing on the overhead projector. We might presume that they have a cognitive question regarding signals of important content that will accept answers like, "Anything written on the overhead is important!" Some educational psychologists would describe this as a mental set. Yet putting the written material in their notes does not, alone, produce learning as measured by frequent quizzes. Why not?

The students in our lectures are searching for information that will constitute test items; they "know" that a successful search will improve their grade. For them, it makes psychological sense to label as "important to this search" whatever appears on the overhead projector. In Neisser's terms, our students have a perceptual schema[11] that selectively extracts information from the lecture environment (whatever is on the overhead projector), attaches a psychological meaning to the information (its importance for grades), and directs subsequent activity in accord with that meaning (get it in the notes). It is unfortunate that, although practically all students have answered the cognitive question about how the activities of the lecturer bear on learning, not quite as many have solved the perceptual problem posed by the cognitive question: "What is the psychological meaning of the material on the overhead?" Hence, their notes may prove somewhat undecipherable when they study for the quiz. Unless they solve this second problem in perception by some other means, for example, by reading the text, a perceptual block about the content to be learned has hampered their learning. And, for those students who solve both perceptual problems about the message conveyed by our use of the overhead projector (a teacher behavior) and the content to be learned, not all proceed to learn what they perceived (for whatever reason). Thus, a discrepancy between notes taken in class and learning demonstrated on quizzes appears frequently, but for quite different reasons.

Implicit in the foregoing discussion are descriptions of both perception and perceptual learning. More formally, perceiving entails selecting and attaching psychological meaning to some subset of the stimuli in our environment. What we already know, the cognitive structure that indexes all the facts, functions, and relations that we have experienced, figures prominently in what we select and how we give it meaning. Indeed, what we cannot relate to cognitive structure is called nonsense, if we sense it at all. The inadvertent social faux pas that is commonly made in unfamiliar cultural settings is a result of being unable to perceive a social cue. We err not because we cannot perceive the cue if we know about it, and not because we cannot react properly if we perceive it, but because we do not perceive the cue at all owing to the absence of its psychological meaning in cognitive structure. When schemata for teachers' cues are similarly absent from students' cognitive structures, the academic faux pas of inadequate learning is conceptually parallel to ours.

De facto evidence exists concerning our ability to learn how to perceive since we can make a proper response as soon as we are told about the cue. Our undergraduate students have learned to copy material from the overhead projector. Their behavioral, and probably mental, responses to a now meaningful stimulus in our lectures represent a relatively permanent change in their behavior following personal experience or imitation of other students' action.[12] Presumably, teachers might enhance their effectiveness by focusing on students' perceptual learning before directing students to learn the curriculum materials. By having a direct hand in tuning students' perceptual schemata to teaching methods, what might have been initial perceptual problems for students could be changed into "rapport" to facilitate learning.

At this point, the distinction between perception and cognition that leads to learning probably seems blurred. Both can produce learning, and both are malleable in that the processes themselves can change with experience. The distinguishing feature is not in the mental process, not in how perception and cognition operate, but in the product of these operations.

The product of perception is a psychologically meaningful representation of a part, not all, of the information in the perceiver's immediate environment.[13] It is important to underscore two qualities concerning this product. First, a psychologically meaningful representation is achieved. This does not mean that the percept is necessarily accurate. Indeed, the common phenomenon in which several eye-witnesses provide different reports of an event lends credence to the interpretation that it is psychological meaningfulness, not veridicality, that is the functional purpose of perception. Second, only part of the information in the environment is included in this representation. We do not perceive the environment by producing a perfect analogue in our minds, from which information is selected. Perceptual schemata serve to highlight meaningful information in the environment; that is the information we perceive, while the rest is lost. That is why, in the previous example, university students in lectures copy information that has been graphically displayed on the overhead projector, but may not learn it. They have perceptual schemata for what the lecturer indicates is important in lectures, but not for the content of the lecture.

In contrast to perception, other cognitive processes that relate directly to learning result in relatively permanent changes in the way information is represented in cognitive structure, and subsequently permit changes in behavior. Presumably, these cognitive processes follow upon perception, but they are not necessarily limited to meaningful representations of information in the environment. The two products are not mutually exclusive either, in that perceivers learn to perceive as a function of changes in cognitive structure and behavior.

Earlier, we defined perception as the act of extracting information from the environment. How do people learn to do this? There clearly are some innate processes involved. For example, a neonate will flinch when an object is perceived as approaching very quickly in the visual field. But most perceptual development important for instructional contexts is learned.

Perceptual schemata are not purely responsive, however. Perceptions are not completely at the whim of the stimulus field; we are not completely passive perceivers. Rather, perception is an active process in which we extract information from the environment. Perceptual learning, then, "refers to an increase in the ability to extract information from the environment, as a result of experience and practice with stimulation coming from it."[14] According to Neisser, this increase in ability is because perceptual schemata are embedded in perceptual cycles.[15]

In a perceptual cycle, as shown in Figure 10-1, a schema directs

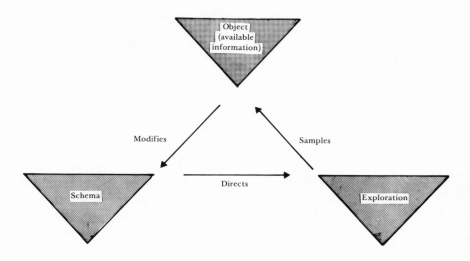

Figure 10-1

The perceptual cycle (from *Cognition and Reality: Principles and Implications of Cognitive Psychology,* by Ulric Neisser [San Francisco: W. H. Freeman and Company, copyright © 1976])

exploration of the environment. The schema defines what information is important. But the schema does not restrict exploration to a single subset of information. If this were to happen, no perceptual learning could occur at all. Rather, in a sense, the schema determines the relative importance of different information, and presumably these differences can range in magnitude from extremely important down to perfectly irrelevant. But the exploration of the environment results in the processing of some information that does not perfectly fit the schema. Hence, the schema undergoes modification. And so it goes.

PERCEPTUAL PROBLEM SOLVING IN LEARNING SETTINGS

We have presented to this point an intuitive argument buttressed, on the one hand, only by a logical linkage between theories of perception and cognition and, on the other hand, by anecdotal observations about how students work to learn from teaching. We know of no research that has addressed directly the issues we raise about students' perceptual problem solving during instruction. If the phenomenon exists, however, there ought to be hints of it in other kinds of research studies. We turn now to relevant but mostly indirect evidence that students do engage in perceptual problem solving regarding content and teaching.

At a general level, a study by Bloom provides some evidence on these points.[16] He asked university students to report on the kinds of thoughts they experienced during instruction. In discussion groups, about 20 percent of the time was spent merely following or trying to comprehend the information covered. For lecture situations, approximately 37 percent of instructional time was filled by these kinds of thoughts. The earlier description of perception as a cognitive activity directed at achieving a meaningful representation of a subset of stimuli in one's environment is synonymous with this activity reported by students in Bloom's research. But beyond general reports of this sort, there is other evidence to suggest that conquering the two perceptual problems we hypothesize to be precursors to learning can significantly facilitate learning.

Perceiving Content in Teaching

Without exception, a teacher must build on what students already know. This follows logically from the fact that psychologically meaningful learning must be related to elements within cognitive structure that learners bring with them to the classroom. It seems essential, then, that perceiving and learning the content of teaching would require students to have some prerequisite information in cognitive structure. This will allow, although not necessarily ensure, the information being presented in teaching to be perceived and linked to previous knowledge in a more permanent way to yield learning. If students could be "preinstructed" so that such prerequisites were salient, then instruction might yield better results.

A study by Larkin and Reif illustrates precisely this approach to reducing students' perceptual problems associated with selecting meaningful information from an instructional environment.[17] These researchers logically analyzed the cognitive state of "understanding" (we would say "perceiving") the content of elementary physics problems about relational concepts (for example, the law of gravitational force). This analysis resulted in a set of preconditions they felt were necessary before students could solve such problems (Table 10-1). Most of these states refer clearly to aspects in our definition of perception in that they entail identifying information provided in a problem, discriminating relevant from irrelevant data according to a criterion, and establishing some psychological meaning (interpretation) for information. This collection of perceptions about a physics problem, when learned by student problem solvers, forms a functional subset of information that can be used to learn the relational concept itself. Thus, Larkin and Reif hypothesized that training students to fulfill these preconditions would increase their learning from text, which should also enhance their overall performance in solving physics problems. We would label training in these preconditions perceptual training, the outcome of which would be perceptual learning about how to perceive elements of physics problems essential to learning principles of physics.

Table 10-1
Summary of preconditions for "understanding" a relational problem

A. State information characterizing the relation
   1. State the relation
   2. Give an example of its application
   3. List properties of quantities in the relation
B. Interpret the relation by using information in various symbolic representations
C. Make discriminations
   1. Applicability
      a. Discriminate between information relevant and irrelevant to finding each quantity in the relation
      b. Discriminate between situations to which the relation does and does not apply
   2. Comparison
      a. Discriminate each quantity in the relation from other quantities.
      b. Discriminate the relation from other relations
D. Use equivalent forms of the relation to find or compare values

Source: Jill H. Larkin and F. Reif, "Analysis and Teaching of a General Skill for Studying Scientific Text" by Jill H. Larkin and F. Reif, *Journal of Educational Psychology,* 68 (August 1976), 432. Copyright 1976 by The American Psychological Association. Reprinted by permission.

The experimental design used by Larkin and Reif unfortunately confounded perceptual training with a personalized system of instruction for trained students versus a typical lecture-discussion format for untrained students. Hence, the differences they report favoring performance of trained over untrained students on physics problem-solving tests are confounded with the kind of instruction students received. The researchers tested for transfer effects, however, by using problems in economics about relational concepts concerning inventory turnover. Comparison of the group means for separate random samples before and after training showed that, on the transfer task, students trained to perceive essential data in a problem statement about relational concepts significantly outperformed untrained students. Larkin and Reif concluded that (perceptual) training improved students' abilities to understand (perceive) the textual statement of the problem beyond the level of understanding achieved by students who had to induce a perceptual strategy on their own.

This study illustrates two important ideas surrounding the role of perceptual problem solving in learning from teaching. First, students can be trained to use a perceptual strategy for selecting information from the instructional environment that is necessary for learning, even for higher-order learning like problem solving. Students left on their own to deal with this perceptual problem about content learned less. Our interpretation of this finding is that perceptual problem solving exists and can be influential in learning. Second, and more exciting, is the finding that perceptual training in one curriculum transferred positively to a second curriculum. Thus, the positive effects of training students to use a functional and generalizable perceptual strategy may contribute to learning beyond the limited context of the training itself and benefit learning in several school subjects.

Another approach to helping students solve the perceptual problem about content to be learned might make use of already existing perceptual schemata to lessen the complexity of content or make salient crucial elements of content. One application of this approach involves directly instructing students about what is relevant before teaching it. This creates or engages a perceptual schema that matches the teaching, rather than taxing the learner to develop a functional schema while also trying to learn the content.

A recent review of research on such preinstructional strategies shows mixed results when learning prose material (rather than the preinstructional strategy) is the gauge of success.[18] In learning from text, for example, providing readers with "explicit" statements about what should be learned quite consistently produces increases in learning the specified content relative to other incidental (that is, not identified) content.[19] It also has been demonstrated that providing students with objectives enhances learning primarily for information that would not have been selectively perceived had objectives not provided a criterion for selection.[20] Students, in this case college seniors, do invoke schemata for selectively perceiving information from instructional presentations without explicit perceptual training. This is supported by the finding of no significant differences in learning for items that were judged important to learn by students given perceptually nonfunctional objectives, like "understand the material in the passage." But, by increasing the saliency of material that otherwise would not meet a criterion for selective perception, that is, by noting it explicitly in an objective, learning was significantly enhanced. Hence, helping students solve the perceptual problem of identifying and selecting relevant information from instructional presentations can supplement existing individual perceptual schemata in beneficial ways without extensive training like that employed in the study by Larkin and Reif.[21]

The beneficial effects of directions to learn particular information are moderated by other variables such as the overall amount of information to be learned, the quantity of information referred to in objectives, the density of information included in objectives relative to the total amount of information, and the specificity of objectives.[22] These variables may account, in part, for the mixed effects induced by preinstructional strategies. Yet, there are at least two other plausible hypotheses for these results that relate to students' perceptual problem solving in trying to learn from teaching. The first is that a preinstructional strategy may not invoke or create a useful perceptual schema because the strategy itself is not well-perceived by the students. It is hard to imagine that a perceptual schema will work if it is not invoked, and few studies of pre-instructional strategies tested this effect directly. Indeed, when high school students were informed about the structure of content they were to learn, not only did they slightly outperform uninformed counterparts after a first attempt to learn, but they kept gaining over them in two later opportunities to continue learning. Presumably, their perceptual schema for recognizing important content grew more efficient.[23]

A second possible explanation for the mixed results obtained in studies of preinstructional perceptual training is that these experiences answer only one of the cognitive questions that bear on learning. If a student can perceive what information is to be learned, the question of what the teaching is telling him to do with that information still exists. It is possible that students not only must achieve meaningful perceptions of *what* they are to learn, but also must face the same kind of issue in coming to know *how* the teacher has structured the experience to promote learning. We turn now to the second cognitive question about perceptual problem solving in learning from teaching.

Perceiving Teacher Intentions

Contemporary views of teaching portrayed in both research and teacher training almost universally presume a one-to-one correspondence between teacher acts and the intended mental responses by students.

For example, if a teacher says, "This is important," it is practically a foregone conclusion that students will somehow emphasize the content referred to by the teacher's statement. Presumptions of this kind are so predominant that virtually no studies have tested directly these kinds of links between teacher behavior and student cognitive processing. Instead, research on teacher effects has examined relationships between teacher behavior and students' learning at the end of a lesson or even at the end of units lasting several weeks.[24] If our conception of learning from teaching is representative of real-world events, answers to research questions relating teacher behavior to learning could get muddled by intervening variations in students' answers to their cognitive questions about teaching.

But, do these presumed teacher-student correspondences really break down? Evidence from several sources suggests that they do. For example, a study by Hughes tested directly an age-old maxim about how to ask questions properly.[25] Student teachers are frequently told to withhold the name of the student they wish to respond to a question until after the question has been asked.[26] The hypothesized effect of this practice is to ensure that all students, instead of merely the named student, attend to and process the information necessary to answer the question. This, in turn, should enhance learning over the case where students are named before the question is asked.

Hughes directly contrasted students' learning, admittedly a distant measure of attention but one for which attention is deemed essential, in an experiment where he taught using the "right" and "wrong" ways to frame questions.[27] No reliable differences in learning were found. It seems that students in Hughes's studies had already answered the cognitive question about how to respond to questions in general, regardless of the manner in which they were framed— name-first or otherwise. What many thought was a powerful cognitive question for students, that is, "Will I have to answer?" was not parallel to how students were perceiving the situation.

Consider another questioning variable, higher-order questions as a second instance of possible mismatches between teachers' intended cognitive responses by students and students' actual answers to their cognitive question about what the teacher intends. Here the assumption is that teachers' higher-order questions will prompt complex thinking by student respondents. Not only will this lift the level of thought in classroom recitations, but students' practice of these cognitive activities should increase their overall ability to "think." At least, that is what is supposed to happen.

A recent review of experiments testing the impact of higher cognitive questions on students' learning supports the disappointing conclusion that the presumed relation is not warranted.[28] Is it possible that higher-order questions are misperceived by students? Two colleagues of ours tested the actual classroom impact of fact and higher-order questions by observing the kinds of responses students made to trained teachers' questions of both the factual and higher-order variety.[29] They found that, although their training procedures were effective in getting teachers to ask more higher-order questions than they had before training, higher-order questions at either time generally did not produce higher cognitive responses by students. Of course, it is possible that higher-order questions do not produce complex thinking because students have not learned the content that must be manipulated to answer such questions. But, given the status of our current knowledge, it also is possible that students simply do not perceive what mental activities the teacher intends to invoke by such questions.

The evidence is skimpy to support our contention that students ask cognitive questions about what the teaching is telling them to do to learn. Beyond the evidence being indirect, it does not provide much information about what really happens in this regard. We attempted to remedy this situation by an experiment in one of our undergraduate classes.

Standing on the shoulders of Larkin and Reif's model regarding the perception of content in physics problems, we examined Marx's lecturing behaviors for his hidden intentions about what students should do to learn from the lecture. We defined a logical link between several structural characteristics of lectures[30] and the mental response we thought students should make to benefit from these clues about "what to do" with lecture content. These relationships are listed in Table 10-2.

Table 10-2

Proposed answers to cognitive questions about the lecturer's intentions

Part of lecture	Lecturer behaviors	Intended mental responses
Preview	1. Names each major concept in the lecture	1. Learn label, listen for different concepts
	2. Gives defining attributes	2. Learn attributes
	3. Gives an example	3. Test ability to recognize concept attributes in a real example, associate label with attributes
Transitions between concepts	1. Names concept just finished and gives an example	1. Review concept label and attributes in example
	2. Signals a change of topic	2. Switch attention
	3. Names new concept and gives an example	3. Review concept label and attributes in example
Review	1. Gives a new example of a concept	1. Analyze the example for attributes, predict what the concept is
	2. Names concept	2. Review concept label, note problem if prediction incorrect

We randomly assigned prearranged tutorial groups to one of five kinds of training (given by Winne) in how to perceive lectures. Three groups were instructed to perceive the occurrence of specific behaviors comprising the previews and reviews of lectures. Three other groups were instructed to perceive these behaviors plus behaviors used in making transitions between major parts of the lecture. We labeled these two kinds of groups "structurally" trained because the students' perception of lecturing was enhanced only with regard to being able to identify the lecturer's behaviors—they were not told anything about the cognitive responses intended by those behaviors.

Paralleling the two varieties of structural training were two kinds of "functional" training. Three more groups of students were instructed about the lecturer's preview and review behaviors, plus the kinds of cognitive responses they should make (either mentally or in their notes) when they observed these behaviors in the lecture. Another three groups of students received functional training on preview, transition, and review of the behaviors of the lecturer.

These two varieties of structural and functional training (that is, preview plus review, and preview plus transition plus review) were intended to alleviate perceptual problems relating to what to do to learn from lectures. To address the cognitive question regarding content in lectures, students in all four training conditions were instructed about what a concept is and how to identify one. All students were taught to recognize (perceive) a concept as a label for a category of real or abstract things that is defined by at least one crucial feature. Tests at the end of the training sessions verified that the students could, in fact, do all of these things when they read a short simulation of a lecture in prose form. We assumed these abilities transferred easily to real lectures, a point to which we return shortly.

Finally, the last group of students served as a control. They participated in a general discussion about things that made for "good" lectures, but were told nothing about the structural or functional items in Table 10-2.

Our hypothesis in this study was simple: students who do not face perceptual problems and carry out the cognitive responses corresponding to the lecturer's intentions for the various behaviors would have simpler sets of things to do in learning from the lecture. In terms of our conceptions of students' cognitive questions in learning from teaching, they should have an easier job of learning because cognitive questions about what the content was and what they were to do to learn were answered in varying degrees by the training they had received.

Over the semester, five quizzes were administered to the class. Training of the students took place right after the third quiz; thus, any effects of our attempts to help students learn by solving perceptual problems should appear as improvements in scores on the fourth and fifth quizzes. We expected some increase in quiz grades for both functionally trained groups, with the control and structurally trained groups' scores changing little.

The results of the study are, at first, an embarrassment to our theorizing. As Figure 10-2 shows, when we use the average marks of students in the control group as a reference, the groups differ little except for a statistically significant and theoretically unsettling decline in scores for the group we had hoped would do best.

We attempted to rescue our theory in the following way. Two weeks after training, Winne went back to the students for "booster" training, that is, a quick review of the material in Table 10-2, and to collect anecdotal reports about how the students were reacting to the boon we had granted them in training. Students in the preview-transition-review functional training group claimed that our training was more a boondoggle. They said that they had no trouble recognizing the behaviors they learned about in training and that they knew what to do when they observed Marx using the behaviors.

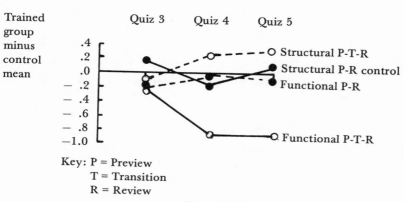

Figure 10-2

Comparison of perceptually trained group means to the control group mean

Unfortunately, doing all that while trying to take notes was impossible for most. Some students disliked the way we had answered the cognitive questions about the lecturer's intentions because it conflicted with a preferred style of taking notes. In other words, the students rejected perceptual schemata we thought were best because they interfered with already well-established schemata with which they were more comfortable. Their rejection was probably less than total, however, which created a bigger perceptual problem because there was competition between the different perceptual schemata. Cumulative effects of this perceptual conflict probably made some of the lecture material confusing, or may even have prevented it from getting to the learning stage at all.

Our naiveté about the malleability of students' perceptual schemata has been adjusted accordingly, but we are even more convinced that perceptual problem solving is integral to learning from teaching since we inadvertently demonstrated that learning per se declines when we made it harder for students to answer their cognitive questions about teaching.

CONCLUSION

We have tried to show how a particular phase of students' mental activities may ultimately affect what they learn. Following upon recent work in cognitive psychology, in particular the seminal work of Ulric Neisser,[31] we have hypothesized and attempted an initial proof that perception is a sine qua non of cognition pertaining to learning from teaching. We posit that during instruction students must solve three problems, or what we have called, after Smith,[32] "cognitive questions." First, students need to develop, or if already developed, bring into use, a perceptual schema for the content of instruction. Second, a conceptually parallel schema must be brought to bear in perceiving the intentions of the teacher's actions (or the textbook's features). Finally, once these perceptual problems are solved, the student must engage in mental operations to bring about learning. The former two cognitive questions are basically problems of perceptual learning, and it was on these problems that we focused our attention.

Perception is an active process of extracting information from the environment and giving this information psychological meaning. It is clear from this definition that we see human learning, in all its manifest forms, to be a process of construction. Psychological meaning does not exist in the environment waiting for a person to absorb it; it is built up inside the mind of the perceiver and thinker, and operates to give texture to the environment. This clearly places us in the "constructivist" camp,[33] with its rather clear implications for the kinds of theoretical questions that ought to guide research. In turn, to the extent that research findings lead to educational programming, we hold the position that educational innovation ought to focus as much or more on the way teachers and students think as it does on the way they behave.

Similar perspectives are held by researchers working in other areas of education. A notable example is the recent work by Anderson and his associates[34] on how people construct the meaning of communications. A striking common element in Anderson's research, Neisser's theorizing, and our speculations is the concept of the schema. According to Anderson, schemata are abstract, personally constructed representations of "generic concepts underlying objects."[35] These representations contain slots for each component of a particular area of knowledge. Metaphorically, one is reminded of the process of chemical bonding, in which certain chemicals fit together like jigsaw puzzles because of the unique nature of their respective molecular structures. If Anderson and his associates are right and these slots in schemata can be identified, we may be able to give directions to reachers about how to teach perceptual schemata to children dealing with learning from teaching, much in the same way that Larkin and Reif did in their study on learning from text.

Our attempts at modifying perceptual schemata for learning from lectures has opened up a new area of research for us. Ultimately, as we have said elsewhere,[36] we believe that research on teaching and research on instructional psychology in general ought to be able to make theoretical statements regarding *how* learning occurs in known situations, as well as *how much* learning occurs under these conditions. Explanatory statements about the processes of learning will require research paradigms that differ from those traditionally used in research on teaching effects. Such modified paradigms will have to have a place for cognitive variables in order to develop a data base for explanations about how learning from teaching occurs. We strongly expect that perceptual processing will be an integral component in these paradigms.

NOTES

1. We also have attempted this task with regard to other elements of research on teaching; see Philip H. Winne and Ronald W. Marx, "Reconceptualizing Research on Teaching," *Journal of Educational Psychology* 69 (1977): 668-678.

2. We have chosen the label "perceptual processing" to describe the mental operations that students use in coming to comprehend the nature of school learning tasks before they engage in learning per se. Some of our colleagues have identified problems with this label, saying that other descriptive names (and presumably somewhat different amalgamations of cognitive events) could be substituted without damaging our argument. We take the position that, at this early stage of relatively unsubstantiated theorizing, it is not profitable to argue about which label is better. Indeed, it is beneficial that different perspectives are taken, since these will help to frame research that contrasts important aspects of how pupils learn from teaching. Thus, we embrace diverse labels for the events we describe as "perceptual processing," but have chosen to use this one label for simplicity.

3. Eleanor J. Gibson, *Principles of Perceptual Development and Learning* (New York: Appleton-Century-Crofts, 1969).

4. Frank Smith, *Comprehension and Learning: A Conceptual Framework for Teachers* (New York: Holt, Rinehart and Winston, 1975).

5. Ulric Neisser, *Cognition and Reality: Principles and Implications of Cognitive Psychology* (San Francisco: W. H. Freeman and Co., 1976).

6. R. Frank Vellutino, Joseph A. Steger, and Gillray Kandel, "Reading Disability: An Investigation of the Perceptual Deficit Hypothesis," *Cortex* 8 (1972): 106-118.

7. Herbert J. Walberg, "Psychology of Learning Environments: Behavioral, Structural, or Perceptual?" in *Review of Research in Education*, Volume IV, ed. Lee S. Shulman (Itasca, Ill.: F. E. Peacock, 1976), 142-178.

8. Donald E. Hamachek, *Behavior Dynamics in Teaching, Learning, and Growth* (Boston: Allyn and Bacon, 1975).

9. For an extended discussion of how these issues of perceptual psychology relate to education, see Robert M. W. Travers, *Essentials of Learning* (New York: Macmillan, 1977), 246-298.

10. Our anecdotal observations about this relation have been confirmed recently in a systematic investigation by Edwin A. Locke, "An Empirical Study of Lecture Note Taking among College Students," *Journal of Educational Research* 21 (1977): 93-99.

11. Neisser, *Cognition and Reality*.

12. The role of imitation is extensive in learning in general, and in perceptual learning. For a comprehensive treatment, see Albert Bandura, *Social Learning Theory* (Englewood Cliffs, N. J.: Prentice-Hall, 1977).

13. Our earlier example about the social faux pas is an instance where perceptual extraction of information from the environment was dysfunctional. Selective extraction also can be functional; see Peter H. Lindsay and Donald A. Norman, *Human Information Processing: An Introduction to Psychology* (New

York: Academic Press, 1972), 1-49, for interesting examples from the physical world.

14. Gibson, *Principles of Perceptual Development and Learning*, 3.

15. Neisser, *Cognition and Reality*.

16. Benjamin S. Bloom, "Thought Processes in Lectures and Discussion," *Journal of General Education* 7 (1953): 160-169.

17. Jill H. Larkin and F. Reif, "Analysis and Teaching of a General Skill for Studying Scientific Text," *Journal of Educational Psychology* 68 (1976): 431-440.

18. James Hartley and Ivor K. Davies, "Preinstructional Strategies: The Role of Pretests, Behavioral Objectives, Overviews and Advance Organizers," *Review of Educational Research* 46 (1976): 239-265.

19. Ernst Z. Rothkopf, "Writing to Teach and Reading to Learn: A Perspective on the Psychology of Written Instruction," in *The Psychology of Teaching Methods*, Seventy-fifth Yearbook of the National Society for the Study of Education, Part I, ed. N. L. Gage (Chicago: University of Chicago Press, 1976), 91-129.

20. Orpha K. Duell, "Effect of Type of Objective, Level of Test Questions, and the Judged Importance of Tested Materials upon Posttest Performance," *Journal of Educational Psychology* 66 (1974): 225-232.

21. It is important to note, however, that the kinds of learning differ significantly across the studies; Larkin and Reif studied problem solving while Duell examined recognition and simple application.

22. Robert Kaplan and Ernst Z. Rothkopf, "Instructional Objectives as Directions to Learners: Effect of Passage Length and Amount of Objective-Relevant Content," *Journal of Educational Psychology* 66 (1974): 448-456.

23. Lawrence T. Frase, "Paragraph Organization of Written Materials: The Influence of Conceptual Clustering upon the Level and Organization of Recall," *Journal of Educational Psychology* 60 (1969): 394-401.

24. For a classic example of this kind of research on teacher effects, see N. L. Gage, "A Factorially Designed Experiment on Teacher Structuring, Soliciting, and Reacting," *Journal of Teacher Education* 27 (1976): 35-39.

25. David C. Hughes, "An Experimental Investigation of the Effects of Pupil Responding and Teacher Reacting on Pupil Achievement," *American Educational Research Journal* 10 (1973): 21-37.

26. For example, see Kenneth H. Hoover, *The Professional Teacher's Handbook*, 2d ed., abridged (Boston: Allyn and Bacon, 1976), 176-177, for several traditional suggestions in this vein.

27. Actually, Hughes did not name students first, but told them that questions would be asked around the room according to the seating chart. Thus, students knew well in advance when they would be the target of a question, which was even more likely than if the name of each student been randomly chosen and spoken before each individual question in the lesson.

28. Philip H. Winne, "Experiments Relating Teachers' Use of Higher Cognitive Questions to Student Achievement," *Review of Educational Research*, in press.

29. Jack Martin and Stanley Auerbach, "Differential Outcome Effects in Teacher Training Research as a Result of Functional versus Structural Behavioral Recording," *Alberta Journal of Educational Research* 23 (1977): 128-137.

30. We based our lecturing variables on a cluster of variables we developed with N. L. Gage, Christopher M. Clark, Penelope L. Peterson, and N. Stayrook, for a study of classroom recitations. See Program on Teaching Effectiveness, "A Factorially Designed Experiment on Teacher Structuring, Soliciting, and Reacting," Research and Development Memorandum No. 147 (Stanford, Calif.: Stanford Center for Research and Development in Teaching, 1976).

31. Neisser, *Cognition and Reality.*

32. Smith, *Comprehension and Learning.*

33. A. Jon Magoon, "Constructivist Approaches in Educational Research," *Review of Educational Research* 47 (1977): 651-693.

34. Richard C. Anderson *et al.,* "Frameworks for Comprehending Discourse," *American Educational Research Journal* 14 (1977): 367-381.

35. *Ibid.,* 369.

36. Winne and Marx, "Reconceptualizing Research in Teaching."

11. Teachers' Thinking

Christopher M. Clark and *Robert J. Yinger*

A relatively new approach to the study of teaching assumes that what teachers do is affected by what they think. This approach, which emphasizes the processing of cognitive information, is concerned with teachers' judgment, decision making, and planning. The study of the thinking processes of teachers—how they gather, organize, interpret, and evaluate information—is expected to lead to understandings of the uniquely human processes that guide and determine their behavior.

The cognitive information-processing approach developed as a logical outgrowth of behavioral approaches to research on teaching that have contributed a great deal to our knowledge of what not only teachers but also students do in classrooms and how this behavior relates to students' learning and attitudes.[1] If the results of such research are to be applied by individual teachers in their classrooms,

This work was supported in part by the Institute for Research on Teaching at Michigan State University. The Institute is funded primarily by the Teaching Division of the National Institute of Education, United States Department of Health, Education and Welfare (Contract No. 400-76-0073). The opinions expressed in this publication do not necessarily reflect the position, policy, or endorsement of the National Institute of Education.

however, adaptations must be made. Each class consists of a unique combination of personalities, constraints, and opportunities. Behavior that is sensible and effective in one setting may be inappropriate in a second setting, and it is the individual teacher who decides what is appropriate and defines the teaching situation. And so, if research is to be put into practice—if general rules are to be applied to particular situations—then we must know more about how teachers exercise judgment, make decisions, define appropriateness, and express their thoughts in their actions.

Several metaphors have been substituted for "teacher" when describing various aspects of this view of teaching. The teacher has been called a processor of clinical information,[2] a decision maker,[3] a planner,[4] a diagnostician,[5] and a problem solver.[6] Whatever the designation, it is the mental processes underlying behavior that are always the focus of study, and research often depends upon teachers' self-reports of their thought processes.[7] Teachers' self-reports have been obtained through a variety of methods ranging from questionnaires and interviews to "thinking aloud" procedures, in which a teacher speaks into a tape recorder while planning, and "stimulated recall" techniques, in which teachers view their own teaching by videotape and attempt to report on decisions and judgments made while teaching.[8]

In addition to the various kinds of self-reports, there are techniques for describing teacher judgment and decision making that have been borrowed from the psychological laboratory, especially policy-capturing techniques through use of the lens model developed by Egon Brunswick.[9] Attempts have been made to write computer programs modeled on the decision-making behavior of expert reading diagnosticians.[10]

What have we learned about the mental lives of teachers? To date, research in this area has been directed toward planning, judgment, interactive decision making, and implicit theories or perspectives, and each of these areas is reviewed here.

PLANNING

Until recently, the literature on planning in education has been mainly prescriptive. Many volumes have been written recommending specific principles for curriculum planning,[11] and most textbooks based on recent methods include at least one chapter on planning. Most of the work in curriculum planning to date has focused on a model first proposed by Tyler[12] and later elaborated by Taba[13] and Popham.[14] This model recommends four essential steps for effective planning: specify objectives, select learning activities, organize learning activities, and specify evaluation procedures. This model is basically a rational means-ends one in which a planner's first task is to decide on the desired ends, or what is to be accomplished, and then to select the appropriate learning activities to accomplish them. Curriculum planning is characterized as a task that requires orderly and careful thinking, and the model is proposed as a rational and scientific method for accomplishing that task.[15]

The only departure from the rational model of teacher planning that has been advocated is the "integrated ends-means model"[16] suggested by Macdonald and by Eisner.[17] They claim that teachers do not begin their planning by thinking about objectives and then proceed to decisions about activities, evaluation, and so forth, but, rather, that teachers first focus on the type of learning activity provided for the students. They argue that objectives arise and exist only in the context of an activity, if students choose their own learning experiences and pursue their own objectives. Thus, in this model, ends for learning become integrated with means for learning, and the specification of goals prior to an activity becomes meaningless.

Although researchers such as Jackson have long pointed to the importance of looking at teacher behavior in the preactive setting, relatively few studies have ventured into this domain.[18] Empirical studies of teacher planning have only been conducted since 1970, and, to date, the published studies can still be counted on one hand.

Zahorik did the first empirical study of classroom planning when he examined the effect of structured planning on teachers' behavior in the classroom.[19] He provided six of his sample of twelve teachers with a partial lesson plan containing behavioral objectives and a detailed outline of content to be covered two weeks hence. He requested the remaining six teachers to reserve an hour of instructional time to carry out a task for the researchers, not telling them that they were going to be asked to teach a lesson on credit cards until just before the appointed time. Zahorik analyzed recorded protocols of the twelve lessons, focusing on "teacher behavior that is sensitive to students." He defined this behavior as "verbal acts of the teacher that permit, encourage, and develop pupils' ideas, thoughts, and actions." Upon examining the protocols of the planners and non-planners, Zahorik noted that teachers who planned exhibited less honest or authentic use of the pupils' ideas during the lesson. He concluded from this that "the typical planning model—goals, activities, and their organization, and evaluation—result in insensitivity to pupils on the part of the teacher."

Taylor conducted a study of teacher planning in British secondary schools.[20] This study examined how teachers planned syllabi for courses, and, as such, it is more a study of curriculum planning than of planning by the individual teacher. By means of group discussion with teachers, analyses of course syllabi, and the administration of a questionnaire to 261 teachers of English, science, and geography, Taylor came to the following general conclusions. The most common theme found across all of the modes of data collection was the prominence of the pupils, especially their needs, abilities, and interests. Following this, in order of importance, were subject matter, aims (goals), and teaching methods. In planning for courses of study, evaluation emerged as being of little importance, as did the relation between one's own course and the curriculum as a whole. Taylor concluded that most course planning was unsystematic and "only general" in nature and that most teachers appear far from certain about what the planning process requires. From the study of syllabi, Taylor found great variation in style, size, and content and concluded that there is little consistency in the role that the syllabus plays.

Through teachers' ratings of the importance of various issues in curriculum planning and a factor analysis of their responses, Taylor identified four primary factors of interest to his sample of teachers. The results generally indicated that, when planning, the teachers tended to consider the following factors, listed here in order of importance: teaching context (for example, materials and resources), pupil interest, aims and purposes of teaching, and evaluation considerations. Rather than beginning with purposes and objectives and moving to a description of learning experiences necessary to achieve the objectives, as the rational planning theorists proposed, Taylor found that these teachers began with the context of teaching, next considered learning situations likely to interest and involve their pupils, and only then considered the purposes their teaching would serve. Also, criteria and procedures for evaluating the effectiveness of their course of teaching were of little importance. These findings led Taylor to conclude that curriculum planning should begin with the content to be taught and the accompanying important contextual considerations (for example, time, sequencing, resources). This should be followed by considerations of pupils' interests and attitudes, the aims and purposes of the course, the type of learning situation to be created, the philosophy of the course, the criteria for judging the course, the degree of pupil interest fostered by the course, and, finally, evaluation of the course.

Zahorik continued this line of inquiry by examining the use of behavioral objectives and the "separate ends-means" model of planning as well as the use of the "integrated ends-means" model proposed by Macdonald and Eisner.[21] He asked 194 teachers to list in writing the decisions that they make prior to teaching and the order in which they make them. He classified these decisions into the following categories: objectives, content, activities, materials, diagnosis, evaluation, instruction, and organization. He found that the kind of decision used by most of the teachers concerned pupil activities (indicated by 81 percent of the teachers). The decision most frequently made first concerned content (indicated by 51 percent of the teachers), followed at a distant second by behavioral objectives (indicated by 28 percent of the teachers).

Zahorik concluded from this study that teachers' planning decisions do not always follow logically from a specification of objectives and that, in fact, the specification of objectives is not a particularly important planning decision in terms of frequent use. He also argued, however, that the integrated ends-means model does not appear to be a functioning reality because of the relatively few teachers (only 3 percent) who began their planning by making decisions about activities.

Only recently has research on teacher planning begun to focus on describing teachers' decision making in actual planning situations. Peterson, Marx, and Clark examined planning in a laboratory situation as twelve teachers prepared to teach a new instructional unit to groups of junior high school students with whom they had had no previous contact.[22] These units were taught to three different groups of eight students on three different days. During their planning periods, teachers were instructed to "think aloud," and their verbal statements were later coded into planning categories such as objectives, materials, subject matter, and process. The following results were obtained from this study: Teachers spent most of their planning time dealing with the content (subject matter) to be taught. Then, teachers concentrated their planning efforts on instructional processes (strategies and activities), and the least amount of planning time was spent on objectives. All three of these findings were consistent with those of Zahorik and of Goodlad and his colleagues,[23] and the third finding resembled results reported by Joyce and Harootunian and by Popham and Baker.[24]

Since Peterson, Marx, and Clark conducted their study in a laboratory situation, with students and materials that the teachers were dealing with for the first time, the results of their study may or may not be generalizable to an actual classroom situation. A study by Morine in a semicontrolled classroom setting, however, showed results consistent with those of Peterson, Marx, and Clark.[25] Morine collected written plans for two experimenter-prescribed lessons (one in mathematics and one in reading) taught by teachers in their own classrooms to subsets of their students. Teacher plans were analyzed according to specificity of written plans, general format of plans, statement of goals, source of goal statements, attention to pupil background and preparation, identification of evaluation procedures, and indication of possible alternative procedures. Morine found that teachers tended to be fairly specific and to use an outline form in their plans, and they paid little attention to behavioral goals, diagnosis of student needs, evaluation procedures, and alternative courses of action.

In a simulated setting, Morine had teachers plan a reading program for fourteen new students. The task was designed to identify the kind of information teachers consider important for planning a reading program for a school year. Information was available from cumulative records for each student, and the resulting plans were analyzed according to the types of information about pupils that teachers requested, grouping procedures used, and the differential use of materials and support services. Morine found that, as a group, the teachers tended to ask for the same kinds of information, were fairly accurate in identifying the pupils' reading levels, and differed little in grouping practices and use of support services.

Yinger investigated teacher planning by means of a detailed case study of the processes involved in one elementary (first-second grade) teacher's planning decisions during a five-month period of instruction.[26] The study was designed to address a need for descriptions and theoretical models of planning processes and to examine the usefulness of certain decision-modeling methods for describing complex decisions as they occur in field settings. To accomplish this, the study used the perspectives and methodologies of both ethnography and information-processing psychology.

The study involved two phases of data collection. In the first twelve weeks of the study, approximately forty full days were spent observing and recording the teacher's activities in both the preactive and interactive phases of teaching. Also during this phase, the teacher's planning decisions were recorded as she "thought aloud" during her planning sessions. The second phase of the data collection further investigated the teacher's planning by observing her behavior in the Teacher Planning Shell (a simulation task developed for this study) and in three judgment tasks examining the teacher's perceptions of her students and instructional activities. Additional classroom observations and interviews were conducted during this phase.

Two central aspects of the teacher's planning and instruction emerged: planning for instructional activities and the use of teaching routines. Activities were described as the basic structural units of planning and action in the classroom. They were self-contained, organizational units functioning as "controlled behavior settings" that were shaped and molded by the teacher to conform to her perceptions and purposes. Seven features of instructional activities were identified (location, structure and sequence, duration, participants, acceptable student behavior, instructional moves or routines, and content and materials) and presented as important considerations in planning decisions.

Teaching routines emerged as another distinctive feature of the teacher's planning technology. Much of this planning behavior could be portrayed as the selection, organization, and sequencing of routines developed as a result of experience. Four types of teaching routines were described in the study: activity, instructional, management, and executive planning routines. Functionally, routines were characterized as methods used to reduce the complexity and increase the predictability of classroom activities, thereby increasing flexibility and effectiveness.

Two models of planning were developed in this study. The first was a structural model of preactive planning that described planning at five levels: yearly, term, unit, weekly, and daily. At each level of planning, the teacher's behavior was described in terms of her planning goals, information sources used in planning, the form that the plan took, and the criteria used for judging its effectiveness. This model was used for identifying different types of planning and for proposing strategic research sites for further study.

The second model of planning generated in this study was a theoretical model of teacher planning. In addition to data collected in this study, the process model was based on the findings of other planning studies and on studies of planning in the areas of chess, musical composition, art, and architectural design. Planning decisions were characterized by processes emphasizing problem finding, problem formulation, and problem solving. In contrast to traditional models of planning emphasizing the statement of goals, the specification of alternatives, and the choice among alternatives, this model placed more emphasis on finding and developing the planning problem and on the design process.

Three stages of planning were represented in the model. The first stage, problem finding, was portrayed as a discovery cycle where the teacher's goal conceptions, knowledge and experience, notion of the planning dilemma, and the materials available for planning interact to produce an initial problem conception worthy of further exploration. The second stage in the planning process was problem formulation and solution. The mechanism proposed for carrying out this process was the "design cycle." In this cycle, problem solving was characterized as a design process involving progressive elaboration of plans over time. Elaboration, investigation, and adaptation were proposed as phases through which plans were formulated. The third stage of the planning model involved implementation of the plan, its evaluation, and its eventual routinization. This stage emphasized the contributions of evaluation and routinization to the teacher's repertoire of knowledge and experience, which in turn play a major role in future planning deliberations.

JUDGMENT

Judgment is thought to be one of the important cognitive processes in the mental life of the teacher. Johnson defines judgment as the "assignment of an object to a small number of specified categories."[27] Cognitive psychologists locate judgment at the end of a sequence of operations within problem solving; it is brought to bear in selecting the most promising alternatives for solving a problem.[28] This view of judgment follows the jurisprudential model of collecting evidence on all sides of an issue and weighing the evidence carefully before reaching a conclusion.

When is judgment important in teaching? At this early stage of research on how teachers think, an empirically based answer to this question is not yet available. The handful of studies discussed below suggests that judgment on the part of the teacher plays an important part in predicting students' cognitive and affective achievement,[29] in predicting teachers' use of instructional moves,[30] in teacher planning,[31] in teachers' recognition of effective teaching,[32] and in selecting instructional activities.[33] It seems likely that judgment is important in many other contexts as well. The brevity of the list is largely because this area of investigation is so new.

To date, three aspects of teachers' judgment have been addressed by researchers. The first involves describing the judgment process, including factors taken into account by teachers and the relative weights given to these factors in reaching a judgment. The second is concerned with investigating the accuracy of teachers' judgments, particularly their predictions of students' achievement or attitudes. The third deals with exploring methodological questions dealing with matters such as how teachers use information of varying reliability and how varying the amount of information available affects the judgment process or judgmental accuracy.

Anderson studied the judgment policies of 164 high school teachers.[34] Each teacher rated thirty-six different hypothetical descriptions of teachers on a nine-point scale ranging from "a very poor high school teacher" to "an outstanding high school teacher." Each teacher rated one of six different sets of profiles. The sets varied the number of teacher characteristics (four, six, or eight) included in the profiles and varied the form of presentation of these characteristics (verbal statements or numerical values). After rating the profiles, each teacher was asked to rate the importance of each characteristic individually on a nine-point scale and to rank the characteristics in order of importance.

The characteristics or "cues" used in profiles for this study were selected by Anderson on the basis of previous research concerning teacher quality.[35] The cues were: homework requirements, interest in individual students, establishment of objectives, fairness in grading, knowledge of subject, clarity of explanations, encouragement of class discussion, and enthusiasm.

Anderson found that the characteristics most important in reaching a judgment of effectiveness were interest in individual students, knowledge of subject, and clarity of explanations. The characteristic least important in these judgments was homework requirements. Teachers who rated verbal profiles were significantly less consistent in their rating than those who rated numerical profiles. That is, the correlations between the level of a particular cue and the rating given that profile by a teacher were more stable when teachers rated numerical profiles. The number of cues available (four, six, or eight) did not influence the consistency of teacher ratings.

Anderson compared teachers' ratings of the importance of cues in their own judgment with their actual use of these cues in making judgments and found strong agreement. This was especially true for cues considered to be least important, namely, homework requirements, encouragement of class discussion, and establishment of objectives. For the cues considered to be most important, however, there were inconsistencies between how teachers rated cues and their use of these cues to judge profiles. For example, enthusiasm was rated and ranked very high, but, when the teachers rated profiles, other characteristics such as knowledge of subject and fairness in grading were considered more important than enthusiasm. This finding indicates that, when making judgments, teachers may base their decisions on a policy that is different from the policy that they report they use.

A study by Shavelson, Cadwell, and Izu investigated the sensitivity of teachers' judgments to the reliability of information received and the teachers' willingness to revise initial judgments when presented with additional information.[36] A total of 164 graduate students in education (119 of whom were teachers) were given information describing Michael, a hypothetical fifth-grade student. (Analysis of the data indicated that there were no differences between teachers and nonteachers; therefore, we will refer to all participants in this study as teachers.) Three types of information about the hypothetical student were provided: father's occupation, the student's use of time, and the student's intelligence. Each teacher was presented with one student description containing either positive or negative information from either a reliable or an unreliable source. After reading the information about the student, the teachers responded to four questions that required an exercise of judgment:

1. What is the probability that Michael will get mostly A's and B's on his report card?
2. In selecting instructional materials for Michael in reading and mathematics at the beginning of the semester, what kinds of texts and instructional aids would you primarily use?
   a. Fifth-grade level
   b. Fifth-grade level or above
   c. Fifth-grade level or below
3. Suppose that, during a mathematics lesson, you asked Michael a question and he hesitated. Would you:
   a. Rephrase the same question in order to clarify it?
   b. Ask a similar question that is easier to answer?
   c. Further explain the problem, then repeat the same question to Michael?
   d. Ask the same question of another student?
   e. Answer the question yourself?
4. How important is it for Michael that you make a point of praising him every time he does good work?
   a. Very important
   b. Important
   c. Somewhat important
   d. Somewhat unimportant
   e. Not important at all

After answering these questions, the teachers were given additional information that was again varied systematically as to reliability and positive or negative valence. This additional information concerned academic ability, curiosity, and attitude toward school. The teachers again answered the same four questions in light of this new information, but without referring to their earlier answers.

The major finding of this study was that teachers were sensitive to the reliability of the information they received and revised their initial predictions of student achievement when presented with additional information. These findings contradict those reported by Tversky and Kahneman, who reviewed studies that examined the ways in which people assess the probabilities of occurrence of uncertain events or values of unknown quantities.[37] They found that people in general were neither sensitive to the reliability of information nor did they tend to revise judgments after additional information was presented.

In the judgment of which kind of instructional material to select for the hypothetical student, the teacher's estimate of the student's ability (that is, the teacher's answer to the first question) was the major factor in making this decision. After additional information had been given to the teacher, however, this judgment was significantly influenced by the teacher's revised estimate of the student's ability, by the reliability and valence of the new information, and by the teacher's original estimate of the student's ability.

The teacher's answers to the questions about instructional moves (questioning and reinforcement strategies) indicated that there was no systematic relationship between descriptions of the student and the teachers' predictions about their own pedagogical behavior. The authors suggest that teachers' responses to these latter two judgment tasks depended on factors not measured in the experiment, such as personal preference for teaching style or philosophy of teaching.

Mondol investigated the possibility of training teachers to modify their judgments by using a form of cognitive feedback[38] coupled with training regarding the relevance of various information sources.[39] Fifty-four teachers in training were asked to judge the likelihood that 108 hypothetical students would be instructional problems in a classroom setting. These descriptions of students were developed by presenting all possible combinations of five descriptive variables: socioeconomic status, IQ, grades, sex, and comments about student personality. For each teacher's judgments, a multiple regression analysis was conducted that produced a measure of the teacher's "judgment policy" (the relative weights assigned to each variable). Teachers then participated in feedback and training sessions in which their judgment policies and the cue variables were discussed. After these sessions the teachers again rated the same set of student descriptions on the same question.

Mondol found significant changes in those teachers who participated in the training and feedback sessions as compared to those
teachers who had no training or feedback. She found that those
with training and feedback made fewer deviations from the optimal
policy at which the training was directed than did the control
teachers (no feedback or training). This change in judgment policy
was largely owing to a more equal weighting of the five sources of
information by the teachers with training and feedback. Mondol
concluded from this study that cognitive feedback and training can
be successfully used to modify judgment policies of teachers. She
concluded, further, that if optimal weighting patterns can be developed for important teacher judgments, training programs could be
developed to facilitate the learning of more effective and efficient
decision making.

One of the difficulties in designing studies of teacher judgment is
to identify those cues or features of the objects to be judged that the
teachers will actually use in coming to a judgment. One approach to
this problem requires that the researchers select features based on
their interests, prior experiences, or reviews of empirical literature
dealing with the phenomena of interest. Another approach involves
selection of cues after informal discussion between the researcher
and experienced judges. A third approach is represented in a study
by Clark, Wildfong, and Yinger.[40] In this study the researchers
attempted to identify the features of activities in the teaching of
language arts that influenced teacher judgment about the quality
and potential usefulness of these activities. Fourteen experienced
teachers in the elementary school examined descriptions of twenty-
six language arts activities in the area of writing. These descriptions
were taken from a commercial catalog of activities in the language
arts. The teachers rated each activity as either high, medium, or low
in attractiveness for teaching in their classroom. After rating all of
the activities, the teachers reexamined each activity rated high and
listed the features that contributed to their judgment of the attractiveness of each. The teachers then repeated this procedure for the
activities rated low in attractiveness.

To identify the important features that influenced the judgments
of this group of teachers, the following procedure was used:
1. Each activity feature identified by the teachers was typed on a
   3 x 5 card; 407 of these statements were produced.

2. Two of the researchers independently categorized each of the 407 teacher statements.

3. The two researchers compared their categorizations of the teacher statements, clarified their own policies for categorization, and negotiated a final set of thirteen categories into which all 407 teacher statements could be sorted.

The features of language arts activities identified by the teachers as influential in their judgment are listed in Table 11-1. These features have been grouped under four headings as they related to: students, subject matter, teacher, and learning environment.

In this judgment exercise, the teachers most frequently mentioned features related to student behavior. Student motivation and involvement was mentioned most frequently as a basis for accepting or rejecting a language arts activity, followed by features of activities thought to influence cognitive and affective outcomes.

In relation to subject matter, the feature most frequently singled

Table 11-1

Features of language arts activities identified as influences on the judgment of teachers

Feature category	Frequency of use
Students	
Motivation and involvement	104
Cognitive outcomes	67
Affective outcomes	44
Subject matter and materials	
Difficulty	68
Fit between content and process	35
Meaningfulness	16
Tangible product	15
Clarity	11
Integration	6
Teacher	
Fit with style	11
Demand on teacher	8
Benefit for teacher	3
Environment	
Fit with behavior setting	19

out was the estimated difficulty of the activity for a particular teacher's class. The frequency with which this feature was mentioned was probably inflated because the language arts activities were intended for students in the upper-elementary grades, while four of the teachers taught in the primary grades.

Half of the activity features that relate to the teacher were concerned with the match between the description of the activity and teachers' predictions of how comfortable they would be in executing it. The remainder of the features in this category had to do with how difficult the activity would be to set up, manage, and evaluate, and whether the activity benefited the teacher in addition to the stated purpose of the activity.

The final category of features identified had to do with how well the activity seemed to fit into the particular classroom organization with which the teacher was working. For example, some activities were judged to be particularly appropriate for use in learning centers.

An analysis of teachers' comments concerning the four activities they rated highest and the five activities they rated lowest indicated that the activity feature contributing most strongly to positive judgments was motivation and involvement of students. The second most frequent influence on positive ratings was the level of difficulty of the activity. The third feature contributing to positive judgments was the fit between content to be taught and the process of teaching involved in the activity. That is, activities rated highest by the teachers were those that increased students' motivation and involvement, those that were low in difficulty, and those that were perceived as good ways to teach the content. In the case of the five activities rated lowest, the most powerful influence identified by the teachers was the difficulty of the activity for students. The second feature that influenced teachers to reject these activities was the amount of demand that the activity placed on the teacher. That is, activities were rated as unattractive if they were seen as too difficult for the students or too demanding for the teacher.

Marx studied the judgment that teachers exercise when they predict cognitive and affective achievement.[41] Twelve experienced teachers taught a series of three social studies lessons to groups of eight junior high school students in a laboratory setting. The teachers had not met these students before the teaching episodes began. After each of the three fifty-minute lessons, the teachers made predictions of the rank order of their students on both a cognitive achievement test and an attitude inventory to be administered immediately after the third teaching session. In addition, the teachers were asked to describe the student behavior or other cues that they used in making predictions about each student.

Marx found that these teachers were not specific about the behavioral cues on which they based their judgments about future achievement and attitudes. The most frequently mentioned cue was "student participation," but the teachers did not identify observable behaviors from which they inferred student participation.

An additional finding of Marx's study was that regression equations using the behavioral cues identified by teachers as entering into their judgments were not good predictors of actual cognitive achievement and results on the inventory of attitudes. The data from one of the twelve teachers studied suggests that teachers' judgments about students' attitudes may be more accurate than teachers' judgments about cognitive achievement. For this teacher, the correlation between predicted student performance on the attitude inventory and actual student performance on the attitude toward self scale was .72. For all teachers combined, the median correlation between teacher predictions and student outcomes was .24 for achievement and .35 for attitude toward self.

Another study of teachers' judgments of students was conducted by Joyce, Morine-Dershimer, and McNair.[42] Ten teachers in the same elementary school were asked to sort cards containing the names of each of their pupils into two or more categories. The teachers were then asked to describe the basis on which pupils were assigned to these different categories. This procedure was repeated several times until the teachers could think of no more categories into which to sort their students. This technique of sorting pupils was used five times during the school year: in September (at the end of the first day of school), November, January, March, and June.

The categories most frequently used by teachers in sorting their students were student personality and student involvement. Other bases for sorting were (in descending order of frequency): student ability and achievement, peer relationships, student performance in a particular activity, and student growth and progress. The high frequency of student involvement as a basis is consistent with Marx's findings and with the findings in the study by Clark, Wildfong, and Yinger.

An additional procedure used in the study done by Joyce and his colleagues was to ask the teachers to predict their students' end-of-year reading achievement. The teachers made these predictions twice, once at the end of the first day of school, and once in November. The most striking finding from this part of the study was that teachers' predictions of success in reading did not differ substantially between September and November, even though the teachers presumably had much more information about their students based on three months of shared experience and the availability of results from a diagnostic reading test. This remarkable stability of teacher judgments contrasts with findings of Shavelson and his colleagues in which teachers did change their judgments after additional information was made available.

In predicting end-of-year reading achievement, teachers were most accurate in predicting which students would be most successful. Teachers were less accurate in discriminating between students who would make average progress and those who would make below-average progress.

INTERACTIVE DECISION MAKING

Interactive decision making refers to decisions made during the act of teaching. The teacher is seen as constantly assessing the situation, processing information about the situation, making decisions about what to do next, guiding action on the basis of these decisions, and observing the effects of the action on students. The fundamental question underlying this work is: how much teaching is reflective, and how much is reactive? The portion of teaching that is reflective is what interests those who study the interactive decision making of teachers.

All studies of interactive decision making by teachers depend on the teacher's self-report of the decision made. The most common method of obtaining self-report data is some variation of a procedure in which a videotape of the teacher's teaching performance is replayed to stimulate recall of the teaching situation. In some studies only short segments of the videotape are replayed,[43] while in other studies the entire videotape is replayed.[44] In the latter case, the videotape may be stopped by the teacher when he or she remembers having made a decision, or the researcher may control the identification of "critical incidents." In most cases, the teacher is asked a standard set of questions after viewing each videotape or segment. The teacher's responses to these questions are audiotaped, and subsequently described either by use of a coding system and frequency counts, by a narrative description of the process, or by a combination of both.

Earlier Studies

The earliest study of interactive decision making by teachers was reported by Clark and Joyce, by Marx and Peterson, and by Clark and Peterson.[45] Twelve experienced teachers taught a social studies unit to three different groups of eight junior high school students. The unit was taught to each group on a different day in a laboratory setting. The students did not know the teacher before they met in the first teaching session.

Interactive decision making was explored by showing four brief (two- to three-minute) videotaped segments from a day of teaching in order to stimulate recall of what the teacher was thinking about while teaching. After viewing each videotaped segment, the teachers responded to a series of questions about what they were doing in the segment, what they were noticing about the students, whether they had instructional objectives in mind at the time, whether they were considering alternative actions or strategies at the time, and whether anything in the situation caused them to change their planned activity or strategy.

A primary finding of this study was that teachers considered alternative strategies only when the instructional process was judged to be going poorly. That is, the teachers were not trying to optimize instruction. Secondly, it was found that the primary cue used by teachers in judging how well the instructional process was going was student participation and involvement. Finally, it was found that teachers rarely changed their strategy from what they had planned, even when instruction was going poorly. That is, interactive decision making rarely resulted in an immediate change in the course of instruction. The interactive decision making of these teachers was more a process of fine tuning and adapting to aspects of the situation that were unpredictable in principle, such as specific student responses.

Morine and Vallance used a stimulated recall task to identify types of decisions made by forty second- and fifth-grade teachers, previously categorized as more effective and less effective.[46] The three major types of decisions identified were: interchanges (decisions relating to instantaneous verbal interaction), planned activities (interactive decisions directly related to preactive decisions), and unplanned activities (decisions to include an activity not originally part of the lesson plan). In general, the researchers found that nearly all of the decisions could be categorized as either interchange or planned decisions (approximately 48 percent in each category) and that there were only slight variations between the two grade levels in this pattern. When responses of more and less effective teachers were compared, no significant differences were found. A general pattern observed in all responses was that teachers focused more on the instructional process than on students' characteristics or behavior when commenting on the substance (focus) of their decisions. When the considerations and bases for the teachers' decisions were referred to, however, the focus changed. In these instances, the characteristics of students carried more weight than the instructional process. Additional findings in the study were that few alternatives to their decisions were mentioned by the teachers and that references to cognitive aspects of the lesson were more frequent than references to affective aspects.

Marland's Study

Marland studied the interactive thoughts of six volunteer teachers, two each at the first-, third-, and sixth-grade levels in two schools.[47] Each teacher participated in two stimulated recall sessions using videotapes of lessons in language arts and mathematics for teachers from the first and third grades and two lessons in language arts for teachers from the sixth grade.

Marland analyzed the transcripts of stimulated recall interviews using two different category systems. The first analysis used a category system developed by Marland himself. Each "thought unit" was judged to fit into one of eleven categories: perception, interpretation, prospective tactical deliberation, retrospective tactical deliberation, reflection, anticipation, information-pupil, information-other, goal statement, fantasy, and feeling.

The second analysis did not involve categorizing every sentence or thought unit in the transcripts. Marland examined the transcripts for instances of psychologically meaningful events: decisions, forfeit decisions, deliberate acts, impulsive acts, cognitive linking, field detachment, externality, internality, principles, beliefs, rules, case histories, and examples of accurate or inaccurate recall by teachers. The results of these two analyses were summarized in terms of the content, of teachers' interactive thoughts, the function of teachers' interactive thoughts, and individual differences in teachers' inter-active thoughts.

Content of Interactive Thoughts. The teachers studied by Marland reported thinking about topics and events in the present, past, and future. Present events included student behavior, teachers' inter-pretations of student behavior, and the teachers' own affective states. Teachers' thoughts about the past included reflections on past events concerned with a lesson and retrieval from memory of factual information thought to be useful in preparing for the lesson, such as personal information about particular students, curriculum content, principles of teaching, and beliefs about children. Topics of teachers' thoughts about the future included tactics to be used next, predic-tions or visualizations of directions the lesson might take, expecta-tions for students' behavior, and learning objectives. Interactive thoughts most frequently reported by teachers were prospective tactical deliberations (20.3 percent), reflections (18.8 percent), perceptions (15.6 percent), interpretations (11.9 percent), and antic-ipations (8.7 percent). Interactive thoughts concerning information-pupil, information-other, and feeling accounted for from 5 percent to 10 percent of the thoughts reported. Relatively few thoughts in the remaining categories of retrospective tactical deliberation, goal state-ment, and fantasy were reported.

Function of Interactive Thoughts. Four functions of teachers' interactive thoughts, according to Marland, account for the majority of the cases. They include correcting or adjusting the lesson when it is not going smoothly; dealing with parts of the lesson that are un-predictable in principle (for example, how to prompt a student who gives a partial answer); regulating one's own behavior by reference to certain principles of teaching; and adapting instruction to individual students. Absent from the teachers' interview protocols were four other possible functions of teachers' interactive thoughts: self-monitoring, verifying interpretations of students' behavior, consider-ing alternative teaching tactics, and optimizing instruction. Teachers rarely gave any consideration to their own teaching style, its effectiveness, or its impact on students. They tended to operate on the basis of hunches and intuition about the cognitive and affective states of students. They did not consider first impressions as hypotheses to be tested by further observation or direct questions. Teachers did think about tactical moves to be made in a lesson, but usually did not consider alternatives. Finally, the teachers did not tend to think about improving an instructional situation unless it was going poorly.

Individual Differences and Interactive Thoughts. An intriguing relationship between an individual difference measure and teachers' self-reports of their interactive thoughts developed when one teacher, who was characterized as having an abstract belief system, was considered more open to making adjustments in expectations held for students than the remaining five teachers, all of whom were characterized as having concrete belief systems. There were no other systematic relationships between teachers' information processing and teachers' presage and contextual variables.

TEACHERS' IMPLICIT THEORIES

Because much of the judgment and decision making that teachers exercise follows from their interpretations of their experience, it is important to study how teachers make sense of their world. The study of what teachers think is based in part on the assumption that, in creating a problem space, the teacher refers to a personal perspective,[48] to an implicit theory,[49] to a conceptual system,[50] or to a belief system[51] about teaching and learning. Thus, the teacher defines such things as the elements of the classroom situation that are most important, the relationships among them, and the order in which they should be considered. Among researchers, the various ways of characterizing conceptual bases carry slightly different meanings. For our purpose, we chose to use the expression "teachers' implicit theories" to refer to this area of research. There are several ways to approach this important area.

The Ethnographic Approach

Janesick used the ethnographic approach to derive, describe, and validate the description of the perspective of a single teacher.[52] The researcher became a participant-observer in the classroom of a sixth-grade teacher for seven months. Extensive field notes based on observations in the classroom and interviews with teachers were analyzed weekly to build and define the teacher's perspective. According to Janesick, a perspective is a reflective, socially derived interpretation of what the teacher encounters—an interpretation that then serves as a basis for future actions. Such a perspective is a combination of beliefs and behavior that is continually being modified by social interaction. It enables teachers to make sense of their individual world, to interpret it, and to act rationally within it.

Janesick found that the perspective of the teacher she studied could be characterized by a concern for creating a stable and cohesive group and for maintaining that group. The teacher made plans and interpreted events in terms of their impact on the "groupness" of the class. Most classroom activities were group activities. The teacher considered himself to be the leader of the group and defined his role accordingly. He modeled and emphasized cooperation and respect for other group members. He designed activities that generated a high level of group consensus.

The Sorting Approach

Another approach to studying teachers' implicit theories was made in the area of reading by Duffy and his colleagues. They had approximately 350 teachers engage in an exercise of sorting propositions about reading.[53] The teachers were asked to sort thirty-six propositions about reading and reading instruction into five categories ranging from "most like me" to "least like me." These propositions, drawn from an analysis of the literature on reading, were identified with five major conceptions of instruction in reading: basal text, linear skills, natural language, interest, and integrated whole. An additional category (confused-frustrated) was added, and six propositions consistent with each of these conceptions of reading were generated.

From among the 350 teachers who completed the exercise, thirty-seven who manifested clear and strongly held beliefs about reading were asked to take a variation of Kelly's Role Concept Repertory Test (REP Test) in order to refine and specify more clearly their conceptions of reading.

In the second phase of this study, eight teachers who evidenced strong belief patterns on the sorting of propositions and on the REP Test were observed teaching on ten different occasions. Ethnographic field notes and postobservation interviews were used to determine the extent to which the teachers' instructional behavior reflected their conceptions of reading. The investigators found that:

only four teachers consistently employed practices which directly reflected their beliefs; these included two teachers who had structured beliefs (basal-linear skills), a teacher who had an eclectic view, and one of the teachers having an unstructured belief system (natural language-interest-integrated whole). Of those whose practices did not reflect their beliefs, two of the teachers having strong unstructured belief systems were found to be smuggling elements of unstructured practices into an administratively imposed program reflecting a structured view. Two other teachers holding unstructured views, however, did not consistently reflect their beliefs; one of the teachers employed practices which, to a large degree, were counter to the unstructured belief system she espoused, while a second teacher operationalized unstructured beliefs only some of the time with some pupils and some activities.[54]

The Principles of Teaching Approach

In Marland's study, described earlier, one of the analyses of the stimulated recall protocols indicated that teachers referred to certain principles of teaching when explaining their behavior in the classroom. These principles of teaching appear to serve the same function as what we have called "implicit theories." Marland's data yielded five principles of teaching that seemed to influence the behavior of teachers profoundly or were mentioned by at least two of the six teachers studied: compensation, strategic leniency, power sharing, progressive checking, and suppressing emotions.

The principle of *compensation* represents an attempt on the part of the teacher to discriminate in favor of the shy, the introverted, the low in ability, and the culturally impoverished. Two of the four teachers who applied this principle were first-grade teachers. This principle figured less prominently in explaining the behavior of teachers in the higher grades. *Strategic leniency,* which is a variation of the principle of compensation, refers to a teacher's tendency to ignore infractions of classroom rules by children seen by the teacher as needing special attention.

Power sharing involves use of the informal power structure existing in the classroom to influence students. The teacher is seen as sharing both responsibility and authority with certain students, which means that the teacher selectively reinforces the good behavior of students perceived as class leaders in order to use their influence on their peers as an instrument for classroom management.

As a teaching principle, *progressive checking* involves periodically checking on students' progress, identifying problems, and encouraging students in low-ability groups during seatwork. In addition to the direct assistance provided, the teacher who utilized this principle also reasoned that she was providing varied stimuli for students with short spans of attention.

The last of the principles, *suppressing emotions,* was derived from teachers' reports that they consciously suppressed their emotional feelings while teaching. They believed that, if they expressed their feelings and emotions, students might be encouraged to do the same, and, if the students became too excited, this would create a management problem.

The Clinical Interview Approach

A fourth approach to characterizing teachers' implicit theories involves the use of the clinical interview. Bussis, Chittenden, and Amarel interviewed sixty elementary school teachers who were attempting to implement open or informal approaches to instruction.[55] The objective of this study was to investigate understandings and perceptions regarding curriculum, children, and the working environment. Each teacher was interviewed for approximately two and one-half hours. Transcriptions of the interviews were coded using a system developed for this purpose.

To describe the implicit theories held by these teachers about the curriculum, the investigators placed each teacher in one of four groups characterized by different "curriculum construct systems." The first group (12 percent of the teachers) was characterized as having "grade-level facts and skills" as a dominant priority. Also, there was little evidence of experiment or change in the curriculum. The second group (22 percent of the teachers) also exhibited "grade-level facts and skills" as a dominant priority, but there was much more evidence of change in their experimentation with the curriculum. Whereas the construct systems of the teachers in group one appeared to be firmly set, the construct systems in group two seemed to be less established, and there was more emphasis on student involvement. In the third group (39 percent of the teachers), "grade-level facts and skills" was an expressed, but not dominant, priority. Broader priorities tended to be dominant, and there was more evidence of a potentially rich curriculum. The fourth group (25 percent of the teachers), showed little evidence of preoccupation with "grade-level facts and skills" and was oriented toward more comprehensive priorities.

The investigators summarized their findings about teachers' understandings of students under three headings: needs and feelings, interests and choice, and social interaction. Within each of these topics, four major "orientations" were used to categorize the teachers who were interviewed.

Needs and Feelings. On the basis of their responses to questions pertaining to the emotional needs and feelings of students, the teachers were grouped according to four orientations: (A) needs and feelings are only remotely perceived and lack reality (20 percent); (B) needs and feelings are perceived as real and their expression as desirable, but they are also seen to be in conflict with learning (15 percent); (C) the expression of needs and feelings is seen as a necessary context for learning (32 percent); and (D) the expression of needs and feelings is seen as integral to and inseparable from the learning process (33 percent).

Interests and Choice. In analyzing the responses of teachers to questions about students' interests and choice, the investigators again used four orientations, the first of which, orientation A, included teachers who did not talk much about children's interests or choices (20 percent). In the few cases in which they did discuss interests they tended to use sex-role stereotypes (for example, boys are interested in science). Student choice was very limited. The teachers included in orientation B believed that worthwhile learning did occur when children pursued their interests, but they permitted students to choose only within elective areas of the curriculum and not in the core subjects (30 percent). Student interest was seen as synonymous with enjoyment. Choice was seen as a process of selection from among a few opportunities presented by the teacher. As in orientation A, these teachers thought about interests and choice in terms of group propensities (for example, the interests of fifth-grade boys) rather than as individual traits or states.

The teachers included in orientation C differed from teachers in orientation B in that they thought about interests and choice in terms of individual patterns rather than group propensities and they were concerned with interest and choice in the core curriculum areas of reading and mathematics as well as in the elective areas (22 percent). They saw students' interests as manipulable by the teacher and easily influenced by factors external to the student, such as peer pressure or the attractiveness of materials. They accepted the expression of interest on the part of the student at face value without probing to discover the meaning of a particular expression of interest. Student choice was seen both as a process of selection from among alternatives and an opportunity for students to exercise responsibility to follow through on their choices.

The teachers in orientation D assumed that interest is a quality of all children and that there is continuity and strength in interest (28 percent). Teacher observation and inquiry were seen as means of bringing out student interests, and teachers perceived their responsibility to be identifying interests already held by students rather than creating new ones. Instead of needs to be satisfied, interests were viewed as useful starting points for investigation into all parts of the curriculum. Because extending interests beyond the initial expression of them was considered to be an important learning objective, these teachers constantly urged students to evaluate the directions in which pursuit of their interests was taking them. They believed it was important to help students develop skill in making good choices as a means of extending their interests, including the decision not to extend a particular interest.

Social Interaction. The teachers were then grouped according to four orientations pertaining to their beliefs about social interaction among students. In this grouping, the teachers with orientation A reported that interaction among students was generally not significant for learning (18 percent). Those in orientation B saw children's social interaction as potentially interfering with learning (5 percent). Those holding orientation C saw children's social interaction as a process in which children instructed one another (for example, as peer tutors) or as a process of learning socially acceptable norms for behavior (37 percent). The teachers with orientation D perceived interaction as a process by which children learn from one another in both the cognitive and social-emotional domains (40 percent).

Based on their categorization of the teachers' responses to the working environment section of the interview, the researchers rated the teachers on the complexity of their views about other adult roles in the formation of institutional policies and the initiative they seemed to be taking in the development of working relationships. In short, they found that in almost every school the aides and parents were much more salient in the teachers' thinking than the principal or school administrators. Ratings of initiative for the development of working relationships was highest for aides and parents and lowest for school administrators, with ratings for the development of a working relationship with other teachers falling somewhere between. A comparison of the teachers' views of the adult-as-resource and the child-as-resource suggested what the researchers refer to as a psychological consistency in thinking about adults and children. For example, teachers who saw no resource value in children also had low mean ratings on developing working relationships with other adults, and the majority of teachers who saw high resource value in children also gave a high rating to developing adult resources. The researchers concluded from these findings that construct systems regarding the development of human resources embrace both beliefs about children and beliefs about adults.

IN CONCLUSION

The studies reviewed in this chapter are in the vanguard of the approach to research on teaching that emphasizes what and how teachers think. Many of these studies raise more questions than they answer, about method as well as about substance. Yet there are a few tentative answers to the question: "What have we learned about the mental lives of teachers?"

On the topic of teacher planning, the available literature suggests that teachers do not seem to follow the "rational model" that is often prescribed in teacher training and in curriculum planning. In particular, the teachers studied did not begin or guide their planning in relation to clearly specified objectives or goals. Rather, planning seems to begin with considerations about the content to be taught and the setting in which teaching will take place. The focus then shifts to student involvement as a process objective. The activity, rather than the objective, seems to be the unit of planning. The model proposed by Yinger further proposes that planning is the progressive elaboration of a major idea, in contrast to the development of a number of alternatives and selection of the optimal alternative from this set.[56]

Research on planning by teachers should focus more on representative field studies of the planning process to complement description and analysis of such planning in highly controlled laboratory settings. Beyond this, there is a need for research on the psychology of planning, as well as descriptions of the process. At this time, we know very little about why teachers plan, how teacher planning changes with experience, and whether individual differences influence the quantity and style of planning. Finally, there is a need for research on the relationship between planning and subsequent action. This last question is perhaps the most promising point of contact between research on thinking by teachers and teaching effectiveness. It is here that the outcomes of planning, both in terms of organizing classroom interaction for the teacher and of influencing student involvement and learning, can be seen.

The findings about judgment on the part of teachers are less clear cut than those about planning. The small number of studies on judgment yields results that are often rich in information about a specific judgmental task, but the uniqueness of these tasks prevents us from making general statements about teachers' judgment at this time. The studies reviewed here involve teachers making judgments about students,[57] teachers,[58] and materials.[59] The evidence is mixed on the extent to which the judgments are flexible and responsive to new information. It is clear that teachers vary as to the accuracy of their predictions of student achievement and the weights that they assign to factors that influence their judgment. Mondol's study suggests that training can be used to change the judgmental policies of teachers.

For future research on judgment to be useful in policy and training decisions, there is need for a greater number and variety of studies on judgments about students, curriculum materials, and other important aspects of the classroom environment. Once a sufficient number of such studies is available, we will be able to make some more general statements about the judgmental process in each of these domains and suggest more systematic and effective strategies in each area.

The studies of teachers' interactive decision making reflect a series of refinements in the method of collecting data about these decisions. The method of conducting stimulated recall interviews has changed from using very short, randomly selected videotaped segments and asking a standard set of questions about each segment to reviewing a videotape in its entirety and giving the teacher control over when to stop the tape and over the kinds of mental processes on which to focus. Another trend has been to move from the laboratory to the classroom. Both developments have made the problems of data reduction and analysis more challenging, but they have also increased the representativeness of the situations being studied.

The few findings available indicate that interactive decision making on the part of teachers occurs primarily at times when students interrupt the instructional process. The teachers studied seemed to monitor student involvement as the primary indication of the smoothness of the instructional process. When interruptions of the instructional process occurred, teachers occasionally considered alternatives, but hardly ever implemented those alternatives. For various reasons, the teachers tended not to change the instructional process in midstream, even when it was going poorly.

The literature on teachers' implicit theories is more eclectic than the other material reviewed in this chapter. There appears to be little consensus. The common thread is the belief that the thinking and behavior of teachers are guided by a set of organized beliefs, often operating unconsciously. The study by Duffy suggests that the connection between a teacher's implicit theory and behavior is a relatively loose one, mediated by circumstances such as availability of resources, peer influence, and characteristics of the student.[60] More research is required on the relationship between the implicit theories of teachers and their perceptions, their processing of information, and their behavior.

Researchers have made a promising start toward understanding why teachers behave as they do. This understanding should grow and develop as more of this kind of research is done. But the most exciting possibility is that the research may bring research on instruction and the behavior of teachers together with that on curriculum and materials. All of these concerns come together in the minds of teachers as they make the plans, judgments, and decisions that guide their behavior. Indeed, the first practical theory of instruction may evolve from research on the thinking of teachers.

NOTES

1. Barak Rosenshine, *Teaching Behaviors and Student Achievement* (Slough, Eng.: National Foundation for Educational Research in England and Wales, 1971); Michael J. Dunkin and Bruce J. Biddle, *The Study of Teaching* (New York: Holt, Rinehart and Winston, 1974).

2. Lee S. Shulman and Arthur S. Elstein, "Studies of Problem Solving, Judgment, and Decision Making," in *Review of Research in Education*, Volume III, ed. Frederick N. Kerlinger (Itasca, Ill.: F. E. Peacock, 1975), 3-42; National Institute of Education, *Teaching as Clinical Information Processing*, Report of Panel 6, National Conference on Studies in Teaching (Washington, D.C.: National Institute of Education, 1975).

3. Richard J. Shavelson, "What Is *the* Basic Teaching Skill?" *Journal of Teacher Education* 24 (1973): 144-151; Christopher M. Clark and Bruce R. Joyce, "Teacher Decision Making and Teaching Effectiveness," paper presented at the annual meeting of the American Educational Research Association, San Francisco, 1976.

4. Robert J. Yinger, "A Study of Teacher Planning: Description and Theory Development Using Ethnographic and Information Processing Methods," unpub. diss., Michigan State University, 1977.

5. John F. Vinsonhaler, Christian S. Wagner, and Arthur S. Elstein, *The Inquiry Theory: An Information Processing Approach to Clinical Problem Solving* (East Lansing, Mich.: Institute for Research on Teaching, Michigan State University, 1977).

6. Bruce R. Joyce and Berj Harootunian, "Teaching as Problem Solving," *Journal of Teacher Education* 15 (1964): 420-427.

7. Christopher M. Clark and Penelope L. Peterson, "Teacher Stimulated Recall of Interactive Decisions," paper presented at the annual meeting of the American Educational Research Association, San Francisco, 1976; Greta Morine and Elizabeth Vallance, *A Study of Teacher and Pupil Perceptions of Classroom Interaction*, Technical Report 75-11-6, Beginning Teacher Evaluation Study (San Francisco: Far West Laboratory for Educational Research, 1975); Yinger, "A Study of Teacher Planning"; Anne M. Bussis, Edward A. Chittenden, and Marianne Amarel, *Beyond Surface Curriculum* (Boulder, Colo.: Westview Press, 1976).

8. Benjamin S. Bloom, "The Thought Processes of Students in Discussion," in *Accent on Teaching: Experiments in General Education*, ed. Sidney J. French (New York: Harper Brothers, 1954), 23-46; Norman Kagan *et al.*, *Studies in Human Interaction: Interpersonal Process Recall Stimulated by Videotape* (East Lansing, Mich.: Michigan State University, 1967).

9. Kenneth R. Hammond, "Computer Graphics as an Aid to Learning," *Science* 172 (1971): 903-908; Leon Rappoport and David A. Summers, *Human Judgment and Social Interaction* (New York: Holt, Rinehart and Winston, 1973).

10. Lois Bader *et al.*, "Observational Studies of Clinical Problem Solving Behavior in Reading Diagnosis," paper presented at the annual meeting of the American Educational Research Association, New York, 1977.

11. Vernon E. Anderson, *Principles and Procedures for Curriculum Improvement* (New York: Ronald Press, 1956); Hollis L. Caswell and Doak S. Campbell, *Curriculum Development* (New York: American Book Co., 1935); J. Minor Gwynn, *Curriculum Principles and Social Trends* (New York: Macmillan Co., 1943); Edward A. Krug, *Curriculum Planning* (New York: Harper and Brothers, 1950); J. Galen Saylor and William M. Alexander, *Planning Curriculum for Schools* (New York: Holt, Rinehart and Winston, 1974).

12. Ralph W. Tyler, *Basic Principles of Curriculum and Instruction* (Chicago: University of Chicago Press, 1950).

13. Hilda Taba, *Curriculum Development, Theory and Practice* (New York: Harcourt, Brace and World, 1962).

14. James W. Popham and Eva L. Baker, *Systematic Instruction* (Englewood Cliffs, N.J.: Prentice-Hall, 1970).

15. Taba, *Curriculum Development.*

16. John Zahorik, "Teachers' Planning Models," *Educational Leadership* 33 (1975): 134-139.

17. James B. Macdonald, "Myths about Instruction," *Educational Leadership* 22 (1965): 571-576, 609-617; *id.*, Bernice J. Wolfson, and Esther Zaret, *Reschooling Society: A Conceptual Model* (Washington, D.C.: Association for Supervision and Curriculum Development, 1973); Elliot W. Eisner, "Educational Objectives: Help or Hindrance," *School Review* 75 (1967): 250-266.

18. Philip W. Jackson, *The Way Teaching Is* (Washington, D.C.: National Education Association, 1965).

19. John A. Zahorik, "The Effect of Planning on Teaching," *Elementary School Journal* 71 (1970): 143-151.

20. Philip H. Taylor, *How Teachers Plan Their Courses* (Slough, Eng.: National Foundation for Educational Research in England and Wales, 1970).

21. Zahorik, "Teachers' Planning Models."

22. Penelope L. Peterson, Ronald W. Marx, and Christopher M. Clark, "Teacher Planning, Teacher Behavior, and Student Achievement," *American Educational Research Journal* 15 (1978): 417-432.

23. Zahorik, "Teachers' Planning Models"; John I. Goodlad, Francis M. Klein, *et al.*, *Behind the Classroom Door* (Worthington, Ohio: Charles A. Jones Publishing Co., 1970).

24. Joyce and Harootunian, "Teaching as Problem Solving"; Popham and Baker, *Systematic Instruction.*

25. Greta Morine, *A Study of Teacher Planning,* Technical Report 76-3-1, Beginning Teacher Evaluation Study (San Francisco: Far West Laboratory for Educational Research and Development, 1976).

26. Yinger, "Study of Teacher Planning."

27. Donald M. Johnson, *Systematic Introduction to the Psychology of Thinking* (New York: Harper and Row, 1972), 339.

28. Allen Newell, "Judgment and Its Representation: An Introduction," in *Formal Representation of Human Judgment,* ed. Benjamin Kleinmuntz (New York: John Wiley and Sons, 1968), 1-16; Donald M. Johnson, *The Psychology of*

Thought and Judgment (New York: Harper and Row, 1955); *id., Systematic Introduction to the Psychology of Thinking.*

29. Ronald W. Marx, "Teacher Judgments of Students' Cognitive and Affective Outcomes," unpub. diss., Stanford University, 1978; Richard J. Shavelson, Joel Cadwell, and Tonia Izu, "Teachers' Sensitivity to the Reliability of Information in Making Pedagogical Decisions," *American Educational Research Journal* 14 (1977): 83-97; Bruce R. Joyce, Greta Morine-Dershimer, and Kathleen McNair, "Thought and Action in the Classroom: The South Bay Study" (Stanford, Calif.: n.p., 1977), mimeo.

30. Shavelson, Cadwell, and Izu, "Teachers' Sensitivity to the Reliability of Information in Making Pedagogical Decisions."

31. Yinger, "A Study of Teacher Planning."

32. Beverly L. Anderson, "Differences in Teachers' Judgment Policies for Varying Numbers of Verbal and Numerical Cues," *Organizational Behavior and Human Performance* 19 (1977): 68-88.

33. Christopher M. Clark, Susan Wildfong, and Robert J. Yinger, *Identifying Cues for Use in Studies of Teacher Judgment,* Institute for Research on Teaching, Research Series No. 23 (East Lansing: Michigan State University, 1978).

34. Anderson, "Differences in Teachers' Judgment Policies for Varying Numbers of Verbal and Numerical Cues."

35. Charles M. Bridges *et al.,* "Characteristics of Best and Worst College Teachers," *Science Education* 55 (1971): 545-553; Robert L. Isaacson *et al.,* "Dimensions of Student Evaluation of Teaching," *Journal of Educational Psychology* 55 (1964): 344-351; Barak Rosenshine and Norma Furst, "Research on Teacher Performance Criteria," in *Research on Teacher Education: A Symposium,* ed. B. Othanel Smith (Englewood Cliffs, N.J.: Prentice-Hall, 1971), 37-72.

36. Shavelson, Cadwell, and Izu, "Teachers' Sensitivity to the Reliability of Information in Making Pedagogical Decisions."

37. Amos Tversky and Daniel Kahneman, "Judgment under Uncertainty: Hueristics and Biases," *Science* 185 (1974): 1124-1131.

38. Hammond, "Computer Graphics as an Aid to Learning."

39. Merlyn M. Mondol, "The Paramorphic Representation of Teacher Decision Making as a Predictor of Inquiry Performance," unpub. diss., Michigan State University, 1973.

40. Clark, Wildfong, and Yinger, "Identification of Salient Features of Language Arts Activities."

41. Marx, "Teacher Judgments of Students' Cognitive and Affective Outcomes."

42. Joyce, Morine-Dershimer, and McNair, "Thought and Action in the Classroom."

43. For example, Clark and Peterson, "Teacher Stimulated Recall of Interactive Decisions."

44. For example, Morine and Vallance, *Study of Teacher and Pupil Perceptions of Classroom Interactions.*

45. Clark and Joyce, "Teacher Decision Making and Teacher Effectiveness"; Clark and Peterson, "Teacher Stimulated Recall of Interactive Decisions"; and Ronald W. Marx and Penelope L. Peterson, "The Nature of Teacher Decision Making," paper presented at the annual meeting of the American Educational Research Association, Washington, D.C., 1975.

46. Morine and Vallance, *Study of Teacher and Pupil Perceptions of Classroom Interactions.*

47. Percy W. Marland, "A Study of Teachers' Interactive Thoughts," unpub. diss., University of Alberta, 1977.

48. Valerie Janesick, "An Ethnographic Study of a Teacher's Classroom Perspectives," unpub. diss., Michigan State University, 1977.

49. National Institute of Education, *Theory Development,* Report of Panel 10, National Conference on Studies in Teaching (Washington, D.C.: National Institute of Education, 1975).

50. Gerald Duffy, "A Study of Teacher Conceptions of Reading," paper presented at the National Reading Conference, New Orleans, 1977.

51. Jere E. Brophy and Thomas L. Good, *Teacher-Student Relationships: Causes and Consequences* (New York: Holt, Rinehart and Winston, 1974).

52. Janesick, "Ethnographic Study of a Teacher's Classroom Perspectives." For a review of studies using ethnographic techniques, see Stephen Wilson, "The Use of Ethnographic Techniques in Educational Research," *Review of Educational Research* 47 (1977): 245-265.

53. Duffy, "Study of Teacher Conceptions of Reading."

54. *Ibid.,* 7-8.

55. Bussis, Chittenden, and Amarel, *Beyond Surface Curriculum.*

56. Yinger, "A Study of Teacher Planning."

57. Mondol, "The Paramorphic Representation of Teacher Decision Making as a Predictor of Inquiry Performance"; Shavelson, Cadwell, and Izu, "Teachers' Sensitivity to the Reliability of Information in Making Pedagogical Decisions"; Joyce, Morine-Dershimer, and McNair, "Thought and Action in the Classroom."

58. Anderson, "Differences in Teachers' Judgment Policies for Varying Numbers of Verbal and Numerical Cues."

59. Clark, Wildfong, and Yinger, *Identifying Cues for Use in Studies of Teacher Judgment.*

60. Duffy, "Study of Teacher Conceptions of Reading."

12. The Generality of Dimensions of Teaching

N. L. Gage

Research on teaching can be concerned with teaching in general, as it applies to all or at least a wide variety of subject matters. Or it can be conducted with a single kind of subject matter, such as elementary school reading. Which kind of research is more advantageous?

This issue arises in the planning of programs of research on teaching. Using the "generic" approach, one looks for uniformity—concepts and principles that apply across all or many subject matters. This approach jumps from one subject matter to another almost as if the subject matter did not make much difference. The "curriculum-

This analysis was prepared at the request of Garry L. McDaniels, then director of the Teaching Research Group of the Basic Skills Division of the National Institute of Education. I am grateful to Ray L. Debus, Raymond P. Perry, and especially Penelope L. Peterson for criticisms of an earlier draft. The paper was part of the work of the Program on Teaching Effectiveness of the Center for Educational Research at Stanford. The program is supported in part by funds from the National Institute of Education, U.S. Department of Health, Education, and Welfare. The opinions expressed in this publication do not necessarily reflect the position, policy, and endorsement of the National Institute of Education (Contract No. NE-C-00-3-0061).

specific" approach, in contrast, is based on the assumption that the subject matter does make a difference—in the kinds of teaching behavior, methods, strategies, styles, and skills that the investigator needs to be concerned with and in the kinds of relationships to significant educational outcomes that he is likely to find.

Further, the issue applies to different grade levels. It applies to various phases of the teacher's work—both preactive (for example, organization and planning) and interactive. It applies to different kinds of outcomes—both cognitive and social-emotional.

In one way, the issue is meaningless. Whenever one does research on teaching, one works in just one subject area—or only a few; at just one grade level—or only a few; with particular phases of the teacher's work and particular outcomes. In this sense, one cannot do research on teaching in general. In another way, however, the issue does make sense. One can choose variables that seem to apply, at least potentially, across the board. Or one can choose variables that take into account the phenomena peculiar to a specific subject matter, grade level, and so on. So one could do research on the teaching of decoding in the first grade by using variables in teaching that apply only to that kind of teaching, rather than variables that apply to teaching almost anything at almost any grade level. The curriculum-specific advocate would insist that only subject matter experts do research on the teaching of that subject matter.

As one examines the literature of research on teaching, one gains the impression that it has been conducted from both of these two major points of view. On the one hand, the major reviews of research on teaching, such as those by Rosenshine and by Dunkin and Biddle, subordinate the role of the curriculum, or subject matter.[1] The orientation conveyed is that the field of research on teaching has been engaged in a search for general relationships between teaching processes (teacher behaviors, teacher-pupil interactions, teaching methods, styles, strategies, skills, and the like) and student achievement or attitude—relationships that are general across, say, various subject matters and grade levels. In making their collations of studies, these reviewers have neglected differences between subject matters and grade levels and have combined studies across these two major kinds of distinctions. It is not clear whether they have done so advisedly and by preference or whether they were forced to do so in order to obtain enough studies in any given cluster to justify some kind of generalization. But the fact remains that, when they brought together the studies on some kind of teacher behavior such as "indirectness" or "criticism and disapproval," they did so without regard to the subject matter and the grade level in which the teaching was going on.

Alongside this kind of review and analysis of research on teaching there has always existed a curriculum-specific literature. One example of that kind of literature is the set of chapters on research on teaching a specific subject matter in the *Handbook of Research on Teaching* and in the *Second Handbook of Research on Teaching.*[2] Both handbooks contain chapters with such titles as "Research on Teaching Literature, Language and Composition," "Research on Teaching in the Natural Sciences," and "Research on the Teaching of Elementary-School Mathematics." In these chapters the research has indeed been brought together in clusters that bear upon the specific problems of teaching a particular kind of subject matter. Similarly, there is the *Journal of Research in Science Teaching,* and there are comparable journals for research on teaching English, mathematics, the social studies, reading, foreign languages, and the like. Professional associations for research on teaching particular subject matters also exist.

The generic approach has similar manifestations. The same two handbooks have chapters representing the generic approach. The first *Handbook* has chapters on teaching methods, the teacher's personality, and social interaction in the classroom. The *Second Handbook* contains a chapter on three contemporary models of teaching—the "behavior-control model," the "discovery-learning model," and the "rational model."[3] All three models are considered without specific reference to any particular subject matter or grade level. And there are journals, associations, symposia, and research institutes with a generic orientation to research on teaching.

The arguments on the generic-specific issue in research on teaching can be put into categories that deal with the generality of learning and teaching processes, the problem of multiplicity, conceptualizations of teaching, and the empirical evidence. After reviewing each of these arguments, I examine some possible ways to resolve the issue.

THE GENERALITY OF LEARNING-TEACHING PROCESSES

It can be argued that research on teaching ought to be conducted without special regard for the particularities of subject matters and even grade levels. In this view, research on teaching is similar to research on learning, which has also in large part been conducted without specific regard to the kinds of categories that are imposed by special subject matters. When psychologists have investigated learning processes, they have been concerned with the learning of concepts, skills, principles, problem solving, and creativity without regard to subject matter.

Thus, Gagné has argued that learning is in principle the same for all subjects and that there are no special principles, laws, or processes that apply only to one subject matter and not to others. In his words, "Learning is not unique to subject matter. There is no sound rational basis for such entities as 'mathematics learning,' 'science learning,' 'language learning,' or 'history learning,' except as divisions of time."[4]

This approach to learning implies that any concept is basically the same kind of thing to be learned, regardless of whether it is a concept in reading or a concept in arithmetic. Thus, the concept of "consonant," as learned in reading, is similar in its psychological characteristics to the concept of "odd" (versus "even") in arithmetic. The pupil presumably learns each of these concepts in basically the same way, and he manifests that learning by his ability to respond to various instances of the same concept by giving the appropriate abstract category or name. When exposed to a collection of instances and noninstances of consonants, the child will show that he has learned the concept of consonant by correctly identifying which instance is a consonant and which is not. When confronted with a series of numbers, the child will demonstrate that he has learned the concept of "odd" by correctly identifying which of the numbers is odd and which is not.

In teaching these two concepts, the teacher might proceed in much the same way, regardless of the fact that one concept relates to reading while the other relates to arithmetic. In teaching the concept of consonant, the teacher might first proceed by giving a definition, such as "a consonant is a letter that stands for a certain kind of sound in speaking—a sound that is made by stopping the air that comes out of your throat by certain movements of your speech organs. It is different from a vowel, which is a speech sound that is created by a relatively free passage of the air out of your throat through your speech organs and mouth." The teacher would then go on to give instances of the two kinds of sounds, that is, of consonants and vowels. Because the vowels are fewer in number, the teacher would probably teach them first by saying that the vowels are the sounds represented by *a, e, i, o, u,* and sometimes *y,* in the English alphabet. All other letters of the alphabet are consonants. Then the teacher would give the children practice in using the concept of consonant by asking them to decide whether a given letter in a series of letters was a consonant or a vowel.

In teaching the concept of "odd number" the teacher might do the same things, except for the details of the subject matter. First, she would define the concept of oddness by saying something like "An odd number is a number that is not divisible by two. An even number is a number that is divisible by two. Examples of odd numbers are 1, 3, 5, 7, and so on. Examples of even numbers are 2, 4, 6, 8, and so on. You can always tell whether numbers that have more than one digit are odd numbers or even numbers by whether they end in an odd or even number. Thus, the number 27 is an odd number because it ends in 7, which is an odd number . . . . " The teacher would then give the children practice in using this concept by asking them to discriminate between quite a few numbers of both kinds. When they had correctly classified the numbers, the teacher would infer that they had learned the concept of "odd" (versus "even").

The same general procedure could be applied to the teaching of many other concepts in reading—grapheme-phoneme correspondence, plural, verb, period, sentence, paragraph, tense, and so on. In arithmetic, the additional concepts would include addition, subtraction, division, digit, fraction, whole number, mixed number, and ratio. In general, the teaching takes the form of defining, illustrating, presenting instances both positive and negative, and requiring discriminations and other applications. The fact that one set of concepts was specific to arithmetic would make no basic difference in the kind of research conducted on the teaching of reading and arithmetic.

Our examples thus far have concerned only one kind of thing to be taught, namely, concepts, in only two different kinds of curriculum, namely, reading and arithmetic. But the argument can readily be extended to many, if not all, of the different kinds of things to be taught in many, if not all, of the different kinds of subject matter. Thus, the teaching of principles in composition should, by this kind of reasoning, be found to be highly similar to, if not identical with, the teaching of principles in science. The principle that the subject and the verb of a sentence should agree in number is, by this kind of logic, basically the same as the principle that one side of a chemical equation should contain the same number of atoms of whatever elements are involved as the other side of the chemical equation. The rule that the final *e* in a French word is silent, unless it has an acute accent, is essentially the same, considered as something to be learned and taught, as the rule that, when distance from the equator increases, the mean daily temperature on Earth tends to decrease.

Nonetheless, in some subject matters, specific teacher competencies have been identified. For example, Lester listed teaching skills in mathematics instruction in *A General Catalog of Teaching Skills.*[5] The skills are specific to mathematics instruction, for the most part, because they require a knowledge of mathematics. At their general level, however, they sound much like skills that would apply to the teaching of any subject matter. For example, one skill identified by Lester is "Identifies student process or skill errors and error patterns." Only when he cites indicators of this skill does it begin to seem curriculum-specific, as when he states that the teacher, after viewing a film or videotape of a student's mathematical activity, should be able to generate a hypothesis concerning possible error patterns and construct a diagnostic activity to test the hypothesis. For these indicators, the teacher would indeed need curriculum-specific skills, because he or she would need knowledge of the mathematics entailed.

Thus these curriculum-specific teaching competencies entail a knowledge of the subject. Yet several studies have shown that the correlation between a teacher's knowledge of the subject and students' achievement in various subject matters is just about zero.[6] On the basis of a complex study employing path analysis, McDonald and Elias speculated that: "A conception consistent with the data is that measures of knowledge of the subject and of [teaching] methodology are antecedents of [teacher] performance, but probably interact with the perceptual-cognitive processes of the teacher to affect teaching performance."[7] And the path from teacher performance to pupil achievement becomes similarly complex.

In his summary, McDonald characterized the curriculum-specific variable of teacher knowledge of subject matter as follows:

Another area requiring refinement in measurement is the pattern of relations between teachers' knowledge of subject matter and their knowledge of teaching methodology. Probably the appropriate procedure would be to consider what is to be taught, working back from this analysis to a description of what a teacher ought to know in order to teach. A clear distinction should, however, be made between knowledge of content and knowledge of process. [In relation to teaching reading, it should be noted that] teachers generally have already acquired basic decoding skills and are competent readers themselves. But they may not, however, be informed about the processes involved in how pupils acquire decoding and comprehension skills.[8]

Thus, the approaches of Lester and McDonald illustrate senses in which certain teaching competencies are highly likely to be curriculum-specific.

Shulman argued in favor of curriculum-specific research on teaching by extrapolating from his research on physicians' diagnostic thought processes.[9] Physicians used hypothetico-deductive methods much more than did the subjects in the experiments on problem solving in the study of thinking by Bruner, Goodnow, and Austin.[10] Shulman attributed this difference in thought processes to the fact that the physicians had a body of knowledge that enabled them to stand the cognitive strain of entertaining several different hypotheses simultaneously. Thus, curriculum-specific research on medical diagnosis yielded results different from those of the generic research on the knowledge-free tasks used by Bruner and his coauthors.

Shulman also noted Brownell's argument in 1948 that, although the same general types of learning go on in all of the various subject matters, the specific types of "arbitrary associations," "skills," "concepts," and "pupil behavior" differ from subject to subject and within the same subject. These differences occur in the "intrinsic relations" among the elements of the subject matter, "the opportunities afforded for the use of previous experience," and the complexity and difficulty of the things to be learned.[11] In short, although Brownell recognized the essential similarity across subject matters of the things to be learned and of the processes by which they would be learned, he stressed the possibly great importance, despite this similarity, of the differences from one subject matter to the next.

Thus, research on teaching and learning should, it seemed to Brownell, be curriculum specific.

Finally, Shulman pointed out that the general approach of the original taxonomy of educational objectives[12] has been converted into a set of several subject-specific taxonomies in a handbook of evaluation that was published fifteen years later.[13] In all these ways, Shulman developed the case for the renewal of curriculum-specific research on teaching. Such research would require the collaboration of subject-matter specialists and psychologists. Left alone, psychologists would continue to follow the spurious general, noncurriculum-specific approach toward which most of them had tended during the preceding few decades.

THE MULTIPLICITY OF CONTEXTS

Another argument in favor of generic research on teaching derives from the difficulty of defining the proper degree of specificity of curriculum-specific research. The problem is readily seen. Just how specific is "curriculum specific"? Is a given curriculum the same as a subject matter, such as reading, arithmetic, science, or social studies? Or does a curriculum also need to be specified as to its grade level, so that we should think in terms of first-grade reading, second-grade reading, and so forth? If this degree of specificity is needed, then, merely with respect to the reading curriculum, we would have eight or twelve curricula, depending on whether we are concerned with reading in eight or twelve grade levels. There would also be eight or twelve curricula in mathematics and in other major subject areas.

If we concern ourselves merely with the five major domains of academic subject matter—language arts, mathematics, social studies, natural science, and foreign languages—then we have specified, even at this crude and gross level of specification, perhaps sixty (five subject matters x twelve grade levels) curriculum-specific fields of research on teaching. To do research in each of these sixty fields implies that we expect to find different relationships between process variables (for example, types of teacher behavior or teaching method) and product variables (for example, types of student achievement and attitude). Thus, we would be assuming and implying that sixty sets of generalizations, or types of relationships, can be found between process and product variables—one set for each of the sixty subject-matter—grade-level combinations.

This degree of complexity will enormously expand the kinds of knowledge to be sought through research on teaching. It will be far from sufficient to have the kind of generalization that is currently attempted in research on teaching—a generalization such as "Degree of teacher enthusiasm is positively correlated with student achievement and favorability in learning from teachers' extended oral presentations (for example, lectures or explanations)." The correlation or functional relationship between enthusiasm and student achievement would need to be reexamined in all of the sixty contexts noted above.

But, of course, even this sixtyfold level of complexity is far from adequate to embrace what is meant by serious formulations of the idea of curriculum specificity. Within each subject matter, the concepts, principles, facts, definitions, types of problems, and the like, must themselves be specified. In this way of thinking, teaching the concept of consonant differs in principle from teaching the concept of plural (versus singular), and both of these differ from teaching the concept of present tense (versus past tense) or the concept of phrase (versus clause, sentence, and paragraph).

Even within a single subject area at a single grade level, the number of things to be learned, into which the curriculum can be analyzed, quickly becomes large. Some applications of this kind of curriculum analysis, as in the attempts on the part of some writers to formulate behavioral objectives for each of the school subject—grade-level combinations, yield thousands of objectives. And each of these thousands of objectives is to be attained in any given grade-level— subject-matter combination, such as first-grade reading, third-grade arithmetic, fifth-grade social studies, or ninth-grade science.

Specified at this level, research on teaching could readily become the search for the good method of teaching a single fact or concept or principle at a given grade level. And methods of teaching would then be studied at the corresponding level of specificity. Research could be done on the ways of teaching the concept of plural versus singular in the first grade, even versus odd number in the second grade, peninsula versus isthmus in the fifth grade, or the concept of moment of force in the ninth-grade science class.

This reasoning should not necessarily be considered a reductio ad absurdum. It is not unthinkable that research on teaching of this kind could yield knowledge about relationships between process and product variables in thousands of different subject-matter—grade-level contexts. This is the program that results when the curriculum is analyzed into the specifics with which teachers and pupils actually work in any given lesson or unit during any single day or week of the school year.

Experienced teachers have often noted that their years of teaching have given them extensive repertoires of effective explanations, demonstrations, illustrations, examples, diagrams, and anecdotes for the myriads of concepts and principles that they teach and the many understandings and skills that they help their students acquire. When it becomes specific, research on teaching may deal with these repertoires of topic-relevant teaching skills. Just as medicine and engineering have not shrunk from these levels of complexity in their research and development, so research on teaching may also need to do the fine-grained work that will yield better ways of teaching a specific skill (such as long division) to a specific kind of pupil (an anxious fifth-grader).

THE CONCEPTUALIZATIONS OF THE PEDAGOGICAL DOMAIN

Another kind of argument on the generic-specific issue in research on teaching stems from the fact that many of the concepts formulated by writers in the field of teaching have served the purposes of those writers without requiring any substantial modification to take account of the specific curriculum or subject matter being taught. When it comes to analyzing teaching into its various "moves," "skills," "methods," "styles," and the like, these writers have been able to formulate concepts that operate well in a variety of different contexts—subject matter, grade level, curricular, and organizational—without modification in terms of the particular context being studied.

This kind of generality shows up in the set of "moves" formulated by Bellack and his colleagues.[14] In a monograph that appeared in 1966 (*The Language of the Classroom*), where they reported on fifteen eleventh-grade social studies classes, they were able to put classroom teaching moves into four major categories: structuring, soliciting, responding, and reacting. During the following decade, that analysis of the types of moves was found useful in about thirty-five related studies describing teaching at every grade level from elementary through college; in subjects as varied as reading, arithmetic,

mathematics, business, science, teaching, and nursing; in six other
countries (Sweden, Finland, Australia, Germany, Canada, and Japan);
and in such varied settings as individualized instruction, mathematics in "open" elementary school classrooms, and early education
programs. In all these studies, the pattern of structuring, soliciting,
responding, and reacting was found to occur in clearly defined
ways.[15]

Another essentially curriculum-generic schema was found appropriate by Hudgins in developing *A Catalog of Concepts in the
Pedagogical Domain of Teacher Education.*[16] This catalog provided a
set of intellectual tools that practitioners could use to isolate areas
of difficulty and subsequently to comprehend and interpret them.
He defined the pedagogical domain as encompassing the settings and
people that influence the content to be taught to pupils and the
methods and procedures used to convey content. The pedagogical
domain includes decisions concerning choice of content and its communication. This domain also includes relationships with other
teachers, administrators, boards of education, and other community
groups. But Hudgins gave priority to those concepts that apply most
immediately to the daily tasks of teaching, especially to the interaction between teachers and pupils. The catalog contains definitions,
indicators, illustrations, and sources for approximately one hundred
concepts of this kind.

Some of the concepts are reception learning (including comparison, definition, description, explanation, fact-stating, generalization, quotation, and summary); productive thinking (including categorizing, comparing, evaluating, explaining, generalizing, and opining);
control of content, such as content organizing (discussion teaching,
lecturing, routine, sequencing, and textbook teaching); process regulating (fourteen categories); and performance rating (three categories). Then it contains chapters dealing with concepts about groups,
including aggregation, classroom group, control of groups, group
alerting, group cohesiveness, and teacher flexibility; group morale; and
group productivity. It considers concepts concerning individuals,
such as achievement motivation, authoritarianism, conformity, self-
concept, sexual status, socioeconomic status, and sociometric status.
Finally, the catalog contains a treatment of the teacher as tutor or
counselor.

The significant feature of this catalog for the present discussion is the striking fact that it gets along without any curriculum specificity whatever. The illustrations of the concepts are, indeed, curriculum specific. They deal with all of the subject matters and grade levels. To illustrate the concept of comparison, the catalog describes an exchange in which "As response to a teacher question following the teacher's presentation on closed plane figures, a pupil says, 'A triangle has only three sides but a square has four.' Such a statement is a comparison inasmuch as the original comparison was expressed in the teacher presentation."[17] To illustrate opining, the catalog notes an occasion on which "A pupil states that he believes that there is life on Mars. He may even speculate as to the nature of such life. He does so, however, in the absence of any very specific evidential criteria."[18] In illustrating the concept of generalization (a statement in which a pupil recounts a general principle, rule, trend, prediction, or conclusion), the catalog offers the following:

A pupil rearranges the following sentence: "They were startled by a school of fish bailing water from the canoe." Thusly: "Bailing water from the canoe they were startled by a school of fish." When asked to cite the rule that he has applied the pupil responds, "You are supposed to place modifying phrases and clauses as close as possible to the words they modify."[19]

Thus, this fairly thorough attempt to catalog types of teacher behavior in the interactive aspects of classroom teaching was made without reference to curriculum-specific aspects of teaching. The catalog itself draws upon and cites a number of similar sources that have made similarly generic rather than curriculum-specific analyses of teaching.[20]

One additional illustration of the way in which the "activities of teaching" can be analyzed without becoming curriculum-specific was provided by Green.[21] He categorized a list of teacher activities as logical acts (for example, explaining, concluding, inferring, giving reasons, amassing evidence, demonstrating, defining, and comparing); strategic acts (for example, motivating, counseling, evaluating, planning, encouraging, disciplining, and questioning); and institutional acts (for example, collecting money, chaperoning, and patrolling the hall). He regarded the institutional acts as not necessary to the activity of teaching. Logical and strategic acts are, however, essential to teaching. Further, the logical acts of teaching should be appraised on logical grounds, while the strategic acts of teaching should be appraised by their consequences for learning.

Subsequently, Green distinguished between "teaching that . . . " and "teaching to . . . . " The former refers to shaping belief and knowledge, while the latter refers to shaping behavior. It involves the distinction between thinking and knowing, on the one hand, and doing or acting, on the other. This distinction is related to that between teaching and training, and Green's analysis leads to the principle that: "In the proportion that the behavior aimed at in training manifests intelligence, it is easier to use the word 'teaching' and 'training' interchangeably; in the proportion that the behavior aimed at does not manifest intelligence, the term 'training' continues to have application when the concept of 'teaching' does not."[22] Green went on to make similar analyses of the distinction between training and conditioning and between teaching and indoctrinating. These distinctions are involved with the degree to which different weights are placed on the grounds of belief as opposed to the content of belief.

The point here is that, at a certain level of analysis, the nature of the curriculum, or the objectives at which education is aimed, becomes important for the determination of the degree to which teaching, training, indoctrinating, conditioning, or instructing is going on. And if "teaching is an activity primarily concerned with enlarging the manifestation of intelligence,"[23] then teaching is more appropriate for certain kinds of objectives than others. If certain beliefs, kinds of knowledge, associations, and the like, are to be acquired on *rational* grounds, then certain kinds of teaching are appropriate. On the other hand, if they can be acquired on arbitrary, *irrational,* automatic, and unthinking grounds—such as the learning of the Morse code or the proper movements for serving the ball in tennis—then different kinds of teaching (or perhaps not even "teaching" at all) are entailed. Thus, by this analysis, we have some justification for a curriculum-specific approach to the definition of teaching and to research on teaching.

THE EVIDENCE FROM PROCESS-PRODUCT CORRELATIONS

The foregoing analysis of the generality-specificity issue rests largely on logical and a priori considerations. Obviously empirical findings should loom at least equally large. Does research actually indicate that relationships between process and product variables—

for example, between some kind of teacher behavior and some kind of student achievement—differ when subject matters differ? When grade levels differ? When cultural groups differ?

This possibility—that relationships between variables differ in magnitude and direction depending on the context—creates the strongest empirical argument in favor of context-specific research on teaching. If a certain kind of teacher behavior has one kind of relationship to pupil achievement in reading and another kind of relationship to pupil achievement in arithmetic, it is obvious that research on that kind of teacher behavior must be curriculum-specific.

Examples of Evidence for Generality

What has the research shown on this possibility? One reviewer of the process-product studies of teaching wrote that, when he looked at two contextual variables—grade level and subject area—by examining the tables in his book on teaching behavior and student achievement, there were no studies available for most of the combinations of grade level and subject area.[24] Nonetheless, none of the available results was particular to any combination of grade level or subject area. For example, the results on teacher questions, clarity, and task orientation were the same for different grade levels and subject areas.

Another instance of generality across subject matters is to be found in the report by Brophy and Evertson that the differences in teacher effectiveness "tended to be rather general across subject matter areas. A teacher who consistently got good gains in language arts ordinarily got good gains in mathematics also, and a teacher who consistently got poor gains in language arts usually got poor gains in mathematics. Few teachers consistently got better gains in one of these subject areas than in the other."[25]

In her evaluation of Follow Through, Stallings reported that similar relationships to achievement in reading and mathematics were found for most variables: length of school day, average time a child spends on the given subject (reading or mathematics), amount and frequency of discussion of the subject matter with adults (teachers or aides), degree of systematization of the instructional pattern in the form of the teacher's providing information and asking a question about that information, and so forth.[26] Indeed, the separate paragraphs in which Stallings summarized the results for reading and for mathematics are worded identically except for the reference in one section to achievement in reading and in the other to achievement in mathematics. The few references to subject matter-specific teaching methods, such as Cuisenaire rods, did not change the general picture of great similarity concerning what teaching variables correlated positively or negatively with achievement in reading and mathematics.

Examples of Evidence for Specificity

On the other hand, McDonald concluded that *no* teaching practices correlated with pupil achievement in *both* reading and mathematics at the second- and fifth-grade levels.[27] With respect to another kind of generality, Brophy and Evertson reported many differences in the direction of process-product relationships between grades one and three and between classes of middle and low socioeconomic status.[28] Stallings reported grade-level differences in the process correlates of achievement.[29] In this volume, the Soars have reported findings that differ according to the socioeconomic status of the pupils.[30]

Tikunoff, Berliner, and Rist compared ten highly effective second-grade teachers with ten much less effective ones.[31] Effectiveness was measured by the mean achievement of the teacher's class in reading and mathematics, adjusted for pretest achievement. The authors made the same comparison for ten more effective and ten less effective fifth-grade teachers. The comparisons were made on the basis of judges' ratings of the classes on dimensions derived from reports on ethnographic observations. Of the sixty-one dimensions rated, twenty-one were "generic" in that they correlated with effectiveness in both grade levels and both subject matters; twenty-five dimensions correlated with effectiveness only in the second grade but did so for both subject matters; three dimensions correlated with effectiveness only in the fifth grade but did so for both subject matters. Similarly, seven dimensions correlated with effectiveness at both grade levels but only for mathematics, and fourteen dimensions correlated with effectiveness at both grade levels but only for reading. Thus, this study yielded results that support both the generic and specific views of teaching effectiveness in some degree.

Overall, the empirical findings seem to favor some degree of both specificity and generality. The findings are not yet abundant enough to support firm conclusions, but they suggest that, when more adequate evidence becomes available, the resulting picture will not be either completely general or completely specific.

We turn now to ways of accumulating more adequate evidence and of analyzing that evidence as it comes to hand. Finally, we shall sketch a hypothetical structure of teaching competence of a kind that seems compatible with the logic and evidence adduced thus far.

IMPROVING EVIDENCE ON THE ISSUE

Presently two paths toward improved evidence on the issue suggest themselves: research on teaching with curriculum packages and the use of meta-analysis.

The Potential of Curriculum Packages

That research on teaching should be conducted within the context of curriculum packages, such as the BSCS (Biological Science Curriculum Study) materials and the SMSG (School Mathematics Study Group) program, has been urged by Rosenshine[32] and by Siegel.[33] Such packages offer the advantage of controlling, from one classroom to another, the materials, sequences, topics, concepts, and activities with which teachers work. Given such control, research workers could focus more sharply on the variations introduced by teachers. They could then attribute variations in student achievement more justifiably to variations in what the teachers have done.

As is well known, the developmental programs that have produced such packages of curriculum materials have not succeeded in controlling the ways in which teachers actually use the packages in their classrooms. As Gallagher put it, after observing in detail the ways in which six teachers taught the same BSCS concept,

The results of this study have confirmed again [the fact] that diversity is the central fact of human existence. In this case, the diversity of six competent teachers is their method of presenting the same curriculum materials . . . . [T]hose interested in curriculum development have not finished their job when they have packaged a cognitively valid and consistent set of materials.[34]

Curriculum-specific research on teaching could proceed either correlationally, by observing what teachers do with the curriculum materials packages, or experimentally, by training the teachers to use those packages in discrete ways. In either case, the findings would be significant for the problem of determining a meaningful position on the issue of generality-specificity.

Here again we face the problem of whether we can hope for knowledge that will have some general value. Curriculum packages abound. Must we resign ourselves to the evaluation of teaching in relation to each package by itself? Or can we hope for generalizations that cut across curriculum packages?

The answer here will have to be determined by experience. But the implications for research strategy as outlined by Siegel are clear and reasonable.[35] We should incorporate both general and curriculum-specific teaching variables into our studies. After we establish generalizations about the best ways to teach with one curriculum package, we can determine the degree to which those findings apply to another package. Such an approach—working our way up from the specific to the general—has the advantage of yielding quickly useful findings at the specific level where teachers work in any given subject in the classroom. With such subjects as reading and mathematics, we could thus obtain from the beginning knowledge that would have practical value, even if it did not yet have scientific generalizability. The opposite procedure, working our way down from the most general level, might make us run much greater risk of obtaining knowledge that might not apply to the practical realities of teaching a specific curriculum to a given kind of student.

Curriculum packages in the future might control teacher behavior so thoroughly that they would leave little room for individual differences among teachers using the same curriculum package. In that unlikely event, the study of process-product relationships in teaching might become genuinely reduced to the study of curriculum package-product relationships. It seems more likely that curriculum packages will always leave enough leeway for variations in teacher behavior to make the study of process-product relationships within curriculum packages worthwhile.

The Need for Meta-Analysis

Closer examination of the ever-increasing literature must be undertaken to sharpen our knowledge concerning generality and specificity. More of the blanks in the subject-matter—grade-level matrix must be filled in with knowledge concerning empirical relationships between teaching processes and educational outcomes.

And, as those blanks are filled in, we should examine the results with the tools of meta-analysis.[36] Such tools allow us to estimate the average "effect size" (correlation coefficient or standardized difference between means) for the relationship between a given pair of variables across a whole cluster of studies that yielded evidence on that pair of variables. Meta-analysis improves on the usual verbal collation of findings across studies or the usual tabulation of the results of individual studies in a cluster. It quantifies the results in the form of an average correlation coefficient or standardized mean difference, so that the overall magnitude of the average result of the cluster of studies can readily be grasped.

To meta-analysis should also be added the procedure of testing the significance of the combined results of a cluster of studies by means of techniques recently brought together by Rosenthal.[37] Especially in a field such as research on teaching, where the expected relationship between any pair of process and product variables is low and where the number of teachers involved in any single study is usually also low (N averaging about fifteen in some clusters of studies), the statistical power of the studies is low[38] and the risk of errors of Type II in statistical inference (inferring that the null hypothesis is true when it is in fact false) is correspondingly great. One way to reduce that risk is to estimate the statistical significance of the combined results of independent studies, as I have suggested. [39] It seems justifiable to expect that this procedure, applied not only to research on teaching but to other areas of educational research, such as the effects of homework or class size, where results have long been considered to leave the null hypothesis intact, will change the picture of what research has yielded.

Thus meta-analysis should substantially improve the process of determining what a body of research means—in terms of the statistical significance and the magnitude of the results. We should be able to penetrate the dark areas where large numbers of studies have been considered to have yielded negative results simply because the statistical significance of weak single studies has been taken seriously.

Beyond providing a better grasp on main effects, meta-analysis should also make possible improved knowledge on the generality-specificity issue. As was shown by Glass, it is possible with meta-analysis to break down the literature on psychotherapy according to types of therapy, types of problems, and the like.[40] Meta-analysis can lead, in research on teaching, to breaking down the studies according to grade level, subject matter, social class of the pupils, and many other variables germane to the generality-specificity issue. Then the average effect size and significance of the combined results in each subcluster can be determined. For example, Hedges broke down studies of teacher variables into subclusters containing only studies performed with elementary school classes and with secondary school classes; the main effects differed significantly in these two subclusters, being greater at the secondary school level. A similar meta-analysis showed that effect sizes were significantly greater in subclusters of studies using teacher-made (and hence presumably more relevant) achievement tests than in subclusters using standardized achievement tests. (In these meta-analyses, grade level and type of test were largely confounded, thus leaving the results questionable, but this illustration of meta-analysis remains pertinent.)[41]

Thus, as research on teaching in many different contexts (grade levels, subject matters, social classes, ethnic groups, and so forth) accumulates, meta-analysis should be applied to the results. What such analyses reveal will illuminate the generality-specificity issue. If the "effect sizes" differ from one context to another, the evidence will favor specificity; the absence of such differences will support generality.

One major question in meta-analysis is that of what constitutes a replication, inasmuch as only replications or "quasi-replications" should be clustered together as the basis for a meta-analysis. Since two studies are never identical, how different can they be and still be considered replications of the same investigation? The answer to this question can be approached by means of the facet analysis proposed by Guttman.[42] Each dimension of a study—its independent variable(s), dependent variable(s), subjects, grade level, subject matter, and even the characteristics of the investigator (for example, the same person, a disciple of the original investigator, a neutral investigator, an opponent of the original investigator)—can be regarded as a facet. And each facet can be considered to have a number of levels.

The importance of a facet can then be judged by the magnitude of the difference made by that facet in meta-analyses of the cluster of replications. Perhaps, if the facet makes a large difference, studies differing on that facet should no longer be considered to be replications. Such results should permit the improved definition of replication in a given research field, beyond the definition based on qualitative analysis of the facets of the replications.

What is likely to be the resolution of the generality-specificity issue—after the further conceptual and empirical work sketched above has been done? It seems worthwhile to state some hypothesis at this point if the further work to be undertaken is to follow something better than the impossible path of trying everything conceivable.

The hypothesis is that teaching behaviors—methods, styles, techniques, and the like—will fall into a hierarchical model, ranging from the highly (if not completely) general to the highly specific. In somewhat the same way as contemporary hierarchical conceptions of intelligence,[43] some dimensions of teaching will make a difference in achievement or attitude or both at each of the following levels of generality (see Figure 12-1):

Level I.   *All grade levels, subject matters, student types.*
Tentative examples of such dimensions are teacher's enthusiasm and teacher-engendered relevant learning time.

Level II. *Major grade-level categories,* such as the pre-school, early primary (grades 1 to 4), late elementary (grades 5 to 8), secondary, and college levels.
Tentative examples of such dimensions are: for preschool and early primary, teacher's warmth; for late elementary, teacher's classroom management and discipline skills; for secondary and college levels, teacher's ability to give well-organized and illustrated explanations.

Level III. *Major subject-matter·categories,* such as verbal (language arts and social studies), mathematical and scientific (algebra and general science), aesthetic (visual, musical, and performing arts), and psychomotor (physical education, driver training, typewriting).
Tentative examples of such dimensions are: for verbal subject matters, teacher's vocabulary and oral-verbal fluency; for mathematical-scientific subject matters, teacher's mathematical ability and the

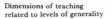

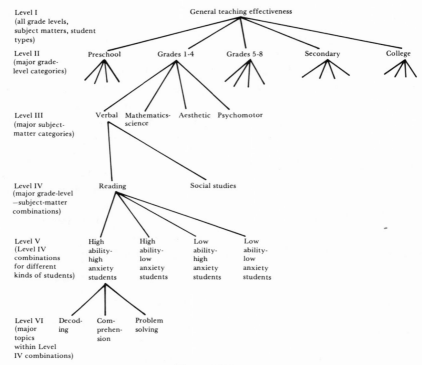

Figure 12-1

**A hierarchical model of the structure of dimensions
related to teaching effectiveness**

ability to organize logical explanations and demonstrations; for aesthetic subject matters, teacher's aesthetic and social sensibility and the ability to support creative effort; for psychomotor subject matters, teacher's visual and auditory perceptual skills and the ability to model desired skills.

Level IV. *Major grade-level—subject-matter combinations,* such as primary-grade reading, upper-elementary social studies, high school geometry, college physics.

Tentative examples of such dimensions are: for primary grade reading, teacher's ability to teach grapheme-phoneme correspondences; for upper-elementary social studies, teacher's ability to guide a student-centered discussion group or organize a role-playing session;

for high school geometry, teacher's ability to present derivations of theorems and detect students' difficulties in following the derivations; for college physics, teacher's ability to supplement and extend textbook explications of concepts, principles, and problem-solving methods.

Level V. *Major grade-level—subject-matter combinations for students at different points on various dimensions,* such as general intellectual ability, academic motivation, ethnic identity, socioeconomic status, sensory and motor abilities.

A tentative example of such a dimension is: for sixth-grade students of ecology who are high in general scholastic aptitude and high in anxiety, teacher's ability to conduct classes with high structuring and low student participation.

Level VI. *Major topics within grade-level—subject-matter combinations,* such as the sound of "th," the Bill of Rights, the Pythagorean theorem, Ohm's law.

The hierarchy has been carried to about the same degree of detail as that explicated for the hierarchical conception of intelligence. It may be that the hierarchy of teaching dimensions will not be established empirically to any greater degree than that attained for the organization of mental ability. But just as *g* (general mental ability) has been relatively well accepted and supported by decades of empirical work, and various group factors (verbal, numerical, spatial, and the like) have been almost as well substantiated and used (in the *Scholastic Aptitude Test* and the *Graduate Record Examination,* for example), so it is conceivable that the dimensions at Levels I, II, and III will eventually be recognized and found useful in the practical work of teacher education.

The view sketched by the present analysis is one that opens promising avenues for theoretical and empirical work. None of the teaching-dimension levels and tentative examples sketched above is completely devoid of empirical support in the research literature of the last decade. Further effort should determine the tenability and weaknesses of the present resolution of the generality-specificity issue.

NOTES

1. Barak Rosenshine, *Teaching Behaviors and Student Achievement* (Slough, Eng.: National Foundation for Educational Research in England and Wales, 1971); Michael J. Dunkin and Bruce J. Biddle, *The Study of Teaching* (New York: Holt, Rinehart and Winston, 1974).

2. N. L. Gage, ed., *Handbook of Research on Teaching* (Chicago: Rand McNally, 1963), chs. 15 to 23; Robert M. W. Travers, ed., *Second Handbook of Research on Teaching* (Chicago: Rand McNally, 1973), chs. 33-42.

3. Graham Nuthall and Ivan Snook, "Contemporary Models of Teaching," in *Second Handbook of Research on Teaching*, ed. Travers, 47-76.

4. Robert M. Gagné, "The Learning Basis of Teaching Methods," in *The Psychology of Teaching Methods*, Seventy-fifth Yearbook of the National Society for the Study of Education, Part I, ed. N. L. Gage (Chicago: University of Chicago Press, 1976), 30.

5. F. K. Lester, Jr., "Teaching Skills in Mathematics Instruction," in *A General Catalog of Teaching Skills*, ed. R. L. Turner (Syracuse, N.Y.: School of Education, Syracuse University, 1973), ch. 7.

6. Edward G. Begle, *Teacher Knowledge and Student Achievement in Algebra*, Report no. 9 (Stanford, Calif.: School Mathematics Study Group, 1972); E. N. Hook, "Teacher Factors Influencing Pupil Achievement in Elementary School English," unpub. diss., Colorado State College, 1965, University Microfilms No. 66-5989; William A. McCall and G. R. Krause, "Measurement of Teacher Merit for Salary Purposes," *Journal of Educational Research* 53 (1959); 73-75; Arthur I. Rothman, Wayne W. Welch, and Herbert J. Walberg, "Physics Teacher Characteristics and Student Learning," *Journal of Research in Science Teaching* 6 (1969): 59-63.

7. Frederick J. McDonald and Patricia Elias, *The Effects of Teaching Performance on Pupil Learning*, Beginning Teacher Evaluation Study, Phase II, Final Report, Volume I (Princeton, N.J.: Educational Testing Service, 1976), 934.

8. Frederick J. McDonald, *Beginning Teacher Evaluation Study: Phase II, 1973-74. Executive Summary Report* (Princeton, N.J.: Educational Testing Service, 1976), 56 [italics in original].

9. Lee S. Shulman, "The Psychology of School Subjects: A Premature Obituary?" *Journal of Research in Science Teaching* 11 (1974): 319-339.

10. Jerome S. Bruner, Jacqueline J. Goodnow, and George A. Austin, *A Study of Thinking* (New York: Wiley, 1956).

11. William A. Brownell, "Learning Theory and Educational Practice," *Journal of Educational Research* 41 (1948): 481-497.

12. Benjamin S. Bloom *et al.*, eds., *Taxonomy of Educational Objectives: The Classification of Educational Goals. Handbook I, Cognitive Domain* (New York: Longman, 1956).

13. Benjamin S. Bloom, J. Thomas Hastings, and George Madaus, *Handbook of Formative and Summative Evaluation of Student Learning* (New York: McGraw-Hill, 1971).

14. Arno A. Bellack *et al.*, *The Language of the Classroom* (New York: Teachers College Press, 1966).

15. Arno A. Bellack, "Studies in the Language of the Classroom," paper presented at the First Invitational Conference on Teaching, Memorial University of Newfoundland, St. John's, May 25, 1976.

16. Bryce B. Hudgins, *A Catalog of Concepts in the Pedagogical Domain of Teacher Education* (St. Louis, Mo.: Graduate Institute of Education, Washington University, 1974).

17. *Ibid.*, 29.

18. *Ibid.*, 49.

19. *Ibid.*, 38-39.

20. Mary J. Aschner and James J. Gallagher, *A System for Classifying Thought Processes in the Context of Classroom Verbal Interaction* (Champaign, Ill.: Institute for Research on Exceptional Children, University of Illinois, 1965); B. Othanel Smith, Milton O. Meux, *et al.*, *A Study of the Strategies of Teaching* (Urbana, Ill.: Bureau of Educational Research, College of Education, University of Illinois, 1962); Hilda Taba and F. F. Elzey, "Teaching Strategies and Thought Processes," *Teachers College Record* 65 (1964): 523-534.

21. Thomas E. Green, *The Activities of Teaching* (New York: McGraw-Hill, 1971).

22. *Ibid.*, 25.

23. *Ibid.*, 32-33.

24. Barak Rosenshine, "Curriculum and Other Contextual Variables," paper presented at the annual meeting of the American Educational Research Association, Chicago, 1974); *id.*, *Teaching Behaviors and Student Achievement.*

25. Jere E. Brophy and Carolyn M. Evertson, *Learning from Teaching: A Developmental Perspective* (Boston: Allyn and Bacon, 1976), 165-166.

26. Jane Stallings, "Implementation and Child Effects of Teaching Practices in Follow Through Classrooms," *Monographs of the Society for Research in Child Development* 40, No. 7-8 (1975), Serial no. 163, pp. 100-101.

27. McDonald, *Beginning Teacher Evaluation Study: Phase II, 1973-74.*

28. Brophy and Evertson, *Learning from Teaching.*

29. Stallings, "Implementation and Child Effects of Teaching Practices in Follow Through Classrooms."

30. See Chapter 5 in this volume.

31. William J. Tikunoff, David C. Berliner, and Ray C. Rist, *An Ethnographic Study of the Beginning Teacher Evaluation Study Known Sample*, Technical report no. 75-10-5, Special Study A (San Francisco: Far West Laboratory for Educational Research and Development, 1975).

32. Barak Rosenshine, "New Directions for Research on Teaching," in *How Teachers Make a Difference* (Washington, D.C.: U.S. Government Printing Office, 1971).

33. Martin A. Siegel, "Teacher Behaviors and Curriculum Packages: Implications for Research and Teacher Education," in *The Handbook of Curriculum*, ed. Louis Rubin (Boston: Allyn and Bacon, 1977), pp. 73-98.

34. James J. Gallagher, "Three Studies of the Classroom," in *Classroom*

Observation, American Educational Research Association Monograph Series on Curriculum Evaluation, No. 6 (Chicago: Rand McNally, 1970), 101-102.

35. Siegel, "Teacher Behaviors and Curriculum Packages."

36. Gene V Glass, "Integrating Findings: The Meta-analysis of Research," in *Review of Research in Education*, Volume V, ed. Lee S. Shulman (Itasca, Ill.: F. E. Peacock, 1978).

37. Robert Rosenthal, "Combining Results of Independent Studies," *Psychological Bulletin* 85 (1978): 185-193.

38. See Larry Hedges, "A Meta-analysis of Studies of Four Teacher Behavior Variables" (Stanford, Calif.: School of Education, Stanford University, 1977).

39. N. L. Gage, *The Scientific Basis of the Art of Teaching* (New York: Teachers College Press, 1978).

40. Glass, "Integrating Findings."

41. Hedges, "Meta-analysis of Studies of Four Teacher Behavior Variables."

42. Louis Guttman, "An Outline of Some New Methodology for Social Research," *Public Opinion Quarterly* 18 (1954-55): 395-404.

43. Philip E. Vernon, *Structure of Human Abilities*, 2d ed. (New York: Harper and Row, 1965).

Index